Contents

About the Author

Louis Columbus has over seventeen years of product management, sales, and market analysis and planning experience, and has been actively involved with e-commerce for the last six years. As Director, Market Research for ZLand.com, Louis actively researches business models of the ASP marketplace, completes competitive analyses of served ASP segments, and completes primary research of early adopter attitudes and preferences for ASP offerings. Louis also has spoken at many industry conferences on the subject of the ASP model and market dynamics of electronic commerce. Previously, Louis was Senior Manager, Gateway Business, where he lead business-to-business electronic commerce initiatives, including the definition of stealth sites, competitive analysis, and coordinating product introductions, in addition to managing content used on gateway.com. While at Gateway, Mr. Columbus also managed the E-5000 Series of workstations. Mr. Columbus also teaches e-commerce and the fundamentals of networking operating systems at California State University, Fullerton and has also taught at the University of California, Irvine. He also serves as a contributing editor to *Desktop Engineering Magazine*, writing on topics of interest to technical professionals. Mr. Columbus has published twelve books on a variety of operating system, hardware, and e-commerce topics. Louis double-majored at the University of Arizona in Marketing & Information Systems Design, and has an M.B.A. from Pepperdine University.

Dedication

To my ever-patient and supportive wife Cheryl for her consistent and wonderful support, and to Alyssa Hope for her wonderful sense of humor and great laugh, which made the efforts seem so fun and enjoyable.

Acknowledgments

Taking the concept of a book from concept to fruition is a process that appears singular, with an author completing the task of getting words on a page, yet is in fact a coordinated team effort among many individuals. From the words on the page to the book in its entirety being delivered to you, there are many contributors adding value along the way. The team at Macmillan has done an outstanding job of coordinating the efforts of technical editors, copy editors, production, and even advance publicity and marketing. Thanks to Loretta Yates, the book has matured from being a simple e-business book to being focused on the Application Service Provider marketplace. Sean Dixon has provided excellent support and direction as well, in addition to the copy editors, Julie McNamee, Kay Hoskin, and Lauren Dixon. The technical editing of a book is one of the most thorough tasks. Thank you, Ankur Laroia, for doing an excellent job on technical edits throughout the review process.

The level of support from Zland.com has been completely unexpected, yet so strong that it enabled this book to get done on schedule and with clarity of striving to serve customers first always. Thank you to all the senior managers at ZLand.com for your enthusiastic reception of this concept and your support as the book was completed. In providing a strategic view of the industry, Glenn Abood has also been a great teacher. Thank you all for giving me the base of knowledge to create this book.

I could have not completed this book without the support and enthusiasm of Rich Wyckoff. His gift of being able to create a department where high levels of achievement are expected then celebrated, his willingness to consider projects that are outside job descriptions yet have the potential to contribute, and the support of diverse opinions that lead to accomplishment, create an atmosphere of achievement.

In learning about the ASP marketplace, I have also had great teachers. Thank you, Dan McCrory, for teaching me about the international marketplace for ASPs and for sharing your extensive knowledge of the industry. I greatly appreciate your assistance and support. Thanks to Bill Junkin for teaching me about international markets and showing me just how global any e-business really is. Thank you, Vince Calandra, for sharing your vision and great attitude with me as I have continually learned about this marketplace. Special thanks also to Rahm Shastry for a great education on Exchanges and partnerships. Thank you for your support of this book as well. Thank you, James McCrory, for your insights and great teamwork during the development phases of this book.

The biggest thanks of all belong to the customers and franchisees of Zland.com, for without you, my experiences within the ASP industry would have not been possible. For the customers I have worked with on success stories, thank you for your cooperation and supportive attitude toward this book. The sales force at Zland.com, specifically John Boulter and Joe Zehnder, has been invaluable in getting the success stories completed. Thank you both for your great support and responsiveness. The Zland.com franchisees are also a great customer group to serve. Thank you all for teaching me about the competitive dynamics of the ASP marketplace and your ongoing support for this book as well.

Thank you, Tauni Oxborrow, for being a great team player and for having a truly "whatever it takes" attitude about helping out while this book was being completed. Your attitude is a great strength and is much appreciated. Thanks also to Chrissy Kelly and Bob Grizanti for their help in getting the graphics together for this book and the assistance with designs. Scott Rasmussen's assistance with researching the various companies and analysis of the market also made the process of creating this book much easier and streamlined the entire process with his contributions.

Thank you Lisa Morgan, Steve Hurdle, Mike Myers, and Scott Lucas for all your assistance and enthusiasm for the book as well. Collectively your focus on the customers in this emerging marketplace continue to be a great way to learn about the ASP model, and the energy level you each have is an inspiriation. Thank you for your contributions to this book and my knowledge of the ASP marketplace.

The research companies listed in this book are the best in the industry at tracking market trends and quantifying them for the benefit of industry participants. Thanks to Kristen Keil of Forrester Research for the outstanding responsiveness and support, and her ability to field the most diverse and detailed questions anyone could be expected to receive. Thank you, Eric Klien of The Yankee Group, for the generosity of your insights and time in helping to shape this book as well, and your contributions in terms of onsite presentations and assistance with market trends in the small business arena. Thank you, Clare Gil-lian, for the most insightful analyses of the ASP marketplace presented. Your presentations have contributed to the insights within this book. The assistance from Meredith Whalen and her insightful comments and presentations continue to be at the forefront of the ASP industry research being done today. I truly appreciate the assistance and responsiveness of Amy Mizoras and her willingness to field any question. Her follow-through is outstanding.

Tell Us What You Think!

As the reader of this book, *you* are our most important critic and commentator. We value your opinion and want to know what we're doing right, what we could do better, what areas you'd like to see us publish in, and any other words of wisdom you're willing to pass our way.

As a Associate Publisher for Sams, I welcome your comments. You can fax, email, or write me directly to let me know what you did or didn't like about this book—as well as what we can do to make our books stronger.

Please note that I cannot help you with technical problems related to the topic of this book, and that due to the high volume of mail I receive, I might not be able to reply to every message.

When you write, please be sure to include this book's title and author as well as your name and phone or fax number. I will carefully review your comments and share them with the author and editors who worked on the book.

Fax: 317-581-4666

Email: quetechnical@macmillanUSA.com

Mail: Tracy Dunkelberger
         Associate Publisher
         Sams Publishing
         201 West 103rd Street
         Indianapolis, IN 46290 USA

Introduction

What Is e-Business?

More than a global communications technology and greater in scope and adoption than television when first introduced, the Internet is changing how products and services are marketed and sold, and increasing the speed of change in many industries. As with any significant change, there are both opportunities and threats. The intent of this book is to provide you with the necessary tools to understand the Internet's impact on your business and its direction. With any significant change, you have the opportunity to either capitalize on it or be reactive and eventually have the technology change your business. Giving you the tools to proactively capitalize on the Internet is the mission of this book. The role of the application service provider, or ASP, as a trusted technology guide is covered thoroughly throughout this book, as are actual case studies from companies who provide ASP-based software and services, in addition to early adopters who have already integrated ASP offerings into their businesses. e-Market Dynamics corporation, a market research firm that specializes in tracking Internet adoption, has recently completed an analysis of adoption rates by technology-produced analysis. Figure I shows the adoption curves by technology. Notice the Internet's adoption curve relative to previous-generation technologies.

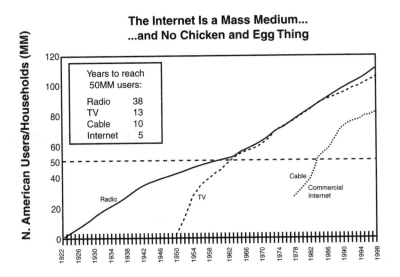

The Internet Is a Mass Medium...
...and No Chicken and Egg Thing

Years to reach
50MM users:

Radio	38
TV	13
Cable	10
Internet	5

N. American Users/Households (MM)

Radio   TV   Cable   Commercial Internet

1922 1926 1930 1934 1938 1942 1946 1950 1954 1958 1962 1966 1970 1974 1978 1982 1986 1990 1994 1998

Figure I   e–Market Dynamics corporation technology adoption curve analysis.

The terms e-business and e-commerce have found their way into the headlines of our evening news programs, newspapers, and magazines. To call a business a pure e-business is to miss the point of the Internet's contribution to streamlining all aspects of an enterprise. e-Business is about taking the strengths of your business and making them even stronger—more available to your customers and suppliers—and ultimately more efficient through the use of online applications. e-Business is taking the strengths of the Internet and applying them to your business. The Internet has grown so quickly because it's a communications platform that is ideally suited for commerce and the streamlining of tasks throughout an organization.

With the first goal of this book being to provide you an overview of what e-business is, the second is to provide you with a framework for seeing how application service providers make e-business happen. With Microsoft, Oracle, and others defining themselves as being in the service business within the next five years as opposed to the software arena, there is a need to understand the ASP delivery approach and the implications for organizations on a global level. This book is focused on watching how many of the larger organizations are adopting the ASP model today, because their adoption rates and approaches to integrating applications over the Internet are indicative of how the overall market will mature.

Who This Book Is Meant For

Developed specifically for technical professionals who are responsible for evaluating new technologies for their organization, this book is meant for intermediate to advanced information systems and business strategy professionals who routinely have the task of evaluating new technologies to determine the impact on their organizations. The terms and concepts throughout the book focus on how existing networking and Intranet technology can be leveraged to best serve your customers. There is also an abundance of market research information throughout this book that provides valuable information you can use to define the direction of initiatives throughout your organization. Information on e-business, including the application service provider role, and ultimately how an organization can capitalize on the Internet are all presented to assist you with your plans, initiatives, and strategies for leveraging the Internet.

How This Book Is Organized

Designed to provide you with a flexible structure for getting up to speed on e-business concepts in conjunction with the ASP model, this book is organized in sections for ease of learning.

Part I: Market Needs Driving e-Business

Part I starts with an overview of the building blocks of strong e-business strategy. Chapters 1 through 4 provide the essentials of e-business, including how the role of application service providers has evolved over time into the force they are today. Chapter 1, "Meeting the Challenge of e-Business with Application Service Providers," includes definitions of e-marketing, e-commerce, and e-operations, as well as an explanation of how ASPs have delivered e-business solutions into some of the world's largest organizations.

Chapter 1 also provides a glimpse into a dominant market dynamic occurring today, which is the migration of value-added resellers into application service providers. Not content with hardware margins anymore, many value-added resellers are actively working to get sales agreements with Oracle, Corio, Interliant, and even Microsoft, to resell these applications over the Internet. These VARs are stabilizing their relationships with clients to provide their valued customers growth paths into the future, and in the process are creating a future for themselves as well. As a result of the influx of VARs entering this industry, there are segmentation strategies occurring rapidly already. This segmentation of the market into small business-focused ASPs that are focused on the mid-tier, and the largest ASPs that are focused on the Fortune 1000 are described in this chapter. You'll also learn how the VARs comprising these ASPs are actually driving segmentation based on the relationships they had with key customers when selling just hardware. This chapter ends with a series of success stories highlighting where the ASP model has been successfully used, and where the challenges exist in using the ASP model within a business.

Chapter 2, "What Drives Application Service Providers (ASPs)?" profiles how the needs of businesses are answered by the application service provider method of software distribution. With the needs of customers comes a definition of business models used by the over 200 ASPs in the world today, given the ASP Industry Consortium's last membership count. The business needs that drive the ASP model to ever-higher levels of adoption include labor shortages in key areas; the rate of technological development, which fuels increasing Internet access times and points of access; the increase in distance learning, which includes application service provider's content and applications; and the increasing need for organizations of all sizes to launch more products in less time. The development timeframe requirements of many companies is now 50% of what it was just three years ago, which translates into getting twice as much development done in half the time.

With a wide variety of approaches to enabling applications, there is a correspondingly high growth of business models that are focused on capitalizing on the opportunities that exist in this industry. Chapter 2 provides an overview of each model, with a focus on how the personalization and accountability are delivering service levels essential for driving e-business adoption in businesses of all sizes. Having accountability for the results of an ASP's work is crucial for the success of a program, as is the offering of personalization options from your Web sites. The business models, which vary in terms of their personal service and personalization, are profiled in Chapter 2. The variety of business models presented in this chapter underscore how competitive the ASP landscape is becoming as well. The breadth of models is covered in detail, showing their relative strengths and weaknesses. At the core of the ASP model is the value propositions of alleviating labor shortages through technology development. The opportunities for distance learning and the ability to get both company-specific and product development information out to regional offices efficiently using the Internet are also reasons that the ASP approach to software delivery is becoming more pervasive. One of the primary drivers propelling the ASP industry to higher levels of adoption is the need for distance learning in companies of all sizes. The need for sharing information on key projects through collaborative tools, sometimes called the e-operations suite of services, is also a critical driver in the overall ASP marketplace. Lastly, one of the key customer segments driving the adoption of the application service provider model are small businesses that are beset with challenges to enable and manage their growth. Chapter 2 also covers this overall focus on growth from the mid-range companies to small businesses.

Chapter 3, "Business Needs Driving e-Business Growth," looks into the needs that are driving e-business growth in the B2B and B2C sectors, and why B2B is growing so quickly. The need for greater time and cost savings, the need for driving a greater velocity of transactions, and the need for serving multiple locations of a growing company with distributed operations all contribute to the growth and acceptance of the ASP model. Chapter 3 also looks at the risks of the ASP model and its implications for meeting needs in businesses of all sizes, thereby rendering a greater return on investment in the ASP model made at the beginning of an integration project. This chapter also illustrates other risks of the ASP model, including the aspects of security of data, adoption rates of key applications, and the issue of Service Level Agreements (SLAs).

SLAs are going to be one of the greatest differentiators for ASPs, so when choosing an ASP be sure to check into what their SLAs are and the terms associated with them. Throughout this book the quantification of trust concept is extensively used. The SLA quantifies the concept of quantification of trust. This chapter ends with a case study of Christopher Radko, a company who is today using tools for streamlining their e-operations tasks.

With the first three chapters looking at the needs driving the concept of ASPs, Chapter 4, "Why Are Businesses Adopting ASPs?" brings the concepts together in greater depth. The chapter shows why companies become early adopters of this model, and focuses on the characteristics of companies that share the traits of early adopters of the ASP model specifically and e-business in general. The "Lessons Learned from Early Adopters" section also looks at the concepts of security and how these companies have been able to develop solutions that alleviate risks of being online with critical data. Application tailoring is also explored in this chapter, as is outbound marketing from sites that have grown from being only unidirectional in communication to being truly bidirectional, to the point of proactively creating and managing expectations with their customers.

Part II: Fundamentals of e-Business

This part explains the many concepts that together define e-business. This part of the book looks first into e-marketing and the implications for being proactive yet considerate in communications to customers, and then works through the e-commerce tools and processes customers of all sizes today expect. You'll also delve into the aspects of e-operations, which include collaboration and integration with legacy databases of all types. In fact, Part II endeavors to provide you with a thorough roadmap for the future of e-business along the dimensions of e-marketing, e-commerce, and e-operations. In short, this section is an e-Business 101 course format, presenting the concepts of what an e-business is by using the building blocks associated with each area defined.

One of the most interesting aspects of the ASP model from a total service experience level is the type of partnerships and the depth of service they provide in the context of the total customer experience. This section also has a chapter devoted to the rapidly growing arena of partnerships in the ASP arena and what their implications are for you.

More than any other type of Web site today, businesses of all sizes are building e-marketing sites to communicate what makes them different, and therefore more valuable, to their customers. Chapter 5, "Communicating Online Using e-Marketing," defines how companies are using an e-marketing strategy to create a unique identity for themselves online, including the implications of managing branding in e-business. Just as everything else on the Web tends to happen much more quickly than in print or other forms of media and communications, the same holds true in branding. It's like working with paint that dries twice as fast. The quickness that the Web provides can actually be an advantage for companies who are looking to get the most out of their e-marketing efforts. Chapter 5 is focused on helping you get the most out of your e-marketing efforts so you can get the feedback you need to further your business.

Looking at more innovative ways of communicating with customers, this chapter looks at how to create customer listening systems, how to drive e-marketing product innovation by creating virtual product councils, and how to get the customer more involved in the development process. You'll also find an explanation of how to define design and site objectives with an ASP for an e-marketing site. You also learn what steps to take to handle the integration of your catalog with back-end systems, including legacy data, which if used in the context of a total marketing effort, can turn into a tool for personalizing your customers' experiences with you. The chapter ends with a case study of how companies are using e-marketing sites to advance their message while getting an interactive dialog going with their customers.

Chapter 6, "Selling Online: How e-Commerce Works with ASPs," looks into the aspects of selling products and even scheduling services via a Web site. This chapter assumes that an application provider will be part of the process of creating an online catalog, so the steps provided in the chapter are consultative to the process of working with another company to create a catalog-driven Web site. As with e-commerce or the sale of products over the web, there is also the need for defining a cross-linking strategy with vendors who are providing products for the catalog, the use of dynamic pricing and auctions, and a plan for defining the day-to-day running of an e-commerce Web site. This is clearly the most important aspect of an e-commerce site development: making it easy to change, easy to manage, and easy to upgrade. This chapter ends with an overview of how you can develop alternate scenarios for growing your e-commerce strategy.

Arguably the biggest reason the Internet gets so much press today is the role it is playing as both a communications and commerce exchange, which also has the potential to deliver significant time and cost savings within companies of all sizes. There is a driving need for collaboration of multinational and global companies with their subsidiaries. Mid-sized companies that have locations throughout a state, region, or country, and small businesses that typically purchase products and services from companies located in different time zones can benefit from having collaborative tools available through their intranets.

In Chapter 7, "Automating Your Business and Information with e-Operations," the need for sharing information in real-time is driving the adoption of a class of applications and services called e-operations. Included in this suite of services (as ASPs are more adept at differentiating themselves through both services and application excellence) are e-procurement, e-logistics, Customer Relationship Management (CRM), and the continual migration of applications from Oracle and others into streamlining data flows. The key metric of performance in this arena is ultimately the return on investment. As the industry matures, the focus will increasingly be on trying to quantify the actual contribution of applications and services to a firm's bottom line. Today the direction is looking at automating information flow with the goal of shortening time-to-market of products for the company adopting the suite of e-operations tools. One of the key points of this chapter is the need to make e-operations map specifically to the needs and legacy structure of a company. As every company has a different set of processes and structure, it follows that e-operations tools need to be mapped to specific needs within an organization. This concept is covered throughout the chapter, because it's important to get a solid foundation for e-operations support at the most basic levels within an organization.

The majority of the time e-business gets mentioned in the press is probably when an alliance has been created between two or more companies for their mutual benefit. Chapter 8, "Understanding Acquisitions and Alliances in the ASP Marketplace," delves into the subject of partnerships. Far from being fraternal, these alliances are often created to either provide technology access for a customer-rich company, or provide a large potential customer base for a promising new technology with little commercial exposure. The end result of these alliances is typically a more robust offering for a lower price for the companies targeted by the alliance or partnership in the first place. There is an overwhelming momentum today for companies to create partnerships, and the ones that are solidly focused on a business model that adds measurable value for the end customer will survive. Strip away all the hype, and you find either a shell of a partnership or a real one, which is generating revenue for both parties and delivering value in the process. This chapter is focused on Cisco's rapidly expanding approach to handling its acquisitions and growth through partnerships. Company profiles in terms of their partnership efforts also covered in this chapter include BroadVision, CommerceOne, Interliant, Microsoft, Sun Microsystems, and Zland.com.

Part III: Architecting and Perfecting e-Business Strategies

With the e-business foundation laid in Part II, this part of the book drives toward the more challenging and correspondingly higher returns aspects of creating an e-business strategy.

Starting with security in Chapter 9, "Planning for Security with Your ASP," this part of the book is focused on how to leverage the investments made by the ASP you choose to get the best performance possible through its data center. This is actually one of the more interesting and often not discussed aspects of the ASP relationship with clients. Many times, companies can derive benefits such as performance reporting services, development of fault-tolerance for beta programs under development, and the fulfillment of SLAs through the data center being an accountable member of the team with ASPs. This chapter also looks into what's involved in migrating databases from your own servers to a data center, the role of ODBC in the ASP model, and the need for having ever-greater levels of fault tolerance and compatibility with your data sets compared with the tools in the data center. The need for checking on the migration tools available on the operating system you're using today is also discussed. Chapter 9 also includes advanced information on the issues of security and quantification of trust.

Being able to build a strategy that lasts saves you the time of having to continually re-architect your roadmap and direction. Chapter 10, "Developing a Scalable e-Business Strategy," provides a series of steps and insights for creating a scalable e-business strategy that focuses on maximizing the differentiation you have in both products and services. As the need for businesses to continually differentiate themselves grows, so grows the need for an ASP to offer services that make it unique. Building an e-business strategy using the feedback from several ASPs can be valuable, and this chapter provides a listing of key success factors for creating a scalable strategy. Ending with a case study from Sun Microsystem's SunTone Program, this chapter looks into the aspects of technology and e-business strategy scalability as a competitive tool.

With scalability comes the need for planning how all the aspects of an e-business strategy hosted through an ASP come together into a cohesive series of steps for accomplishing your ultimate e-business objectives. Chapter 11, "Pulling It All Together into an e-Business Strategy," provides a framework for handling the role of application integration over time with your sites. This framework includes the implications of having a Virtual Private Network, offering applications over it for specific audiences within your organization, and having an intranet developed by the application service provider you partner with. You'll also learn to show how the components of an e-business strategy change over time and how you can take advantage of the change. Lastly, this chapter provides a look at what actual e-business strategy looks like from several companies actively developing their various e-marketing, e-commerce, and e-operations individual initiatives. There is also a case study of Buy.com to show the progression of its e-business strategy in conjunction with the focus on renewed branding of the popular Web site. This chapter delivers what the final result of the study of an e-business strategy is all about: building a consistent, scalable, and actionable e-business strategy.

Anything that gets measured gets better. It has to because there is a focus on it, and that's the idea of this last chapter. Chapter 12, "Knowing You Are Doing It Right: Measuring Results," starts with an overview of the metrics of success in measuring the performance of a Web site. By looking beyond the common metrics often quoted in the industry today, the chapter provides insights into how you can create your own metrics for measuring the performance of your Web site and the ancillary e-commerce being generated from it. You'll also find a helpful reference of tools, some free and others available for a fee, which provide you a starting point for defining how you will measure the performance of your site. This chapter provides insights into how to use customer listening systems, including questionnaires and surveys of all types, to accurately measure customer satisfaction with your site. There is also a case study that profiles how the metrics of commerce applicable to Gateway.com and others actively are used in creating product direction and positioning objectives. You'll learn how to use the Web as a bidirectional, dynamic channel of communication for gauging the needs of your customers and thereby ensuring their satisfaction levels. This chapter's goal is to provide the framework for providing that level of feedback from your efforts on your Web site. As with any metric, there also needs to be the sharing of expectations with your ASP, and having the quantified set of expectations written into the Service Level Agreements (SLAs) with your ASP to ensure the highest performance possible while maintaining scalability and room for expansion.

Market Needs Driving e-Business

I

1

Meeting the Challenge of e-Business with Application Service Providers

CHANGING HOW COMPANIES SERVE their customers and compete for new business, the Internet is proving to be an area of commerce that delivers responsiveness at higher levels than was possible ever before. In an age in which businesses that would have taken years to build are created and grown in a matter of months, the essential components of any strong business—which include excellent service, measurable results, and the ability to stay focused on the customer—are essential for these companies to continue growing. For years companies have hired experts to provide services that would have taken significant investment to develop in-house. The emerging class of e-business providers, the application service providers, is fulfilling the need for e-business strategy development and execution, freeing companies to focus on perfecting what they do best. This book aims to provide you with the guidance necessary to create an e-business strategy and first decide whether the application service provider model is right for your organization, and then second, what steps you need to take to make sure you get the most impact in working with an application service provider.

How e-Business Is Changing the Way Companies Compete

The Internet augments the tools your business can use for overcoming challenges to accomplish goals, but it also presents an entirely new series of challenges for you to contend with. Think of it as a tool for communicating more frequently than was previously possible due to time and distance constraints. At its best, the Internet gives you the flexibility to serve more customers in less time, generate entirely new classes of customers at diverse and remote geographic locations, and provide feedback to them on issues they care about. By increasing your communication capabilities, the Internet can strengthen the relationships you already have with your customers; however, as with any tool, you need to use it correctly. If you do, you can make the most of your existing strengths and extend the capabilities of your business. The Internet has great leverage and is quickly challenging other forms of communication as the fastest-growing communications technology ever.

Staying focused on what you and your company do well while extending your strengths and messaging via the Internet is the essence of e-business. e-Business represents a new set of tools that gives your company the chance to compete more effectively than ever before.

The effects of e-business strategies in companies are often immediate and noticeable. This is most visible in highly competitive industries, travel for example, in which customer satisfaction coupled with speed and accuracy of execution is everything. Service and personal communication is critical. The increasing role of e-business strategies in the travel industry alone shows that businesses are now more focused than ever on competing for the customer.

Competition in many industries is taking on an entirely different series of characteristics than before because of e-business. The increasing use of e-business tools by start-up and small businesses is creating an entirely new type of competitor. This emerging class of competitors could be called "hyper competitors," in that their growth is dictated only by the speed of their combined e-business and traditional approaches to gaining customers. Additionally, established mid-tier and higher-end competitors are either piloting e-business programs or launching entire e-business initiatives. To anyone outside the industries experiencing this level of competition it looks as though these companies are abandoning their core strategies and are going to the Web with aggressive e-business strategies. Taking a closer look, it's apparent that the companies with the largest e-business initiatives and efforts actually are leveraging what they do best—their core competency—with the latest tools on the Internet through e-business providers.

e-Business has the potential to give your company the chance to focus on what it does best while using e-business applications, tools, and techniques to compete more effectively for revenue. At the same time, you can drive costs out of the processes used for doing business.

Contrary to the misconception that undertaking an e-business strategy means drastically modifying your business, nothing could be further from the truth. An e-business strategy delivers its greatest value when the applications, tools, and techniques of e-business strengthen the core business and its focus on customers.

It's All About the Customer

The speed and accuracy of communication that is possible using the Internet is unmistakable. World events, such as the fall of the Berlin Wall, the development of entirely new countries within weeks, and the nearly instant newsfeeds from anywhere to anyone with a browser, continually underscore the rapidity with which information is communicated today. Email is a classic example of how communication can be instant and unmistakable in intent—even more so than phone conversations—across literally thousands of miles in seconds.

Information is now immediate. If it's personalized to you it has an even greater impact because it speaks to your interests. The Web has proven itself a powerful communications tool that is able to handle commerce as well.

The ability to have immediate information, communicate quickly, and provide personalized messaging all have implications for your business. The fact that many companies are now having to modify production processes to return their focus to the customer instead of to operational efficiencies is further evidence that e-business is affecting every business, every day. Although your company might or might not have an e-business strategy today, it is undoubtedly being affected by the quickening pace of change made possible by accelerated communication via the Web. Customers want to communicate with you via email; people at trade shows, conventions, and even dinner parties ask for your company's Web site address. Your competitors, even small ones that appear to be regional in focus, have Web sites up, and some are taking orders. International competitors once thought to be either uncompetitive or out of touch with local markets suddenly have the potential to sell anywhere, anytime. e-Business is making competition global and providing opportunities for businesses everywhere to compete in markets not accessible before.

e-Business strategies are really all about creating more opportunities for your company to increase revenues and decrease costs. It's about extending your existing business with the latest applications, tools, and techniques to get more done in less time and save money in the process.

There is a common perception that e-business is e-xpensive and tends to take the focus of companies away from their customers and place the focus into the processes (which need to have a customer focus in them anyway). The fact is, however, that the winning e-business strategies are simply focused on building lasting relationships with customers and slicing waste from manual processes. Many companies are working with application service providers (ASPs) that provide the necessary applications, tools, and techniques for driving the parts of an e-business strategy. The role of the ASP is one of technology partner, and is described in detail throughout this book.

Two of the best examples of how companies are using e-business strategies to better serve their customers are Dell Computer and Gateway, direct PC marketers. Dell, at last count, has generated over $750 million in revenues from its Web sites alone in the last full fiscal year. Gateway's extensive e-business programs are also commonly used by many of the leading colleges and universities for ordering PCs and supplies online. What is fascinating about each of these companies is their absolute commitment to having the customer drive their processes internally. You can see that commitment when touring the production floor at Gateway Computer in North Sioux City, South Dakota for example. Orders placed on the Web site the night before are built during the first production shift, which starts at 3 a.m.. These workers, over 4,000 of them, take individualized PC orders and, working in teams, create configurations to the customer's exact requirements, down to the software being loaded, even the addresses that will be used for making the PC plug into a corporate network. Each PC is then tested to specific requirements and then boxed and shipped, in many cases for delivery within 24 hours. Gateway also tracks how many PCs are delivered by the "promise date," which is when the customer was promised the PC. Climbing in performance, Gateway now ships nearly all PCs on or before their promised date.

The customer pervasiveness is evident even in the customer service organizations of these companies. Technicians answering phones and email inquiries are given star status, with vacation trips and awards for outstanding service to customers. Program managers who handle the communication programs with customers on one hand and with engineering, marketing, and development organizations on the other also have the option of bringing in additional materials to meet a customer's need. The focus on the customer is unmistakable.

The direct model of selling PCs illustrates how the voice of the customer needs to permeate a company for it to grow. The role of e-business is that of communicating with customers and giving them the chance to communicate their needs to you. The applications, tools, and techniques available in e-business also are aimed at saving production costs. Gateway, for example, uses its intranet to coordinate production schedules between departments, material planning, and even scheduling the delivery of PC parts and components to the factory. This all leads to cost efficiency because Gateway doesn't need to keep inventory sitting around in warehouses, and can instead use its financial resources for serving customers more efficiently over the phone, in its stores, and on the Web. Gateway is using e-business to extend its capability to reach more prospective customers and serve current customers more responsively.

Personalization Is King

The ongoing competition between larger, multinational banks and their smaller, regional counterparts is an interesting battle of slogans. The larger banks talk about global breadth, the capability to serve you from Sri Lanka to Stockholm. Smaller banks have countered with the more personalized approach of knowing you by name, not by account number, and precisely tailoring financial programs to your needs. Of these two approaches, the latter is definitely winning as the need for personalized service is skyrocketing. For example, Compass Bank, a small bank in the southeastern United States, started out by having as many satellite offices as possible, many located in the smaller communities and cities throughout the southern United States. The satellite offices were able to complete complex transactions while maintaining people on staff to give personalized service to every customer at the bank. Lines were only two or three people long even during lunch periods. Not surprisingly, Compass Bank is one of the highest growth banks in the United States today. The bank's growth is directly related to its personalized approach to handling the needs of customers. This great competitive virtue can actually be accentuated by an e-business strategy.

The ability to be unique and personable on a Web site is going to define the winners and the losers in the coming five years of widespread e-business adoption. One of the best sites is the legendary amazon.com. Called by investment analysts the *stickiness factor of a site*, the capability of a site to retain customers is considered crucial in developing ancillary business models that complement and grow a core business. One of the best approaches to "stickiness" is the My Yahoo! portal, which gives you the flexibility of creating online stock quotes and news categories, and even alerts when your friends get online. It's free as well, which is true of all sites offering personalization. Plan to personalize your e-business strategy to make customers stick with your site.

When looking for an ASP, focus on the aspect of personalized support. There are literally hundreds of ASPs, some focused on the largest corporations and some focused on specific vertical markets. This issue of personalized support is critical for your e-business strategy to be successful.

e-Responsiveness

Because the transfer of information is immediate, responding to customer needs is essential for a company to grow. Having the capability to respond quickly and accurately to meet the needs of your customers can spell the difference between holding onto them or losing them to a competitor. The role of e-business is to provide your company with the capability to take responsiveness to your customers to entirely new levels of performance. Working with ASPs that focus on how to empower companies to facilitate communication with customers, you can create applications that increase your company's responsiveness. The "hyper competitors" mentioned at the beginning of this chapter are taking personalization and responsiveness to new levels, and earning customers in the process. Because e-business is about extending the strengths of your company, service and responsiveness will increasingly be the factor that differentiates growing companies from companies that are merely hanging on.

When customers can get instant stock quotes, instant weather, instant response on bank account queries, and even instant greeting cards, the expectations are that your company will be able to keep up. That's one of the aspects of e-business that is very real and immediate: Being responsive to customers can drive up the loyalty to your company. ASPs are working every day on the challenges of taking businesses to the next level of responsiveness, which means your company can potentially leverage off the ASPs' development efforts so you don't have to do it all yourself. The ASP model is getting customers because many companies don't want to re-invent the wheel; they want to learn from ASPs that do these tasks as part of their core business.

Taking on the task of measuring how satisfied your customers are with your level of responsiveness is critical. What gets measured, gets better, and throughout this book I provide metrics that give you the opportunity to better gauge the results of your e-business strategy.

Strengthening Your Competitive Advantage Through Application Delivery

By working with e-business experts at an ASP, you can have an e-business strategy that ensures your company's competitiveness and at the same time keep your efforts focused on serving customers. In working with these companies, it's essential that your expectations and application needs be clearly communicated. Taking your company's needs and defining them in the context of a services/product roadmap is crucial. Although many of the companies you work with as a supplier or customer have service and product roadmaps, you should have your own roadmap before fully starting an e-business strategy and working with an ASP to implement it. Figure 1.1 shows an example of a product roadmap.

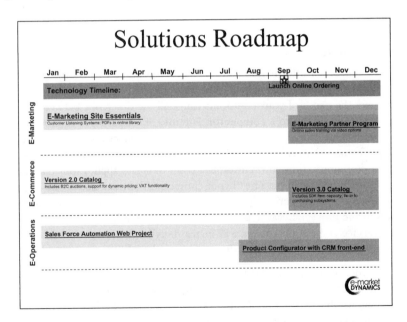

Figure 1.1   Having a roadmap gives your customers and suppliers a good idea of what your plans are and how they relate to your product strategy.

The role of the ASP increasingly will be seen as critical in the delivery of applications, tools, and techniques in addition to providing insights into how to build a Web site that is responsive to customers' needs. Having this roadmap will provide you with the flexibility and freedom to quickly make decisions on which direction to take your e-business strategies.

Steps to Building an e-Business Roadmap

One of the key factors that is shared across all successful ASP implementations is a simple, clear direction of how the ASP's product offerings contribute to the accomplishment of the clients' objectives. A roadmap is one of the essential communication tools for graphically describing the direction your company wants to take with its e-business strategy. Often roadmaps are referred to and even drawn on white boards, yet taking the steps to actually create a document not only provides a great communications tool but also brings closure to any issues in your company as to what belongs on the roadmap. It is both a consensus- and communications-building document.

The following are the steps for building a successful e-business roadmap:

1. Start with your existing product roadmap, and if you are a services business, a map of your existing services. For each product or service planned, define the needs being addressed in your current and potential customer base. These needs are those of your customer—and the value that your product or service brings to them.

2. Actively visit your customers and get an idea of how they are using the Internet for other tasks. Ask them how you could be using the Internet to make their transactions with your company more streamlined. These customer interviews can be conducted both in person and over the telephone. It's a great idea to actually visit a few customers a week to get first-hand impressions of what their thoughts are on how your company could develop tools to serve them better over the Internet.

3. Query your product marketing, product management, sales, operations, and production teams for information on customer feedback they have heard for product ideas. One company found the best ideas for new products and services came from the operations team, which worked hand-in-hand with customers to solve their connectivity challenges.

4. Work with industry analysts such as International Data Corporation, Gartner Group, The Yankee Group, and Forrester Research. All these companies actively track e-business trends and emerging markets, so working with them can provide market forecasts by key area. You can find International Data Corporation at www.idc.com. You should also check out The Yankee Group at www.yankeegroup.com and Forrester Research at www.forrester.com.

5. Develop a pro-forma product roadmap and make the priorities clear for your e-business strategy. When you have reached this point it will be easy to answer quickly the question of what the top three priorities are for your e-business strategy. Be clear and concise with the figures and logic because this document defines the direction you'll give to members of the ASP team you'll work with.

6. Begin building consensus for the roadmap internally with the teams that assisted with input in addition to your senior management and the board of directors if necessary. These teams are cross-functional teams that are responsible for making the project move along to completion. The purpose of this step is to get the focus on the future direction the roadmap shows for the integration of e-business into your business. The roadmap at this point is very clear and accurate, with figures substantiated from the research companies mentioned earlier in this list.

7. With the consensus completed, use the roadmap to begin evaluating ASPs that can assist you in making it come to fruition. For example, if your company is primarily serving consumers and has a sizable catalog of items, you need to find an ASP with catalog expertise and the ability to scale. Taking the priorities from the roadmap and building a short RFP is a good way to get all the bidding ASPs and even Web site developers on the same level. Although the work to this level looks formidable, it will provide a strong sense of continuity to the responses you get. You'll get a much better idea of what each ASP has to offer and cut through conjecture as to what each can truly deliver.

8. Have each of the three finalist ASPs and consulting companies provide suggested pricing for the roadmap completion and comments on whether they can beat your deadlines. This will give you a good idea of which ASP has technology, strength, and flexibility.

9. As the ASP decision is being finalized, the roadmap becomes a vision of what needs to be done. It's truly a beginning with the end in mind, which makes the closure on tasks much easier. The finalized roadmap is a document that is apt to change as your customers' preferences change over time, and modified within time horizons in which changes can be made. The important aspect of a roadmap is that the applications listed will have metrics associated them, giving you the chance to measure how well you are serving your customers based on the direction chosen. The best roadmaps are living documents, reflecting the changing tastes and preferences of the customers it's intended to serve.

It is crucial that you develop an accurate and effective product roadmap, because you need to anchor your business and its expectations clearly before engaging an application service provider. The roadmap becomes a compass that provides direction for your company's e-business strategy. Many of the companies that have integrated e-business strategies into their companies *without* a roadmap have had to create one eventually out of the need for clarity of direction. The roadmap represents your expectations in writing for the application service providers to bid on and fulfill.

Exploring the Building Blocks of e-Business with an Application Service Provider

It's best to look at e-business from the standpoint of its key attributes. The ability to quickly and accurately communicate with customers is what differentiates those companies who have successfully taken on an e-business strategy relative to companies who have not. An essential element of any e-business strategy is leveraging the instantaneous nature of communications on the Internet to understand customers more accurately than has been possible in the past. In many respects, the e-business strategy you develop will actually be a communications strategy.

e-Marketing

The most basic of e-business components, *e-marketing* is focused on getting an identity online. It's sometimes called "brochureware" and is typically an HTML version of the company's brochures and product descriptions. Many companies are taking the brochureware concept a step further and focusing on providing PDF files of their most popular brochures for use by customers. e-Marketing is all about using one-way communication to establish an identity online.

Typically, a company just beginning on the Internet starts with an e-business strategy that focuses purely on this aspect of its site. The outcome of this type of strategy is typically getting leads via in-bound telephone calls or faxed orders. This area of e-business is getting the most competition by far.

Companies that do Web hosting, ISPs that provide Internet access, and Web site developers are getting into this arena. The outcome of all these companies entering this space is that the price of Web sites is dropping quickly. By early 2002, a pure e-marketing site, even to the level of one you pay for today, will be free. Because there is no real commerce happening on the site, the business models of companies offering e-marketing are based either on upselling into e-commerce solutions or using advertising as the basis for generating revenue. Clearly even Web site developers, many of whom are also in other businesses, are also driving down the cost of a strong e-marketing site.

Site prices are dropping in e-marketing due to two major factors. The first is the advent of the click and build companies such as `bigstep.com`, `freemerchant.com`, and others that offer small businesses the chance to create an e-marketing site on their own free in exchange for having a banner ad in place. The second is that small businesses are realizing that having a Web site is more than just having a Web site developer who can create HTML pages for purely marketing purposes. As a result of this second market dynamic, the early adopter small businesses are going with ASPs who can integrate both a catalog and an intranet into the total Web presence. Take the two market factors together and rapid price degradation results in the e-marketing arena. Any company just focused on e-marketing today will have a tough future. That's where the concept of the ASP really is getting traction with the small business community; the ASPs are seen as being able to handle a company's present and potential needs, whereas the present e-marketing suppliers are increasingly being seen as a "point" and not a complete solution.

In this market area, the application service provider supplies a breadth of more robust tools than would be available for a Web site developer. The ASPs see this area as the eventual "loss leader" in the marketplace and are gearing their product strategies toward e-operations and collaboration tools. Given the market dynamics that are favoring the customer, free e-marketing sites are going to become increasingly available over time. Watching how ASPs differentiate their free offerings from their premium services is valuable from the standpoint of seeing how best to use your budgeted resources for extending an online strategy. The following sections provide a list of items you can use to check into the depth of an ASP in this area.

Online Surveys

Recall that the essence of any good e-business strategy is the capability of a company to serve its customers more responsively and in the process get to know them better. This is clearly necessary and is possible using online customer surveys. If an ASP has a product offering in this area, it's probably the result of the ASP doing surveys itself. Make sure the ASP you are considering has the tools available to get you in touch with your customers.

Lead-Generation Tools

The need to feed your sales force leads is crucial for the long-term growth of your company. Does the ASP you are looking to partner with have the capability to generate leads from the sites it is hosting? Be sure to check to see whether the ASP has a track record of providing these types of tools.

Email-Management Programs

The ASP should provide email auto-response capabilities that enable you to define the messages being sent back. The need for generating an accurate and timely response, even to emails, is critical.

ShockWave and Flash Templates

You want to engage and get your Web site visitors interested in your company and its products. The ongoing development of ShockWave and Flash templates is one of the areas in which e-marketing focused ASPs are differentiating themselves. These templates provide for the appearance of a custom designed e-marketing site at less than a third of the cost.

e-Commerce

The capability to handle transactions online is one of the most vital areas of e-business. *e-Commerce* is mainly focused on the task of completing transactions online. The key e-commerce aspects to consider when selecting an ASP to partner with include the ASP's relative level of security offered, its experience with fraud verification, whether the ASP has international expertise, and whether the ASP sees auctions in their future. In short, you need to determine the level of the ASP's experience and whether they are capable of scaling with your business. The e-commerce aspect of your e-business strategy is the most crucial, because this is the method of generating revenue. Here are the key issues you need to work through with an ASP before using them for an e-commerce solution for your business. To begin thinking about e-commerce in your e-business strategy, consider asking your potential ASP candidates these questions:

How many years of experience do you have in the e-commerce arena?

For which companies have you successfully completed a catalog? Which are customers today?

What is your direction on auctions? (You should be looking for an answer that includes dynamic pricing and the eventual integration of auctions into a catalog.)

What percentages of the catalogs you've developed are business-to-business? What percentage is business-to-consumer?

What is the top catalog limit in terms of number of items? What's the typical size of the catalog you deploy?

Do you have real-time links to Federal Express, UPS, and others for checking order status for my customers?

Can you integrate Federal Express directly into the catalog you are building for me?

How long does it take for your company to create a catalog of 100 items? Can I integrate PDF files into the description fields of the catalog?

These are just a few questions you need to ask an ASP before getting started on the broader topics of your catalogs. Start by viewing your business as a global enterprise because the Internet opens up opportunities for getting customers on a global level very quickly. One company, for example, started selling chocolates online and quickly had over four times the number of customers in a matter of months, three from outside the United States. e-Commerce makes a global economy a reality.

e-Operations

The e-operations area is where the most value can be obtained from an e-business strategy and where cost reductions through the use of the Internet are possible, because it is in this area where e-business strategies get the greatest leverage from the Internet. *e-Operations* consist of e-procurement, e-logistics, and customer relationship management. The focus within e-operations is to use the technologies that serve as the basis of the Internet to make transactions more efficient, to share information more adeptly, and to facilitate the completion of supply chains. Keeping in mind that e-operations are focused on the collaborative aspects of communicating, this area of e-business is poised for the fastest growth of all areas. Throughout this book there will be many examples of companies who have adopted applications in the e-operations arena for streamlining internal processes.

One of the major differentiators of e-operations relative to e-marketing and e-commerce is that the latter two are focused on maximizing sales, whereas the former is clearly focused on driving down costs to increase the return on investment or ROI. The key metric of success with e-operations is the development of a sound strategy for maximizing the ROI for core functions in your business.

Application Service Providers Deliver e-Business Solutions

The role of the ASP is to be an enabler of tools for businesses of all sizes to use in streamlining their businesses. The tools provided by ASPs make transactions and communications with other organizations and within your own organization more efficient. Here is a brief history of how ASPs have evolved and their delineation by segment served.

Where Do ASPs Come From?

Many people look at the ASP model and say that is harkens back to the timesharing days of the first mainframes. Although the concept of renting applications is not new, the pricing approaches and the availability of the applications via a commerce-enabling technology is. For the first time, a business can check inventory at any time from any Internet connection in the world. Executives can check sales order status and net sales for a given month at any moment, anywhere. This is the differentiating aspect compared to the days of timesharing. Feedback in the ASP model from the hosted applications is immediate and available anywhere. The availability of data 24/7 is transforming businesses more every day, and the approach to distributing software through this model is one of the prime drivers.

Where do the ASPs come from? What are their core competencies? The first series of ASPs evolved out of the VAR channel, others from software companies, and still others from companies that are adept at serving a specific vertical market. What unifies all these companies is their focus on how best to provide responsive service to their customers. The customer and service become the differentiators, with the product being customized in many instances to the exact requirements of a customer. The world of the ASP is one of providing the latitude of options to their customers—it is not a one-size-fits-all world, and personalization is crucial. With the concept of the customer relationship being the asset, here are definitions of how companies have evolved into ASPs.

VARs Migrating for Margin

The value-added reseller or VAR has long had its relationships with clients as its top priority. Increasingly, these companies are being squeezed on margin from the direct sales of servers, workstations, laptops, and desktop computers from Dell, Gateway, Micron, and others. With more and more small businesses favoring the direct model and inbound sales calls to their offices to save them time, the VAR is left with the challenge of re-engineering itself into a viable entity for the future. Many have embraced the role of ASP and several have had much success. What's required for them is the adoption of Web expertise and the capability to create trust in that expertise. They must make the customer see what was once a hardware expert is now a software expert. Companies who have done this successfully include NovaQuest, now WebVision, and Avcom, which is now affiliated with WebHarbor.

Software Companies Seeking Channels

From the largest software companies in the world, including Microsoft, to the smaller vertical market companies, all are interested in pursuing the ASP approach to service revenue as opposed to product sales. Many CEOs of companies working with packaged software are actively working to get away from the high level of dependence on operating systems and get to a Web-based strategy to alleviate the time constraints of updates, the massive challenge of handling the updates in conjunction with operating system upgrades, and the need for testing applications on various hardware platforms. It's a great opportunity to simplify a software business when the Web is used as the delivery mechanism. With licensing revenue for many mid-sized and greater companies, the application service provider approach to distributing applications makes the pricing matrix for a publisher easier to maintain. From the software publisher's perspective there are many benefits, with just two provided here.

Differentiation in the ASP Arena

With so many companies in this area, what makes each unique? One of the most efficient approaches to differentiating them is to look at their market orientation, which is provided in each of the following sections of this chapter. The market orientation and with it, pricing structure, product strategy, level of services offered, and the level of consulting and custom engineering, vary significantly by the size of the customer base. The following profiles by size of customer base are useful to look at as a baseline for evaluating which ASPs you can use for your business.

Small Business Focus and Personal ASPs

Characteristics of ASPs that serve this market include the following:

- ASPs many times are started as service businesses themselves, giving them the capability to better understand the needs of their predominantly service-oriented business customers. From the heritage of serving customers, the ASPs understand how service businesses work.

- This is the segment that the click and sell Web site developers are aiming at. The click and sell companies are focusing on e-marketing for the small business.

- Many times the legacy or history of the company includes being purely a Web site developer, which means the sites developed were purely e-marketing in focus, and many times were built completely in HTML, not XML or dynamic HTML for quick updates.

- Many times small businesses do not have the funds to pay for a customized Web site. It is very common in this area of the market to find Web site developers and ASPs that will work for equity in the customer's company. It's fairly common to see ASPs who have stock in companies that are intending to go public and need a world-class site to get noticed.

- Typical prices for a Web site are below $5,000 and the customer has the ability to edit contents any time he wants. This is particularly true of ASPs using the Notes platform in addition to Java. This pricing is indicative of ASPs that have competitive offerings for mid-size and smaller companies. The pricing associated with going with larger ASP providers, such as Oracle, typically are in the six-figure and even seven-figure range.

- Small businesses need to have one-on-one support, and the companies capable of providing hands-on support and accountability to the small business person will flourish in the coming years. The capability to assist the small businessperson with all types of e-business issues, not just the immediate ones regarding a site, will be a differentiator well into the future.

Mid-Market ASPs and the Evolving VAR

This is the land of the VAR. ASPs serving the mid-market come from the ranks of VARs that are quickly changing their business models to be more competitive with their customers. The common characteristics of ASPs in this market include the following:

- Many VARs are reinventing themselves into ASPs, many times using the applications from IBM and Oracle to create a new series of tools for their customers.

- This market area is where e-operations is getting the majority of new customers, as the core functionality of applications created for Fortune 1000-level accounts are being continually migrated tot this market segment.

- Expect to see increased competition for mid-market business from EDS, Oracle, and others as the need for having a personalized approach to getting tasks completed with customers increases.

- e-Operations innovation for the mid-sized business will drive demand for these solutions in small business. ASPs offering these applications and services will have technology alliances with other companies to create value for their collective customers.

Top-Tier ASPs: Oracle and SAP in the Fortune 1000 market

When looking at the highest end of the market, the delineating characteristics of ASPs are as follows:

- Cycle to implement is typically the longest in this segment, as is the sales process. With a CIO buying into a pilot project, the adoption time can be cut into a fraction of the time given additional resources.

- Top-tier ASPs typically have an enterprise approach to project management and have teams of analysts that provide expertise in providing legacy data in the development of an ASP solution.

- Applications are almost always a mix of e-commerce and e-operations, mostly focused on the ability to ship items directly from an order on the Web site. Integration to the back end of a corporation is the goal of this approach.

- Increasingly, ASPs serving this market segment do process re-engineering at the same time they are creating links into the back end of corporations to fill orders from catalogs, and also provide key metrics of performance for the site.

Internet Pulse Check and Metrics: Dominant Trends and Predictions

A roadmap for your e-business clarifies to everyone what the key goals and objectives are for your company getting on the Internet in the first place. There are many metrics you can use for evaluating how your ASP initiatives are fairing. This section provides insights into those tools and directions for how to use them.

Key trends, which are driving the ASP marketplace and the breadth of offerings from ASPs you will have to select from in creating your e-business strategy, are driven by the market factors discussed here.

Personal Productivity-Focused ASPs Will Emerge

The introduction of ASPs that offer personal productivity applications over the Internet will make the ASP marketplace grow at a quantum pace. Microsoft's Office

Online initiative is one of the first groundbreaking efforts in this area, in which the entire Office Suite is provided over the Internet. This program within Microsoft has been in a beta test phase with several of the industry's best-known ASPs for over a year. It's also received the endorsement of International Data Corporation, one of the world's leading market research companies.

Considered by many to be a bandwidth issue, providing office suites online is going to be one of the most competitive aspects of the ASP industry for years to come. With Sun Microsystems offering StarOffice free for the downloading from their Web site for the UNIX, x86, and Linux platforms, the competition is going to be fierce for the desktop of the connected professional. Sun's approach of making their office suites available free is driving the download rates into the millions of copies and prompting many smaller, cash-stretched companies to embrace the Sun architecture for their online office suites. Sun Microsystems has done its homework in making the filters for importing and exporting Microsoft Word and Excel-based files compatible with StarOffice. The best news for existing and potential application service providers is that Sun and Microsoft will continue to deliver the highest value possible for the lowest price. Competition in the personal productivity segment is going to drive down the price of these tools rapidly.

Application Service Providers Are Transforming Themselves from Building Sites That Sell to Sites That Save on Costs

One of the most challenging aspects for the first application service providers was defining their identity relative to companies that just provided static HTML pages. Companies that produce HTML pages are commonly called Web site developers. They range in size from many employees to just two or three people working out of their garage. There continues to be the need for accurately defining the differences between Web site developers and application service providers, with the latter clearly having the capability of providing tools and applications that streamline operations and are scalable. HTML is, by definition, not scalable, whereas applications, tools, and techniques delivered by the application service providers you choose to work with need to have the capability to scale their applications in response to your customers' needs.

The ASP Model Will Transform Software Companies into Service-Based Companies

The direction Microsoft, Oracle, IBM, and many other companies are taking with the ASP model clearly shows a fundamental shift in the business models of software companies. Embracing the model, these companies are transforming into services businesses. Steve Ballmer, the recently announced CEO of Microsoft and longtime Senior VP, has actually made the comment that Microsoft is busily transforming itself into a services business. The efforts with Microsoft Office Online underscore the coming shift in Microsoft's strategy. Oracle's Larry Ellison, CEO and founder, has stated many times on CNBC and even at trade shows over the last year that 50% of his company's revenue will be from the Oracle Online product store. IBM's many initiatives in the e-business marketplace have transformed this once hardware-centric company into a company literally defining e-business with each new initiative they roll out.

Syndication of ASP Applications in a Year or Less

The industry's top analysts are predicting that there will soon be ASPs in the market-place that specialize in taking the applications that are already developed and creating a customized look to them for their business customers. This will be one of the primary market drivers allowing e-businesses to enter the ASP marketplace with the simple act of an OEM contract. An OEM (Original Equipment Manufacturer) provider creates customized applications for someone else. The OEM providers of ASP applications, in effect syndicating their applications, will be one of the primary drivers making the cost of adopting an ASP solution drop quickly in the most competitive arenas of product offerings. The syndication-focused ASPs are now in the finalization stages of their application development and will no doubt have major partners when they launch their companies.

VARs and Software Companies Will Become ASPs Themselves

Look for companies that have in the past just sold PCs and networking to become resellers of applications delivered through the ASP model. Although this is national in scope today it will be increasingly apparent at a local level within the coming year or less. That expertise with the ASP model is worth more to companies than the capability to resell hardware. There's more value to customers in the knowledge of e-business. VARs will be redefining themselves with an e-business focus throughout the first decade of the new millennium.

Brick and Mortar Companies Will Embrace the ASP Model

In an effort to differentiate themselves from other brick and mortar companies, many are starting to investigate bundling in ASP services for their business customers. The first step in this area is Staples offering human resources and accounting applications via the ASP model at aggressive prices. The prime target of many of these brick and mortar companies is the 0–100 segment of small businesses, which have enough people on staff for their core businesses, yet do not have the bandwidth for handling ancillary functions. The role of brick and mortar companies offering the ASP model will continue to increase as small businesses begin trusting the ASP model as a delivery mechanism for their applications.

IBM Re-Focuses on Small Businesses with a Personalized ASP Approach

Bolstering its role in the ASP industry today with both the Magic Box Server advertising and promotional programs, Lotus Notes integration strategies with ASPs, and the development of ASP-based solutions using XML and Java, IBM is definitely looking to be a dominant force in the ASP industry for years to come. Look for IBM to provide a personalization component for its ASP-enabled applications by 2001. The focus on creating a personalized commerce experience for IBM customers' end users will be designed as a portal and will be customizable by the customer.

Yahoo! and Dominant Portals Will Enter the ASP Marketplace

Today you can see on the Yahoo! and Excite sites the embracing of "utility" applications, which are just the beginning of their adoption and offering of larger, more business-focused applications. These utility applications meet the fundamental needs of companies to keep track of meetings (calendar functions), communicate (free email), and customize information (MyYahoo.com for example). Look for all the major portals to be ASPs within the next 18 months or less. The fact they are all offering personal productivity tools today actually makes them one of the pioneering ASPs in the personal productivity area. Further, the global presence of these portals is also going to drive demand for localization productivity applications much faster than a single company taking on countries in a sequential approach. The portals, with their global presence, will be some of the first large-scale ASP providers for the average consumer in addition to small business.

Click and Sell Sites Will Be Integrated to the BackOffice Level

There is a series of companies that specializes in the development of e-marketing only sites today, or aiding organizations in the sale of their products over the Internet. These companies have Web sites that provide for the development of a Web site, including the look, colors used, navigational aspects, catalog, and increasingly, the back-end processes typically called BackOffice functionality. Clearly this class of company is interested in delivering greater value over time, and is actively working to create a breadth of applications that can assist with communication processes within a company as well. Looking to create long-term customer retention with their current base, these click and sell companies will be offering accounting, data migration, and other tools to allow their customers to tie back to critical online data from their businesses.

Total Solution Providers Emerge and Battle VARs, Direct PC Sellers

The emerging class of Network Outsourcing and Desktop Services (NODS) is quickly gaining momentum in the low- and medium-levels of the market. Yet the competition in the hardware aspect of these total solution providers is tough, as many potential customers in these markets are actually more interested in having in-bound sales approach them due to the time constraints of running their businesses. Having a single point of contact to provide network connectivity, applications, hardware, and even data hosting is asking any business to trust a single provider with virtually the entire company. The loyalty of businesses to Dell and Gateway and their e-commerce engines is a force these total solution providers will need to deal with. Companies in this area include Everdream and Centerbeam, two well-known companies in the ASP industry that have outstanding management teams. There will be those companies that will adopt the model proposed by these companies, yet for companies offering this service, look for them to OEM syndicated applications to scale their product offerings for their customer bases' diverse needs.

Quantification of Trust and Security

Despite the continual efforts to secure the Web, there are challenges emerging on the average of once a week. Security, and with it the quantification of trust in transactions, is critical for the growth of the entire industry. The focus on making transactions secure is going to be one of the most challenging aspects of the growth of the ASP industry. The focus on quantifying transactions is also going to be the focus of companies who strive to grow through being aggregators of transactions handled by several other members of the supply chain in the past. This is a critical issue that is discussed in detail throughout Chapter 9, "Planning for Security with Your ASP."

Resources for Tracking the ASP Marketplace

As you consider which application service provider will make the best partner for your e-business strategy, review the information sources described in the following sections. These are the industry's leading sources of information. If you are looking at a specific ASP, be sure to get the names of other customers the ASP has served and check its references.

Where to Start?

You might be looking at the ASP industry and seeing this literal mountain of information to sift through to get an idea of what this market area is all about. You don't have to be so daunted by the task because the media and research companies have already taken the mountain of data in this area and made it into an easily traversed terrain. The intent of this book is to provide you the stopover points in the ASP landscape that are worth checking into. But before beginning a tour of the key areas of the ASP marketplace, here are places to visit on the Web to get up to speed and stay current with the ASP industry.

There are also research companies listed that can provide you with the necessary figures and market data to make creating a business plan or even a prospectus (sometimes
called an S1, a document you need to file with the Securities and Exchange commission for going public). In the development of an S1 the credibility of the research
providers is essential, for example. So let's get started with a look at the industry associations, followed by the media companies' approach to providing ASP information,
and ending with the research companies who are adept at sizing the direction and size
of this marketplace. Research companies occasionally offer free ASP-related information on their sites, yet the typical subscription for a full service is $20,000. Obviously,
if you are thinking of creating a business plan and actually launching and running an
ASP, these research companies are definitely worth the investment, especially Forrester
and The Yankee Group.

Industry Sites You Need to Visit Often

Start with the ASP Industry Consortium located at `www.aspindustry.org` or alternatively at `www.aspconsortium.org` (both URLs go to the same site). This is the best site
to check on a daily basis to see the goings-on in this industry. There is a significant
amount of information available free to non-members, including several market sizing
reports that are free for the downloading. The purpose of this site is to provide a central reference point for anyone wanting to learn about the ASP industry. In the
Resources section of this site you'll find a FAQ document, a series of investment and
market research documents free for the downloading, and a listing of industry information sources. The ASP Industry Consortium to date has over 300 members, and has
subcommittees working on best practices, research, education, and membership
focuses. If you are going to be actively involved either as an ASP or by covering the
ASP industry for your company, be sure to visit this site every few days to check on
what's new.

Another great site for checking in on the activities of the ASP industry is WebHarbor.
com (`www.Webharbor.com`). This is the best site for getting up-to-the-minute feeds on
press releases from participants in the ASP industry. This site's focus is on providing a
clearinghouse for information on the ASP industry, and it has a search engine for finding ASPs by functional area. Their publication area is one of the better ones on the
Web dealing with the ASP industry. WebHarbor.com also sponsors an industry newsletter called *ASP Industry News*, which is located at `www.aspindustrynews.com` and is
accessible through the publication area of the WebHarbor site.

One of the first and most-visited sites is from ASP News & Review at `www.aspnews.`
`com`. If you are going to track the ASP industry, then get a subscription to the newsletter offered by this company. It's the industry standard of newsletters in this area and is
written from a perspective of both Europe and the United States. It's delivered
monthly via PDF, which makes it easily read online or printed and read offline. The
content on this site provides an international perspective of the ASP industry.

Definitely worth visiting, the ASP News site is considered one of the most-watched in the industry for international developments in the ASP industry. Custom reports are reasonably priced at this site as well, delving into specific topics surrounding the ASP marketplace. You can find the monthly newsletter at `www.aspnews.com/review.htm`.

Aimed at CIOs and intermediate to advanced IT professionals, ASP Island located at `www.aspisland.com` is comprehensive in content and useful for checking on events happening in the ASP community. All the sites listed here have calendars, yet the presentation of events along the lower-right section of the front page of this site make it easy to stay current with conferences and seminars relevant to this industry.

ASPStreet.com at `www.aspstreet.com` captures the eclectic nature of the ASP industry with its portal appearance and tabs for providing information on events, ASP resources, RFPs, directory of the site, archives, and a logon screen for gaining access to membership-based content. You can spend hours on this site reading about alliances, announcements, new products and services, and initiatives that are occurring the in the ASP industry. This site is comprehensive and provides quick poll results, which are great for getting an idea of the current dynamics in the ASP vendor community.

SearchASP.com at `www.searchASP.com` also has a portal-based approach to providing information and has a running survey on one of the sidebars, which queries businesses that are adopting the ASP model into their core processes. This is a comprehensive site, with content well-organized into specific categories for ease of navigation. This site also can be configured for login to more detailed content for no charge, in addition to email updates when content on the site changes. This site should be part of your top ten list because the content is in-depth.

Covering the Citrix-based thin client area of the industry, which has thin clients as an orientation, Thin Planet at `www.serverbasedcomputing.com` offers a wealth of content on thin platform ASP solutions and is tied in with the Digital Island Web site. Its coverage of Citrix-based solutions is one of the most thorough in the industry.

There are literally tens of hundreds of other sites that cover the ASP industry, yet the ones mentioned previously have the most successful track records and longevity when it comes to handling the formidable task of staying current with the ASP industry. As more and more sites containing content on the ASP industry emerge, be sure to check the e-Market Dynamics corporation Web site at `www.emarketdynamics.com`, which will include updates to this book. e-Market Dynamics specializes in tracking small business adoption of the Internet and the role of the ASP in small businesses.

Media Companies and Their Contributions to the ASP Knowledge Base

The continuing popularity of the ASP model and the idea of taking software and turning it into a service business intrigues many members of the IT community, including the press who routinely write for this audience. Presented here are several of the key sources of information you can routinely use for staying current on the ASP marketplace.

The first is ZDNet, which has an entire area of their site under *PC Week* dedicated to tracking the latest news with regard to ASPs. You can find the ZDNet Resource Center dedicated to the ASP arena by going to the PC Week page at `www.zdnet.com/pcweek` and selecting ASP from the Resource Centers area. This is one of the best resources on the Web for information from a broad cross-section of the industry.

Capturing the market dynamic of companies who are migrating from being VARs into the application service provider role with their customers, CMP Publications is busy generating insights into this market dynamic on their Web sites `www.CMPnet.com` and `www.varbusiness.com`. Both of these sites are read regularly by everyone who works in IT distribution channels. The continual re-definition of Ingram Micro, for example, is covered well in this publication and its Web site, in addition to extensive coverage of success stories from VARs that have successfully re-invented themselves into application service providers. The "war stories" told by VARs is one of the most interesting aspects of this site, as is the legacy of NovaQuest (now WebVision), and the continual adoption of an e-commerce intermediary by the industry leaders in distribution including Tech Data, Merisel, and Ingram Micro.

A sister publication of *VAR Business* is *Computer Reseller News*, which can be found at `www.crn.com`. This is the bible of the computer distribution industry, the *PC Week* of that aspect of the industry. The continual redefining of business models in the distribution channel arena has led to this publication taking on an ASP-centric focus in terms of content. It's a great site for the latest information affecting the IT industry supply chain.

CNET's `www.news.com` and the main site, `www.cnet.com`, have interesting information on the ASP marketplace from a consumer perspective. The News.com site is one of the best at presenting headlines in the industry as they happen, and I have seen analysts use `www.news.com` as their home page.

Check Out These Research Companies for In-Depth Market Statistics

First, The Yankee Group's small business practice is one of the best available for tracking the dynamics of the ASP industry and is considered to have a strong understanding of the dynamics of the ASP industry as it relates to businesses with fewer than 1,000 employees. You can find their Web site at `www.yankeegroup.com`. The Yankee Group extensively covers the focus on the integration of application service providers with businesses in the 1 to 1,000 employee segment.

Forrester Research is considered one of the best research companies at showing the integration of application service providers with other business models that comprise e-commerce, e-procurement, and e-logistics. This company has analysts who have a solid grasp of the application service provider marketplace and its relevance for corporations of all sizes. Clearly the most responsive of research companies in this list, Forrester Research provides its clients with a service called Research Answers in which clients can write in questions for an automated response from a series of analysts online. If you are considering writing a business plan and eventually going public with your idea for an ASP, consider getting a subscription to the *Forrester Custom Filter*, which is very affordable in the realm of research companies. You can find Forrester at www.forrester.com. Forrester is indispensable for market data and tracking evolving trends in e-commerce.

The venerable Gartner Group also includes one of the better-known companies in the research community, Dataquest, which it acquired several years ago. The Gartner site is one of the better ones at providing a preview of their content for the reader. You can find the Gartner Group at www.gartner.com. This is the largest research company tracking the ASP industry, and they have built a sizeable customer base with CIOs on a global scale who look to Gartner analysts for insights into which technologies to integrate. This is also one of the best companies at conceptualizing market dynamics through a quadrant model they use. It's also one of the higher-priced services, yet it is one of the best. Customer service is excellent, as is the availability of data online.

The research company that clearly has the widest breadth of coverage on the IT industry is International Data Corporation located at www.idc.com. Considered to have the greatest depth of technological expertise and a very strong track record in the ASP services area, IDC is clearly the state-of-the-art research company that provides a level of analysis not present in other providers. IDC's focus on production of research seems at times to overshadow responsiveness. This is a powerhouse research company, which can clear entire fields of questions. Overall this is one of the world's leading research companies with a depth of analysis not found anywhere else in the industry.

Summary

The role of application service providers in your e-business strategy is critical and will most certainly change as the industry matures. This chapter's goal is to provide you a foundation on which you can build strategies for getting the most out of e-business. With e-business being defined as the integration of Web benefits, the ancillary roles of e-marketing, e-commerce, and e-operations are defined in this chapter as a starting point. The role of the ASP as provider of applications in each of these areas continues to evolve, so check the resources listed in this chapter at least once a week or more. It's also a good idea to subscribe to the newsletters mentioned in this chapter in addition to getting on the email distribution lists in each of the information exchanges mentioned in this chapter.

2

What Drives Application
Service Providers (ASPs)?

CONSIDER THE BUSINESSES AND SERVICES you interact with on a daily or weekly basis. The fundamental value proposition of these companies is that they are in the business of saving you costs, time, and ultimately, making your company more efficient as a result. Conversely, how many times have you thought that having an online PR clipping service for your business, or having the capability to review financial statements that are accurate up to the minute, anytime, anywhere, would be of great value? How many decisions have been delayed due to lack of accurate information or any information at all?

There is an irony to the fact that the Internet is making millions of pages of content available to you and your organization yet does not at present provide a suitable means of succinctly analyzing that content and presenting the results for your use. Analysts and information strategists in companies are tasked with taking the wealth of information and content on the Internet and then creating valuable analysis from the many sources of information.

Underlying the irony that the information explosion actually makes the decision process more difficult, there is also the expectation by many that anything on the Web is actually easier to create and maintain than printed media. Although this may be true with e-marketing based sites, this is certainly not the case with e-operations based applications that rely on tying together with legacy applications in existence before the Internet.

The company looking to use an application service provider first should see the market drivers that are shaping the direction of the ASP market and its participants. The most proactive and visionary customers today will actually help define the direction and depth of offerings in this industry. ASPs are in many respects working toward a model of efficiency by having little customization in their service and product suites. It's a continual challenge for an ASP, because it needs to customize the application to the client, yet for internal purposes, it also needs to get efficiency out of production and operations by streamlining delivery.

As with any emerging market and corresponding driving technology, there are challenges of managing expectations both of delivered products and services, and the support associated with them. The intent of this chapter is to explore the market dynamics of the ASP arena that are shaping product offerings, including the proactive role customers play in this industry. Of all Internet-based marketplaces, the ASP arena is marked by product strategies developed both with and for customers in real time. The need for being a responsive resource is an underlying assumption and core value, which is included in the business models explored in this chapter. The core concept of the ASP model is service, and within service there is the opportunity to differentiate on customization or personalization, responsiveness, scalability, and upgradability of applications as the needs of a customer grow.

Exploring Business Models

The capability to deliver applications via the Internet to virtually any desktop with Internet accessibility is alluring to both software developers and investors alike. Creatively working to integrate the aspects of the Internet with those of advanced application development technologies including XML, Java, and Enterprise Java Beans, ASPs are creating entirely new classes of software almost monthly. Further, the continual focus from IBM on Notes as a development platform works to bring time-to-market advantages to those companies willing to aggressively pursue product strategies both with internal development staffs and with partnerships.

One of the core values, which define a successful business model over another, is the capability of the model to scale for partner's inputs and contributions. The most successful business models are capable of scaling to take into account a focused reciprocal approach to bringing business and new opportunities to each business participating. The continual evolution of Linux, for example, shows a model of association, which drives the sum total of efforts to produce a robust operating system. The cost savings of working with Linux have attracted many ASPs to that operating system. The capability of a business model to create a win/win situation for each partner involved is very powerful. On a consumer level, this model is the basis for EBay.com, in which there are tens of thousands of partner sellers that generate traffic in the millions of visits.

There are several ASP business models that are starting to emerge from the ASP market arena. Here is a review of each of the dominant models that continue to be successful in generating customers and recurring revenue streams.

Companies That Offer e-Marketing Sites Online

Often called by ZDNet and others the "click-and-sell" sites, this class of company provides all the necessary tools for creating an e-marketing and e-commerce site online. As the fastest growing of business models, this area has attracted many competitors; Bigstep.com and FreeMerchant.com are two market leaders. The business model of these sites focuses on the development of thousands of online customers, charging them nothing for creating their sites, and charging only for completed transactions. The larger click-and-build sites are increasingly looking to partnerships for creating a comprehensive product suite. In the near future, it is feasible that a business will be able to get a free simple e-marketing site, catalog, and even a click-together simplified HR application using the tools on these sites. The key aspect of these click-and-sell sites is their capability to generate customers for the more expanded applications that can enable collaboration and cost savings throughout an organization.

It's apparent that the click-and-build companies are very successful at attracting new customers for their offers of free e-marketing sites. With over 880,000 business users now communicating the competitive advantages of their companies online free, click-and-sell companies are rapidly creating an entirely new class of application service provider. This class of ASP is aimed at the companies that are either unsure of needing an online presence and don't want to spend the funds, or smaller companies that just want to experiment with online marketing and don't have the funds to hire an ASP or Web site developer. Click-and-sell companies are in the business of offering companies a free online presence for making their e-marketing sites visible to the outside world, including sales catalogs. These click-and-build companies make their money on advertising revenue for banner ads and also on catalog revenue, accruing 5% of monthly sales on items sold through a catalog.

What makes the click-and-sell site a leader in the area of business models? It has the following key strengths, and also the following challenges. First, for the strengths, a click-and-sell site is free, which draws thousands of users to the site for e-marketing and e-commerce tasks. The click-and-sell sites generate revenue by the costs per transactions fulfilled from the catalogs online with customers, and the advertising revenues generated by showing potential companies the size of the customer installed base. The limitation of this business model is actually the limitation it places on its customers. Customers cannot, for example, create customized templates; they cannot create a customized look either. The catalog is useful yet does not provide the necessary tools for creating a truly in-depth and industrial-strength trading center. Lastly, the click and sell sites require branding on their customers' sites and also have limited search engine optimization capabilities.

Furthermore, on the topic of marketing and analytic tools, many of these sites do provide approaches to checking the number of hits, where they came from, and the number of orders placed. They are finding it difficult to quantify the number of hits to a specific URL, as many of these companies require a URL that has their name in it. Figure 2.1 shows an example of a Web site created with Bigstep.com.

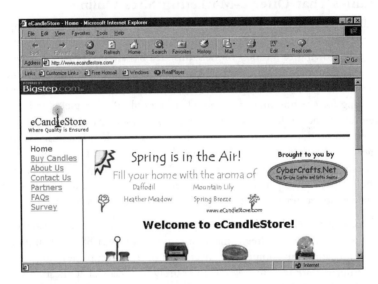

Figure 2.1   A small business site created using one of the click-and-sell sites.

Search Engine Optimization

Many businesses, after getting their sites online, find no one comes to visit. This is both frustrating and a challenge for companies, which is the reason for the pervasive advertising of URLs throughout our daily lives—everything from commercial jets to crock pots. Although advertising is prohibitively expensive, you can use *search engine optimization* to get a Web site listed on search engines, which uses a unique approach to embedding metatags into a Web page so the search engines will find it more often. Companies such as ZLand.com offer this service and have had very successful results. One example is of a chocolate manufacturer who had a Web site with his products listed and found very little traffic. In fact, the site was not even breaking even. The chocolate producer used the search engine optimization from Zland.com and was picked up in a search engine by a regional department store looking for more chocolate suppliers in its area. As a result, the chocolate company has seen nearly a doubling in revenue in the last six months.

In summary, the click-and-sell sites, although free for e-marketing and nominally priced for e-commerce tasks including catalogs, are not the industrial-strength sites needed by many larger organizations. Companies in this arena have either limited or often no capability for importing or exporting data. There is also the limitation of only a few pages of templates to generate a Web site, and the added issue of the URL having the name of the click-and-sell company in the site's address. Despite these limitations, this business model continues to grow for the following reasons:

- Click-and-sell companies give businesses the opportunity to learn about their Web site needs and develop catalogs in real time, without a staff.

- Instead of going through a long, drawn-out production cycle, you can create a basic catalog in a matter of minutes.

- A business with many divisions that wants to test the Internet as a communications vehicle can do so in a matter of minutes for no cost.

- New products and business ideas can be tested quickly and without cost.

- Partnerships from the click-and-sell companies promise to bring e-operations tools into their overall product mixes within the coming years. Bigstep.com has more partnerships than any other click-and-build company. Although e-marketing is the strong focus of these companies today, they do realize that e-operations is the direction of the future.

e-Business Accountability and Relationship Selling

One of the interesting insights that comes from spending time with CEOs of businesses is that they as a group see the potential of the Internet as an avenue for generating additional revenues. These CEOs also see the Internet as having the potential to minimize their costs through more efficient communication. For the vast majority of businesses, the idea of having orders placed for their products over the Internet and even leasing applications seems futuristic and great in potential, but the issue of trust is still crucial. How can I trust that the application will provide the right information at the right time? And what about the orders on my site? How can I make sure the orders are all correct? What about the HR records I update over a weekend for a new hire? These questions and more require a singular point of accountability for the businessperson. The point of having a trusted guide, a person to go to, who will provide guidance and consultative advice is invaluable for the businessperson looking at the ASP model. Relationships are what this model is all about, with the revenue stream being driven by both monthly lease fees and upselling to customers as their needs change. This model focuses on how to be a long-term asset to a customer.

Long the domain of EDS, IBM, Oracle, and others, this approach to one-stop personalized selling of e-business solutions is needed for businesses of all sizes. One of the most interesting dynamics of companies that are using this approach to provide ASP services is that relationships, once created and sustained by solid performance on commitments and ongoing trusted communication, turn into customers who migrate from the most simplistic Web sites to the most complex. Taking the personalized approach to providing e-business solutions, over time, creates trust. From the foundation of trust created, many CEOs begin adopting e-business solutions to solve their problems. No other business model in the ASP arena can personally take responsibility for developing a customer over time. The e-business expert is the trusted guide and can eventually assist customers, if they choose to take the advice, to drive for cost reduction in their companies, creating a collaborative intranet in the process.

With the personalized approach resembling a technology-savvy concierge in a great hotel, the business model of e-business accountability and relationship selling also needs to singularly focus the internal operations on the needs of the customer. This perspective, with many technology and pricing decisions surrounding the service aspect to the customer, makes this model "high friction" in terms of having a strong e-business expert be the evangelist internally for the customer. When a company has an e-business evangelist inside an ASP looking out for their needs, the execution will be strong and the relationship will grow.

The need for guidance and the benefits of providing it for businesses is evidenced by many of the leading software companies embracing the ASP model. The ASP model is a service business that requires responsiveness in e-business experts. With service being the differentiator, the voice of the customer must permeate both an ASP provider and the companies using e-business solutions. One of the real strengths of this model is that the voice of the customer comes through via e-business experts who rightly evangelize solutions for their customers inside the company. For example, Oracle Online continues to grow as an ASP, providing e-business experts to customers who are adopting Oracle solutions.

On a global scale, the most attractive segment for ASPs is small businesses. There are 4 million small businesses today in the United States alone according to The Yankee Group. With a projected 4% growth rate, this will turn into approximately 5 million businesses by 2003. Reaching into this segment does not make sense for the larger companies that have cost infrastructures that prohibit their servicing smaller businesses cost efficiently. Using a franchise model, Zland.com focuses on bring local e-business experts to small businesses around the world. The focus on being a one-stop shop for the small business is critical because the bandwidth in companies below 1,000 is already stretched thin. The need for having a resource for handing off critical tasks is essential for growth of e-business strategies in these companies. Without the help of an e-business expert or consultant, the tasks necessary to create an e-business strategy wouldn't get done.

Figure 2.2 shows the approach one ASP, Zland.com, is taking in providing personalized support through the ASP model. The role of the e-business expert as trusted guide is critical, especially in smaller companies in which the focus needs to be on doing a minimum number of tasks for maximum results. That's the true traction of this business model: It provides efficiency for small businesses to get their online objectives accomplished.

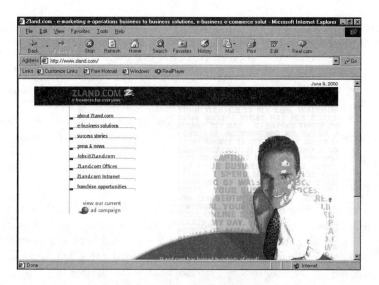

Figure 2.2   Zland.com uses a franchise model for providing personal accountability to customers multinationally.

With the strengths of personal accountability, focus on the customer for the long-term, and the capability to span applications for e-marketing, e-commerce, and e-operations areas, the relationship selling model is adaptable for many types of customers. The shortfalls of this model are succinctly explaining the value proposition of the relationship-based model and simplifying pricing and options. Overall, this model shows great promise because the relationships with customers are the asset, and the product innovation is used to further serve the evolving needs of customers as their businesses change and hopefully grow.

The Community Model

Starting as a Web site used for auctioning off Pez dispensers, Ebay.com is now a fully functioning corporation with a market capitalization of over $200 billion. Using a community-oriented concept of creating online areas where people with similar interests can bid on items of interest, Ebay.com has risen to be a standard in B2C commerce. What's interesting is the business model initially focused on taking a percentage of the transaction for a processing fee, and is now a model that includes revenue streams from advertising, partnerships, and international expansion.

The community business model is well suited for B2C commerce, in which people cruising the Web for pleasure can quickly get a handle of the pricing for items of interest. Further, the community model creates specific market segments within itself, further segmented by purchasing behavior. This provides Ebay.com with additional advertising opportunities as well.

Clearly the strengths of this business model include the capability to quickly distance yourself from competitors through a loyal customer base. With Ebay.com being the premier B2C site for auctions, it's entirely feasible that given its market leadership, Ebay.com will also create a B2B auction site. There is an unmet need in the B2B market today for an industry-wide auction site. If Ebay.com does address this market need, they will have the benefit of already having several million customers to which they can market B2B applications. It's possible that Ebay.com will eventually branch into B2B commerce, even possibly creating a sales exchange in antiques for dealers to actively trade their items. Clearly this model provides a direct connection into e-procurement and e-operations because these areas of the ASP product suite are focused on collaboratively working with departments within a company to drive down costs.

Another company using the Community Model is Agillion, which is delivering e-operations applications via the ASP model. Agillion's community of customers uses the forms-based interfaces for entering Customer Relationship Management-oriented data. It's a low-end approach to bringing Customer Relationship Management, which is the managing of customer data, to the masses. Agillion is actively working to bring value to its communities by streamlining the user interface and the introduction of data interoperability with Microsoft Outlook, GoldMine, and other contact management and scheduling software. The role of the Community Model will be one of creating a "buying club" using the approach to spread the benefits to all members. It's possible that Agillion will eventually turn into one of the online accounting companies that already compete for companies looking to outsource accounts payable and receivable.

What then are the downsides of this model? First, the product strategies are definitely evolutionary as opposed to revolutionary for this model because the risk of losing customers diminishes with every successful migration from one product or service offering to the next. Secondly, this model needs to have a strategic plan or vision guiding it; it does not respond well to impulsive and aggressive moves because companies basing their businesses on it require an element of stability. The service proves 24/7 availability of critical data.

The Distribution Model

Taking a page from the world's leading distribution companies, there is a dominant class of ASPs acting as application aggregators, taking entire series of applications and enabling them over their platform. FutureLink is one such company that focuses on bringing in applications from many different companies to add value to their customers. The distribution model in effect aggregates applications into a cohesive product strategy for customers to choose from. Just like other distribution-oriented models, this one looks at the velocity of transaction rentals and the breadth of products that can cover the chosen markets.

What's crucial about this model is the role partnerships play. For FutureLink, the role of Citrix, Compaq, and Microsoft are crucial because the technologies these companies provide serve as the foundation of the delivery approach FutureLink uses for providing applications. Each of these partnerships provide specific technologies that are essential for FutureLink to deliver leased applications to customers.

The drawbacks of this model include the shortcomings of many Internet-based distribution and selling companies, which are primarily being accused of "hollow" business models that don't have a true delivery of value over time. Specifically, companies that are consistent in the value they deliver over time with a business that would have succeeded on the Internet or without it are the ones making progress both in market share and profitability. The role of the Internet is then one of streamlining these already solid business models to enable even greater growth. The need for building a robust BackOffice for serving up the applications, and the capability of the BackOffice of a distribution company to scale is also critical. All the investments in scalability and development of applications, including their testing, makes the distribution model very expensive to operate. For companies adopting this model, they must rely on the velocity of transactions and breadth of application leasing as the prime revenue generators.

The Promotion and Advertising Model

A multitude of companies on the Internet have the development of a large readership or viewership to drive up advertising prices as their primary business model. One of the more unique companies in this arena is Buy.com, which until recently was selling its products below cost and attempting to make up the difference in advertising revenues. This assumes that the products being sold have a relatively flat demand curve that tends to trail off, thereby leading to more visitors once a "cliff" on the price has been reached. This happens on certain products, which have limited supply, but with much competition in key areas of computing products, this doesn't tend to work all the time. Upon its IPO early in 2000, Buy.com first told everyone in interviews that its model would now include for-profit products. This was refreshing to the analysts who track the company.

With the advertising model in full gear at other companies such as Yahoo!, it's apparent how a market leader for premium pricing, leading to other media strategies, can leverage the model. Yahoo! has been focusing on driving content into their site, thereby creating an ever-greater value for visitors using the search engine features of this portal to find sites of interest. As Yahoo!'s traffic has grown, so has its market capitalization, which stands at $91 billion at the time of this writing. Yahoo! is actively working to create television, printed, and online content as part of an overall media strategy.

The Software to Service Model

The gauntlet has been thrown down by Larry Ellison of Oracle to other software companies to change their business models from software sales to application leasing.

At the same time, Oracle is saying it will use its exclusive value-added resellers as the e-business experts to provide ASP services. Yet the direction Larry Ellison has set is clear; he commented to *Internet World* during October, 1999 that 50% of his company's revenues would be generated from Web-based sales. This is an aggressive goal and is quickly being pursued with the Oracle Online application suite of Web-enabled applications for large and medium businesses.

What's so intriguing about this model are the implications for companies that have built their sales and support organizations and processes to support sales tasks instead of service tasks. Microsoft is in the midst of this transition as evidenced by comments and anecdotes from Steve Ballmer during the close of the 4th quarter, 1999. With the Microsoft Office Online pilots underway and the efforts to streamline licensing, Microsoft is working to get their business model turned into a services-based model as quickly as possible. Using their extensive resources for marketing and development, Microsoft can be expected to lease all components of Office online before the end of 2000.

The strengths of this model include the capability to create recurring revenue streams, leveraging the Internet to deliver the value. This is also a business model that focuses on the development of longer-term relationships than has been possible in the mass sales approach from before. The third aspect of this model, which is going to be interesting to monitor in the coming years, is the implications for OEM partners of these companies. With the direct model turning these companies into service businesses, will the direct model in effect give the end customer a complete decision of which operating system on which computer? The dynamics of OEM pricing and the very nature of the relationship will change between Microsoft and its OEM partners. There will be a migration of ancillary business models of companies also serving Microsoft.

The weakness of this model is that it does not require the size and scope of an organization needed for traditional application publishing and sales. The re-engineering of companies such as Microsoft and Oracle is expected to be gradual yet significant. Coupled with the Department of Justice ruling on Microsoft and its migration to a service-based business model, the ruling to potentially split up Microsoft could be the best solution for how to streamline internal processes to re-engineer the company internally. What the Department of Justice can do through their ruling is what the market would have potentially done within three years as well. Clearly the transformation of Microsoft and the other larger software companies is at hand. Many of these larger companies have pricing structures favoring larger customers, and these companies are challenged to scale down to smaller businesses as the cost-per-sales call for larger corporations is too high for the larger players in this market. For example, it costs companies such as Oracle $165–$200 per sales call.

The VAR to ASP Model

Starting from the same foundation as the E-Business Accountability and Relationship Selling Model, the VAR to ASP Model also relies heavily on relationships with customers. Many VARs first established their relationships with leading Fortune 2,000 companies by selling them networks, software, PCs, and servers over the last 15 to 20 years. The effects of the Web as a change agent on industries are felt strongly in the PC and information systems VAR arena today. Although companies including Dell and Gateway have acted to change distribution, the VARs are now in position to retain the most valuable asset they have: their customer relationships. To that end, VARs are becoming application service providers through partnerships with Oracle, Great Plains Software, SAP, and many others. The VAR today is taking on the role of sales channel for the higher-end ASP applications, which require both project management and a strong voice inside their companies on behalf of the customer.

The strengths of this model include its capability to serve larger corporations through pre-existing relationships with companies they have known for years. Another benefit of this model is that many VARs have experience with training, support, and the development of product expertise internally, making them self-sufficient. The down-side of this model is that it really doesn't give the VAR complete control of its own destiny unless the strategy is to learn from the larger players and then embark as an ASP on its own. Many VARs are in fact doing just that. This model is focused on high service and low margin, as the applications are resold, netting a sell-through margin to the VAR.

ASPs Focusing by Segment

Watching the ASP marketplace evolve is synonymous to watching a kaleidoscope against the noonday sun; as new colorful companies emerge, some disappear and still others reshape themselves. The constant, however, is that small businesses and their needs are actively shaping the types of applications being offered. The capability of an ASP to focus on a vertical segment and capitalize on serving the segments' needs with a variety of products drives product breadth. Many ASPs are looking to small businesses with operations tools that lend themselves well to a per-seat pricing strategy. Nearly all the ASPs in this market area are first focusing on the number of employees in a company as primary segmentation criteria. Figure 2.3 shows how ASPs are segmenting themselves by size of company.

Because the business model for most ASPs starts with a single per–Web-site charge for creating an e-marketing presence to a specific per-seat charge for e-operations applications, this segmentation is pervasive throughout the industry. Per-seat charges on a per-seat basis for leasing an application with slight variations in the breakout of employees—these classes give ASPs the insights needed for creating entirely new product strategies by market served. The need for accurately gauging the needs in each of these areas is typically accomplished through focus groups and customer surveys sponsored by ASPs.

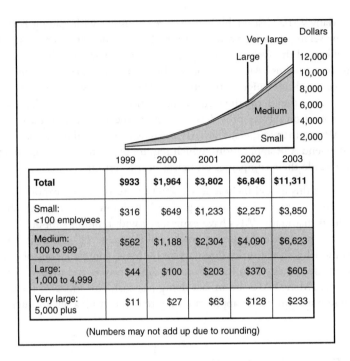

	1999	2000	2001	2002	2003
Total	**$933**	**$1,964**	**$3,802**	**$6,846**	**$11,311**
Small: <100 employees	$316	$649	$1,233	$2,257	$3,850
Medium: 100 to 999	$562	$1,188	$2,304	$4,090	$6,623
Large: 1,000 to 4,999	$44	$100	$203	$370	$605
Very large: 5,000 plus	$11	$27	$63	$128	$233

(Numbers may not add up due to rounding)

Figure 2.3   ASPs segmenting themselves by number of employees is a common approach to market segmentation in this marketplace.

Secondary segmentation is from the standpoint of early adopters, mainstream users, late adopters, and laggards. Clearly customers in the early adopter area dominate the ASP arena. Figure 2.4 shows a distribution of ASP customers by class, projected in 2003. The early adopter plays such an important role in this marketplace that they are discussed in a later section of this chapter.

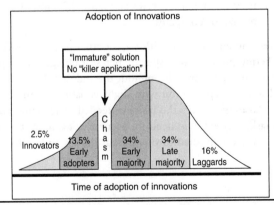

Figure 2.4   Defining segmentation by customer behavior is another approach to defining this marketplace.

A third perspective on segmentation is on technology preferences. Admittedly this is not often used because the market is still maturing. Yet there are certain customers who are focused on scalability and security, have a staff of people who can handle Java programming (in larger corporations), or have a series of Notes applications internally already. This is a criterion that will develop over time as the market stabilizes.

Turning Challenges into Opportunities

Taking the problems of other businesses and providing solutions has long been the basic focus of service businesses. In the ASP industry, taking on the challenges of creating an e-business strategy and accompanying Web site is the service proposition of application service providers. This holds very true in the ASP arena, because the focus of ASPs just entering the marketplace today is on small- and mid-sized companies. The key to the ASP marketplace and its dynamics is seeing the perspective, by ASP, of how they perceive your need and the broader market need. Companies that communicate this, sometimes called a *value proposition*, are US Internetworking, Verio, Zland.com, and Intel with their hosting services. Because a new ASP is announced practically every week, it's imperative that the value proposition be examined to see how the company sees itself. Is it a technology or marketing-focused company? Is their focus on the latest gadget or the ability to go the distance with a customer? One of the best tests of a value proposition is to check and see how many times, if any, the customer is mentioned in their statements and the vision of the company. You can learn quite a bit just from reading a paper presented by their CEO, for example.

Yet at the basis of the driving change of ASPs is the capability to fulfill service commitments. *Service Level Agreements* (SLAs) are crucial for the long-term growth of the industry. SLAs are covered in later chapters of this book as well. A Service Level Agreement is actually a quantification of service performance. The ASP's industry term for the contract, which states overall levels of performance to be delivered, is defined in SLA agreements.

Small Business Driving Innovation

Think about a small business you deal with on a periodic basis. Perhaps you are one yourself. What are your challenges? What are the tasks that take the most time yet don't really provide the greatest return? This is the inflexion point for ASPs targeting companies of all sizes, but the small business marketplace is a driving force because its needs are both more immediate and more acute. The small business demands of delivering products to its customers, managing revenue and growth of receivables, and of handling all the paperwork for hiring and having people on payroll are often outsourced. First these tasks were sent out to companies such as ADP and others for fulfillment. With the growth of the Internet and its availability everywhere, these same tasks can easily be completed internally as well. The need for accurate information internally and instantly drives the ASP model, along with additional factors presented here.

Labor Shortage Means HR Outsourcing

With an unemployment rate hovering at 4% nationally and 2% in the tech centers of the United States, companies are increasingly looking to do more business in less time, with the same headcount or even less. Holding onto employees is difficult, and handling all the paperwork is also daunting. As more companies enter the ASP arena this will be a primary focus for them. This will be an area that will see significant product and service changes in the coming years.

Technology Development

Scaling applications on a global level is the foremost challenge of any ASP today. Because, by nature, this marketplace is focused on a one-to-many approach to providing application services, the need for having headroom in the BackOffice capabilities of a provider is crucial. This area is changing so quickly that if you were able to get the best minds of this industry together for a week and record the transcript, certain aspects of the conversation would be obsolete in the six weeks it would take to fully appreciate and analyze their insights.

With the ASP marketplace changing so quickly, the answer to handling this is getting a partnership in place with each of the companies who are acting as technology generators or technology developers. For the business looking at the ASP model, it's important to realize that those partnerships its ASP has are critical for the success of both the ASP and its customers.

Distance Learning

This is one of the key factors driving this marketplace to quick adoption. One of the characteristics of early adopter companies of the ASP model is their configuration as a business. The overwhelming need to communicate across broad geographic locations is a key driver for adoption of the ASP model. Taking the faster growth companies with revenue growth over 15% per year, there is the corresponding need for having online training available on a 24/7 basis as employees and their offices are constantly being added throughout regions of the world in high adopter companies.

Saving on travel costs and lost time when associates are out of the office, distance learning is making significant inroads into corporations worldwide. The ability to complete training at any location, anytime via a browser makes this approach to teaching and instruction one of the fastest growing areas of the IT industry. According to International Data Corporation, training completed over the Internet, sometimes called distance learning and even e-learning, is growing at over a 100% compound annual growth rate through 2003. This is attributable to the fact that the delivery of courses over the Internet is becoming increasingly accepted. In addition, there is an emerging class of ASPs that are focused on serving the needs of companies that want to learn more about how to program in Java, XML, and C++. Another trend driving the adoption of e-learning is the introduction of corporate and private universities that are entirely Web-based.

Cross-Functional Communication

At the heart of e-operations, cross-functional communication is the need that tools aimed at dropping costs of manufacturing and operations focus on as a differentiator. Just how collaborative an application is depends on the time and cost savings it achieves. As companies grow and change through stages of communication patterns, the need for having an electronic representation of these patterns of information needs to be planned for. This approach to planning needs based on communications flow, using the Internet to augment its efficiency, is ultimately how the ASP model will be judged in five years.

Internet Adoption in Small Business

These are the trailblazers of the ASP arena, those companies stepping out and becoming the first adopters. In this section you'll get a glimpse at who these companies are and why they chose to be among the first to integrate ASP applications into their companies.

Who Is the Early Adopter?

By definition, this is a company that jumps into the latest technologies looking for the benefits to accrue over time for their firms. In the case of ASPs, the early adopter shares these common characteristics across international boundaries:

- These companies have several remote locations, with the median number being four or more. The focus of these regional offices is on sales and customer service, and there is a challenge to any sized businesses to have both the information and culture disseminated to these remote offices.

- Companies that are early adopters also have fewer than 15 years of experience. Consider that Microsoft was founded in 1975 and waited until 1986 to go public. At the time of their IPO, Microsoft annual sales were $197 million and they had 1,153 employees—a far cry from their $19 billion in sales for 1999 and their 31,396 employees today. Also consider Cisco, which shipped its first product in 1986. Since then, Cisco has grown into a multinational corporation with more than 20,000 employees in more than 200 offices in 55 countries.

- Typically have a higher revenue figure compared to non-adopters because these companies have found how to integrate technology into their companies.

- Have predominantly service-based businesses that are B2B focused. ASP applications are seen as tools for handling responsiveness to the customer base.

- Have a higher per-PC count than the non-adopters and have an intranet in place before adopting an ASP solution.

- Have a tendency to work with other companies that are also early adopters and compare results, especially on the service dimension.

Channels of Delivery

One of the major differentiators by ASPs is their approach to distributing services to their clients. From the largest companies, there is the model of the e-business consultant along with a deployment team, which provides the key aspects of program management and testing. Increasingly, this model is being focused on smaller businesses as well. The channel dynamics of VARs trying to hold onto their customers while migrating the business model of a hardware reseller to focus on the Internet is a challenge. To see how the channels of delivery vary by ASP, check out CMPNET.com and also VARBusiness.com; both sites capture information on the VAR to ASP transition.

Click-and-Sell Convenience

Potentially one of the delivery approaches that will change e-marketing and e-commerce in the short-term, click-and-sell companies are intriguingly taking the Dell model and bringing it to the ASP model. What is not found in personal time with an e-business expert is made up for in the time efficiencies of creating a Web site unattended while online.

Case Study: Why Trigon Electronics Chose an ASP Solution

Trigon Electronics uses its Web site to deliver timely product information to its dealers, maximizing sales productivity in the process. Dealers are very enthusiastic about having product literature in the form of data sheets available 7 days a week, 24 hours a day online.

In addition to serving its dealers with timely information, Trigon Electronics finds that its Web site is a valuable tool for projecting an accurate image of its business.

Providing Security Products to Many of the World's Best-Known Companies

Trigon Electronics earned a significant market share in the security industry by evolving products to meet the needs of customers. Trigon has built a solid reputation in the security marketplace, starting with gate openers and electronically enabled security products in the early 1980s and advancing to intercom replacement products today. Some of the world's leading corporations use Trigon's products, including Bay Bank of Boston, Citibank, General Motors, Ford Motor Company, Kaiser Permanente, and Xerox. These companies and many others have Trigon products installed in their offices, and in many cases, at ATM locations.

Trigon's rigorous production standards include the use of stainless steel cases and adherence to military spec standards of reliability and electromagnetic interference ratings. A 22,000 square foot production facility in Silver Lake, California, where security products are produced to exacting specifications, complements Trigon's selling efforts worldwide.

Online Information for Closing Sales

Selling security products to many of the world's best-known companies required that Trigon build a strong, smart, dealer channel that understands how to sell and install security products. The company's ZLand.com-based Web site at www.trigonelectronics.com serves as a communications tool for making sure dealers around the country, and soon around the world, have the product information and literature they need to be successful. Substantial incremental business has resulted. "The Web site saved many sales for me by providing the information I needed when I had to have it," said a Trigon dealer during a recent sales conference.

Trigon chose to use the Adobe Acrobat format to distribute its product literature, installation instructions, and product guides online due to the pervasive support for this file format.

Dealer Locator Provides Dealers with an Online Presence and Cross-Linking Capability

Ron Edde, National Sales Manager with Trigon Electronics, championed the Web site and drove the creation of solutions tailored to the needs of dealers. Drawing from his experiences in the publishing industry, Edde was able to get much of the product literature online for immediate use by dealers nationwide.

Trigon and its dealer network are starting to view the Internet as a marketing tool, and the ZLand.com-provided Dealer Locator is winning strong support in the dealer network. "Having the option of including a dealer's Web site address is a great feature. Several of our dealers already have Web sites, and the painless approach to including their email addresses and URLs is great," Edde commented.

The Dealer Locator is also introducing dealers to opportunities for generating referral business over the Internet. Dealers also like having a specific page in the Dealer Locator for their particular business. The ability to optionally add an email address and a URL gives those dealers an online presence and an opportunity to cross-link traffic between Trigon and themselves.

Online Product Descriptions, Photos, Specifications, Part Numbers, and Programming Instructions

The Customer Lounge area of the Trigon site provides a central reference point on the site for dealers and OEM customers to find product descriptions, photos, specifications, part numbers, and even programming instructions. The Customer Lounge also provides dealers with assistance in getting the Adobe Acrobat files up and running. The online Customer Lounge is the first step in what Edde sees as a continuing adoption of technology to better serve Trigon dealers, making it possible for distribution partners to create entire presentations for pursuing opportunities.

Edde is confident that the Web site clearly can provide even more valuable information to dealers in the future by leveraging the multimedia aspects of the Internet. His vision for the future of the Web site includes having product and sales training materials online in streaming video. "The ability to visually communicate a product's key selling features and benefits will be a powerful sales tool for us in educating our dealers. I can see where we will want to explore having streaming video product training as well. Dealers will be able to get up to speed online at their convenience," Edde commented.

"One of the dealers recently told me that the Web site met the need for having product information delivered quickly, giving him the opportunity to be responsive with quotes and answers to customer questions," Edde concluded. "He really summed it up when he told me that Trigon's site is fantastic!"

Summary

Finding a need and filling it is a good basic business axiom seen again and again within technology/market innovations. The market for leaseable applications over the Internet continues to grow and mature as the needs from all classes of businesses continue to outpace existing staff and resources. The ASP model is the "release valve" for companies growing at a rate faster than their infrastructures can support. In many cases, the early adopters of the ASP model are companies needing the tools immediately on a global level. As these needs continue to change the landscape of international business, the ASP arena will also continually change to reflect unmet needs.

3

Business Needs Driving
e-Business Growth

To FULLY APPRECIATE THE IMPLICATIONS of an e-business strategy for your organization, you must consider first the challenges facing you and your colleagues today and then think of their solutions. One of the most prevalent challenges is fostering an ongoing dialogue with your customers about what they want in future products. Because urgent tasks tend to squeeze out the important, this is often talked about but doesn't actually happen often enough. Bringing your customers into the development process is critical for the development of future services and products that will effectively serve customer needs. Using the Internet for this task is one of the best applications of the Web. Perhaps the most important aspect of using the Web outside your company is communicating with customers. The communication process makes sure the direction of all the systems in the company are contributing to meeting the needs of customers. Studies have shown that companies using technology to stay in touch with their customers are far more effective and ultimately more profitable than others that have not used technology for handling tasks.

Much of the media coverage of the ASP model focuses on the benefits companies are obtaining from bringing collaboration and operating efficiency to client organizations. Within three years or less the ASP model will be seen as a service business instead of a product-oriented one. The combination of creating and bringing collaborative tools to market in conjunction with a service-centric model brings the delivery of ASP models to an entirely new level of professionalism and performance. For ASPs, the delivery and support for e-operations applications are becoming more of a consultative approach to working with you.

This chapter focuses on the needs that are driving companies of all sizes to adopt the ASP model, and the implications of bringing in an ASP to handle mission-critical tasks in the e-operations area.

What's Driving Business-to-Business Growth?

By far, the majority of ASPs today are having the greatest success in selling to companies engaged in business-to-business services, with commerce between businesses being the largest proportion of demand in ASP-enabled commerce. Clearly, all the innovation in the ASP arena is due to the early adopters in the business-to-business aspects of e-business. The continued growth of e-business globally will be primarily driven by business-to-business electronic commerce, as the graph from Forrester Research in Figure 3.1 shows.

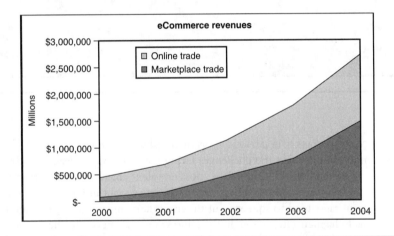

Figure 3.1   The business-to-business marketplace is projected to grow exponentially in coming years.

Inevitably, when you look at a graph showing the aggressive growth of this marketplace, you have to ask what underlying factors make the forecast appear realistic and attainable by an industry. Being accurate and credible about the direction of a market is the currency that research companies trade with. Being able to show their forecasts as reliable has implications for each company's reputation when it comes to venture capitalists and the contributory role they can play in getting business plans up and running. The role of market research in the ASP marketplace has been, at its best, the quantification of market opportunities, risks, and growth rate. At it's worst, the market research on the ASP marketplace has made the opportunity appear too confusing for the general investment community to get behind with financial resources and cause growth. International Data Corporation, Forrester Research, Gartner Group, and The

Yankee Group all have excellent reputations with investment companies. You can get insights into the ASP marketplace from these companies via their free research offerings available on their Web sites. International Data Corporation has a free research report on the ASP marketplace that is downloadable in exchange for your contact information, for example. The other research companies also offer free market research on the ASP marketplace from time to time. Each of these research companies has a specific strength:

- IDC (www.idc.com) is strong at analyzing the overall trends driving the ASP market, with particular emphasis on case studies of mid-tier (over 1,000 employees) and larger organizations adopting the ASP model.
- Gartner (www.gartner.com) is the CIO's reference point for the ASP market arenas, and has some of the best information available on advising companies on how to ensure the highest level of security for data.
- Forrester (www.forrester.com) has a great view of the key trends affecting the market, and is the strongest in terms of responsiveness and customer service.
- The Yankee Group (www.yankeegroup.com) excels at analyzing the interaction of ASP vendors and their offerings for small businesses.

Figure 3.2 shows how The Yankee Group is forecasting the growth of the ASP marketplace in U.S. small business with attention paid to the very small (2–19 employees), small (20–99 employees), and medium-range (100–499 employees) classes of small businesses. In general, many research companies agree that a small business is defined as a company with between 1 and 1,000 employees.

With the best handle on small business adoption, The Yankee Group is adept at handling the intricacies of bringing analysis to the needs that ASPs have in small businesses. In further analyzing the market and defining the relative level of adoption by service area of the ASP model, The Yankee Group has done an excellent job of segmenting uses of Web sites by their role in the definition of e-business. The highest rates of adoption are in e-marketing, as more and more companies turn to a fundamental Web presence to maintain competitiveness in their chosen markets. There is a market dynamic of small businesses that will migrate to e-operations applications quickly, as the level of trust grows for integrating applications throughout an organization. Figure 3.3 shows the relative level of adoption of e-business by application area.

With the need for communicating the value proposition of products and services, and the fact that there is little downside risk to having brochures online, e-marketing is the most saturated area in e-business. This is also the area in which companies most often change their direction and select one approach over another for sending their message to their customers. For the second major application area, e-commerce, the relative level of adoption is still somewhat low because companies must trust Web sites for generating revenue and for the completion of fully featured catalogs and ordering tools. Taking the concept of the Web into a fully collaborative tool and streamlining processes—in effect becoming a tool for redesigning processes in a company—the continuing development of e-operations services and products will drive the maturation of this marketplace.

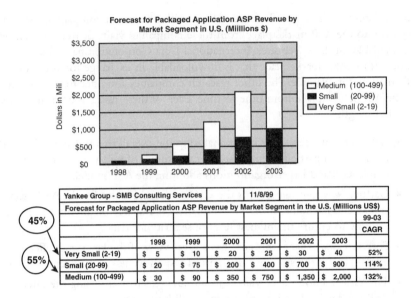

Yankee Group - SMB Consulting Services				11/8/99				
Forecast for Packaged Application ASP Revenue by Market Segment in the U.S. (Millions US$)								
								99-03
								CAGR
	1998	1999	2000	2001	2002	2003	
Very Small (2-19)	$ 5	$ 10	$ 20	$ 25	$ 30	$ 40	52%
Small (20-99)	$ 20	$ 75	$ 200	$ 400	$ 700	$ 900	114%
Medium (100-499)	$ 30	$ 90	$ 350	$ 750	$ 1,350	$ 2,000	132%

45%

55%

Figure 3.2   The Yankee Group is the leading research company tracking small business
adoption of the ASP model in the United States.

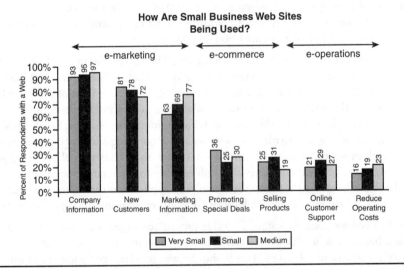

Figure 3.3   The Yankee Group's small business research shows that the majority of small
businesses in the United States have adopted e-marketing sites, with e-commerce being
the second most-used application area.

Market Dynamics That Drive Growth Assumptions

With the ASP marketplace still maturing at a rapid rate, it's important to realize there are wider market dynamics driving its growth trajectory and the nature of what type of industry it will be in the future. It is common, for example, for the presenter at an ASP Conference to ask all the people to raise their hands who are actively shopping for an ASP solution and have come to the conference to gain insights. In the conferences I attended while writing this book, potential customers routinely were less than 10% of the audience. Fully the majority of audiences at industry events are vendors looking to understand the market dynamics in greater depth or are companies interested in selling their services to the ASP community.

> If you want to pursue your knowledge of the ASP arena by attending a conference, be sure to get in touch with Ziff-Davis Events or ZDNet Events in addition to IDC's AppSourcing Forums, which are also very good at providing insights into the marketplace. These conferences have strong speakers on the first day so plan to have a full first day and listen closely to their comments. If you are going to be the person handling the ASP implementation in your company, you'll find these conferences a valuable tool for getting the "straight story" of the ASP industry. Typically the sales pitches are minimal, and there is more of a candor of what has worked and what hasn't in the midst of industry peers for these companies. You'll also see how the market dynamics covered in these conferences are at times almost self-fulfilling in defining this marketplace. Further, if you happen to have venture capitalists speaking about the ASP model in the context of value propositions, the clarity and frankness they bring to these events is welcome. Having a venture capitalist talk about sustained value is like getting a window open in a stuffy room: Their frankness is refreshing.

In analyzing the forecast of ASP adoption, keep in mind that many research companies, in creating their market models and garnering the resulting revenue figures for this marketplace, make the assumptions described in the following sections.

Challenge of Awareness

Arguably the single biggest issue for the ASP industry's forecasts is the need for continually developing awareness. There are many companies that offer services that are comparable to the ASP model, yet the companies do not specifically call themselves ASPs. Instead they call themselves ISPs with hosted services. The lack of awareness in this market is comparable to the first days of the Apple Macintosh, where Guy Kawasaki became the consummate evangelist and marketer. Clearly the ASP industry needs to have the focused, passionate efforts that Apple first showed in its Macintosh application software efforts. The ASP industry is in need of evangelists who can increase the awareness of potential customers. As someone who is looking at the ASP model, be sure to check in every once in a while at the sites listed in Chapter 1, "Meeting the Challenge of e-Business with Application Service Providers," to see the key messages of the ASP model and the current issues.

Challenge of Infrastructure

In defining the relative growth of this market, many research companies are focusing on the growth of the underlying Internet infrastructure, with several (including IDC) looking at the wireless Internet access points that are increasing the distribution points of applications being hosted. This is one of several forecast assumptions, which has the highest potential of affecting ASP demand due to its capability to increase total available market size.

Tendency of the ASP Arena to Be Vendor-Driven Today

This marketplace is highly fragmented and, to a large extent, vendor driven. That explains the high concentration of companies attending these conferences and typically the low customer counts. This is a vendor-driven marketplace right now and as such, it gives customers the flexibility of defining their own solutions as the market itself is defining what it will look like. It's a shopper's market as customers are much sought-after and the investment community is continually stressing customer satisfaction through service-level agreements and enhanced satisfaction with delivery of services.

Collaboration and e-Operations to Dominate the ASP Industry

Growth will be globally based with collaborative applications driving the majority of the demand. The migration from e-marketing to e-operations applications is going to have a pronounced effect on those firms that are only focused on the e-marketing side of the e-business equation. Many will become system integrators and will migrate their businesses "upstream" away from a purely e-marketing focus. Others will become providers or intranets, reselling e-operations applications as well.

Velocity of Change in the ASP Marketplace Is Faster Than Predicted

The transition of companies from using the Web for providing information to selling products is occurring faster than many analysts projected, with e-operations—using the Web for driving the costs of production and development down—being the dominant trend in coming years. The focus will be on driving the costs out of products and redefining the channels of distribution through more efficient commerce. This is the factor driving the forecasts of e-operations and e-procurement as the highest-growth areas of e-business today. Driving costs out of processes and streamlining them is pervasive across all sizes of business on a global scale. The concept of e-procurement is based on streamlining supply chain purchasing electronically.

Top-Tier Companies Driving Acceptance of the ASP Concept

Credibility of the ASP model is being enhanced by the efforts of AT&T, HP, IBM, Oracle, Microsoft, SAP, Sun, and even hardware companies including Micron, Compaq, and Dell with their hosting initiatives. The accumulated effect of these companies getting behind the ASP model will be seen during the coming years as customer trust is exemplified through high adoption rates of tools that bring together organizations in efforts to drop their costs. When the adoption rates by ASP product area are tallied years from now, the relative effects of Sun, with their Star Office in the personal ASP market arena, for example, will be illustrated by measure of market share. Market share estimates are just becoming available for personal productivity and other areas of the ASP model.

Global Reach of the ASP Model Now Apparent

Increasingly, business models are being focused on international opportunities, requiring 24/7 availability and fault tolerance. Creating a catalog in multiple languages, for example, is easier for a small business to outsource than to take internal resources to complete. The dual needs of being up 24/7 and being localized for the needs of a given country or region of the world are market factors driving the demand of the ASP model on a global level.

Increasing Importance of Quantifying Expectations Through the Definition of Service Level Agreements (SLAs)

Quantification of ASP performance is already a major contributor to the growth of the ASP model because it is creating more trust through the quantification of performance levels. The Service Level Agreements (SLAs) now being introduced into the ASP arena are also taking the mystery and open promises out of the sales equation. The SLA will actually be one of the stronger tools for getting the ASP model accepted by companies hesitant to sign up due to lack of assurances in the past. This quantification of performance will translate into a higher level of trust than would have been possible before, thereby creating increased demand for e-operations tools that are used for driving down costs and increasing efficiency in organizations.

Looking at Needs as Market Drivers

The market research companies tracking the ASP industry are looking at the mix of both the larger technology issues intersecting and influencing the purchasing decisions of organizations. The key needs driving this market are explored in this section. These are the customer trends that ASPs are responding to with their product and service designs. In the end, an ASP is actually a service business—and the needs described in the following sections are the "pain points" they are focused on solving.

Shortage of Trained Staff and Professionals

Not being able to find the right information systems person at the right time in organizations has become an almost universal need that is targeted by many ASPs. With the increasing number of excellent job opportunities in the IT community, there is also the issue of turnover and holding onto the associates already onboard. Being able to extend the breadth of what existing IT staffs handle is possible using the ASP model as an outsourced resource. The ASP model is being built to allow existing IT staffs to manage it with a minimum amount of interruption to existing priorities. Being able to offload the development and maintenance tasks is one of the key benefits of the ASP model when it comes to the shortage of workers today. Consider that there are 10 IT jobs for every 3.3 workers available and you can see the need for having an ASP model that can compensate for the shortage of trained IT staffs and professionals.

Distance Delays in Conducting Business

It's interesting to see that the early adopters of the ASP model defined in detail in the next chapter are primarily choosing ASP-based solutions due to the wide geographic coverage their companies have. With many companies having locations throughout a region or at international locations, having an ASP provide access to members of an organization anytime is a compelling solution.

Companies that have distribution channels are in effect dealing with distance delays in formation delivery as well. The ASP model is used successfully in many companies that rely on distributors to cut down on the time delay of getting information into the hands of salespeople in the distribution channel.

With the distance delays comes the fact that over time documents tend to be inaccurate because inevitably there are multiple versions of documents created. Putting documents up on a server to make them accessible to everyone on the intranet site provides an instantaneous competitive advantage for many companies.

Coordinating communications across a wide distance is one of the essential needs in organizations of all sizes that the ASP model is adept at meeting. Because this communication requirement is so pervasive in many of the faster growing companies, the ability to collaborate on projects and development programs on a global scale is already possible today. This need has pushed the scalability of the ASP model to new levels of responsiveness.

Time Savings in the Services Sector

With the velocity of transactions in many industries accelerating, especially in the PC industry, the need has arisen for real-time pricing, availability quotes, and order status reporting within seconds of the query. Automated banking on payment gateways also requires the ability to complete transactions in seconds. The ability to design order status and customer query systems online for instant access is one of the benefits of the ASP model. Several countries are experimenting with kiosks, which will have high-speed connections to the Internet to provide banking and public transportation scheduling and status information.

Cost Savings in Manufacturing Industries

The essence of an e-business strategy is the potential it provides for driving costs out of a business and streamlining a business model. When e-business strategies were introduced in several industries, the benefits were readily apparent. The rapidly changing scope of the PC industry's channels of distribution is a testament to the power of the Internet to change entire supply chains. Streamlining commerce is quantified through the costs savings achieved. For example, the capability to order parts and even subcontract for assemblies to be produced outside your plants saves you the time of managing both the production of these items and the continual reconfirmation of orders. The potential for cost savings by collaborative information sharing through selling and supply chains is significant. Increasingly, e-business will be known as the cost savings achieved through the streamlining of commerce electronically; the e-marketing aspects of unidirectional communication will become commonplace in the coming years. The real benefit of an e-business strategy will be in driving costs out of processes and enabling more efficient communication throughout organizations.

Velocity of Transactions Drive Inventory Turns

Every growing company needs the ability to drive more transactions through its Web site and ultimately through its organization. Handling these transactions, fulfilling customer orders, and also tracking the customers' purchasing statistics is a big challenge. Companies as diverse as EDS and SAP are taking on this challenge with industrial-strength tools for handling *customer information management*, sometimes called CRM or *customer resource management*. Smaller companies that have built strong applications on diverse platforms are assuming the challenge as well. The ASP model is acting today as a unifying thread across the largest solutions in this market and the smallest applications because customers' data is needed on a 24/7 basis. This is sometimes called an "always on" data strategy.

The essence of the e-business strategy you are creating is how you can increase the speed and responsiveness of a given transaction. Using an ASP's solution for driving increased responsiveness to your customer through more efficient processing gives you a strong building block to customer retention and eventual loyalty.

ROI of an Investment in ASPs

The financial returns of investing in the ASP model must be quantified. Metrics are being generated in the industry today to look at the total cost of ownership and the role of service level agreements in generating returns on the investment in an ASP. Throughout this book the ROI (return on investment) is mentioned to bring the quantified benefits of the ASP model into focus.

You should look at an e-business strategy from three vantage points. First, it is a communication channel for getting the word out to customers and partners about your new offerings and the implications for your business. Second, it is the revenue generation expectations of your business relating to the Web. Third, it is cost reduction through efficiencies and the streamlining of commerce using the Web. Taken together, the investment in an ASP to give your company the capability to compete effectively along these three dimensions becomes measurable after the customer base has adopted the e-business strategy you're offering. Over time many companies track their ROI per sales program and track cost reductions typically by the increased number of transactions completed and revenue achieved.

What's Driving Business-to-Consumer Growth?

Convenience, time savings, personalized shopping experiences, learning, career development, and finding jobs are just some of the reasons consumers are adopting the Internet, and in a sense, creating their own e-business strategies. Many companies are using the Internet for communicating who they are and their strengths, with many using online banking and travel sites for handling business and vacation travel. Although the consumer sites, including Amazon.com and others, are generating the majority of media coverage today, business-to-business electronic commerce will far outpace consumer-based e-commerce in the coming years. B2B commerce will ultimately surpass B2C commerce, due to the fact that what gets measured gets better, and B2C commerce is not as amendable to an ROI as B2B commerce is. Consortiums of companies can drive adoption of new technologies faster and with greater force than can consumers.

Eventually, the ASP model will be used throughout the consumer community as well. Yahoo! and its utilities, including a calendar, is just the first phase of what IDC is calling personal productivity ASPs. The implications of this class of ASP are provided in this section. Personal productivity applications are specifically built to replace desktop applications. For example, Microsoft Office Online is a suite of applications that are enabled over the Internet for lease by Microsoft through a series of specially selected VARs. The entire StarOffice initiative is also the same class of ASP-delivered application suite.

Trust and the Internet Experience

The quantification of trust is more pervasive in a B2B e-commerce strategy compared to B2C e-commerce approach as the applications making up the B2B e-commerce arena are differentiating themselves based on the ability to quantify performance and trust. The ability to drive fear out of transactions when a person is skittish about ordering via credit card over the Internet becomes a cultural issue instead of a purely technological one. Just as companies are doing today, the early adopters in the consumer arena are also experimenting with the benefits of being online. The capability to use the Web to secure leisure time is one of the biggest motivations for the early adopters in the consumer arena. As the size and scope of jobs are changing as the economy itself changes, everyone wants greater control over their time. That's one of the most alluring aspects of the personal productivity ASP model: the capability to assist consumers to control their time and complete tasks when they want to. Yet at the basic level of all this change remains the issue of trust. As better authentication programs are developed and as generations embrace e-commerce more than before, the issue of shopping online will become cultural instead of purely a new adopter trait.

ASPs and Delivering a Personalized Shopping Experience

Delivering a personalized shopping experience to both B2B and B2C customers is a competitive advantage you can obtain through the expertise of an ASP. The precedent set by companies such as Amazon.com, American Airlines, Expedia, and others has created the expectation that personalization will be a requirement for Web sites from this point forward. Planning for personalization is a potential differentiator that makes the shopping and use of any Web site more memorable than those sites not offering this feature.

Security of Data at Hosting Centers

Having a secure, trusted server for your information is crucial for the long-range growth of your e-business. As you compare ASPs and their offerings, be sure to drill into the hosting locations and their fault-tolerant features, including their capability to have your data online 24/7 with no interruption of service. Companies such as Exodus Communications have fault tolerance and enhanced security features typically found in the best of hosting centers. Taking on the e-operations aspect of your e-business strategy at times may require you to put your data on a secured server at a remote location. Actually visiting the hosting site is always a good idea and a useful test to see how committed an ASP is to being responsive to you as a customer.

Adoption Rates of Key Applications

Look through the applications an ASP offers to see which are heavily adopted and which aren't; also, investigating the relative success or failure of the application is essential. You must have this honest and frank information to make the right decision on an ASP. Because there isn't a Consumer Reports on ASPs yet, you can first check with the success stories on an ASP's site to see how other companies are using the applications. You can also check in with the ASP Industry Consortium (www.aspindustry. org) to see whether the ASP you are considering using is involved with any committees and also whether it has won any industry awards. The ASPire Awards (from the front page of the site www.asp.industry.org) from the ASP Industry Consortium recognizes excellence in application delivery to meet customer needs. The awards are a good place to start looking at solutions.

Case Study: How Christopher Radko Drives a Successful e-Business Strategy

The challenge for many companies whose products are highly seasonal is to generate sales throughout the remainder of the year. Christopher Radko's approach to building a Web site with the tools from its chosen ASP, ZLand.com, shows how one company in the holiday ornaments business has taken on this challenge using the tools of e-commerce.

Focusing on the critical Christmas selling season, Christopher Radko turned to an ASP to quickly enable all aspects of the Radko electronic commerce goals for 1999. Hundreds of ornaments can now be previewed, priced, and ordered via www. christopherradko.com. The site also provides a listing of key distributors and shops, including their Web sites.

Combining Craftsmanship and Sound Business Practices

The impetus for Christopher Radko's company occurred in 1983 when the family Christmas tree, laden with thousands of antique glass ornaments from Europe, tipped over. Vowing to replace the thousands of broken ornaments, Radko made it is his quest to find true glass ornaments that would equal the quality of the ones broken. After designing several himself and having them produced by local craftsmen, he soon found friends interested in purchasing them. In addition, Radko had the opportunity to travel to Europe, where he found many antique pieces that reflected the same crafts-manship found in the family heirlooms he was so intent on replacing. Yet before he could deliver them to his home, friends asked if they could buy one or several of them.

What began as an effort to replace family heirlooms grew to become a business with 4,000 total designs to its credit, over 700 of them featured in the 1999 Christopher Radko catalog. To produce these ornaments, the company has more than 1,500 people working in cottage factories in Poland, Germany, Italy, and the Czech Republic. Instead of going door-to-door to sell his products, Radko today has 3,000 accounts, including the venerable retail giants Bloomingdale's, Neiman Marcus, and Marshall Fields. One of Radko's many accomplishments is the recruitment of Walt Disney and other key customers as OEM partners. Christopher Radko now creates customized figurines for Walt Disney, F.A.O. Schwartz, Starbucks, Marie Osmond, DC Comics, and several of the world's leading department stores.

Complementing all these efforts is the firm's latest communications and commerce vehicle, its Web site, developed in conjunction with ZLand.com. Unlike the traditional retailing media for seasonal items such as ornaments, the Web serves Christopher Radko and its customers 365 days a year.

The ASP's approach to catalog building made it possible for Christopher Radko's 1999 catalog to get online quickly, in time for the 1999 holiday selling season. On the Web site there are hundreds of ornaments that can be previewed, priced, and ordered online. The site also provides a listing of key distributors and shops actively selling ornaments, and includes listings of their Web sites as well.

The ASP-enabled catalog architecture provides Christopher Radko with the flexibility to add key marketing messages and images of these ornaments. Examples of the custom work Christopher Radko has done may be found among the Disney Catalog ornaments, including Winnie the Pooh, for the 1999 Disney Christmas Catalog. An example of the craftsmanship that Christopher Radko brings to its ornaments is apparent to online shoppers in the details in this ornament.

Today's online customer can even listen to the Radko Holiday Song online, in addition to checking order status and finding ornaments that are appropriate for each season. Christopher Radko's ASP-designed Web site is making a seasonal product line accessible to customers all year long, while sustaining the business with ornament products that cross the highly seasonal barriers experienced in the early stages of the company's life.

Summary

The adoption of the ASP model is driven by the need for businesses to work more efficiently together, driving costs down and the level of collaboration up. This chapter has profiled those driving needs in detail and provided a glimpse at how market research companies are looking toward the intersecting of large, more macro-like trends to impact and be impacted by customer behavior in the ASP adoption arena. The role of the early adopter is making an indelible imprint in the market today. To understand why the ASP marketplace is growing the way it is, it's important to view the early adopter organizations and see how their influence is shaping this industry. This group is profiled in the next chapter.

4

Why Are Businesses Adopting ASPs?

CERTAIN NEW ADOPTER COMPANIES and selected members of the industry press continue to see the idea of outsourcing new applications as the wave of the future when it comes to delivering applications. Enabling applications over the Web is all about bringing businesses time to value, or competing effectively by providing customers greater opportunity for revenue or greater reductions in costs. The ASP model is actually following what the IT industry has known for quite a while: Taking the most common tasks and delegating them to the people with a core competency for getting results in those areas is the best approach possible to getting more done in less time. That's the essence of this delivery model: It gives organizations of all sizes the opportunity to focus on their core business models without being distracted by systems issues and the very real need for building systems that will scale.

This chapter focuses on actual companies that have adopted the ASP model, and provides insights into their motivations for getting an ASP involved with their businesses. One of the foundational elements in the growth of e-business is the quantification of transactions, and over time, the building of trust in electronic transactions. This trust factor ranges from building a simple e-marketing site to a full implementation of an integrated warehouse and shipping solution. For example, one of the key lessons learned from Jeff Bezos and his Amazon.com efforts is that building a robust order-fulfillment system is the best approach to building an e-commerce strategy. Amazon.com quickly received attention from Yahoo! and also the Wall Street Journal, resulting in a 10-fold increase in sales. By having a focus on the fulfillment aspects of his business, Bezos was able to scale rapidly as his business grew.

Case Study: How Tamura Corporation Is Using ASP-Enabled Applications

Tamura is one of the world leaders in the manufacturing of components. Tamura's complex components and the need to get the latest information out are the most important aspects of selling them, hence the need for getting the latest technical info onto the site in PDF format.

Developed to provide Tamura's distributors and customers with the latest technical specifications, the company is focusing on how to compete more effectively for business in its channels of distribution. Tamara decided that using the Internet for communicating with its distribution partners and sales offices would alleviate the bottleneck that occurred when trying to get information out quickly. Because Tamura's sales force was included in the most recent information, the overall effectiveness of the entire team increased with the greater flow of information. They reacted enthusiastically to the external Web site, as did internal employees who now have a place of their own on the Web—Tamura's intranet.

Tamura is a high-volume, world-class designer and manufacturer of power-conversion and magnetic products. The company owns and operates 26 factories worldwide, which build over 1,000,000 telecommunications, audio, and power transformers daily and 2,500,000 wall plug-in power sources monthly. Tamura's factories are certified to ISO 9001/9002 and are BSI licensed. Tamura products meet the toughest international agency requirements.

Tamura sells directly to large OEMs and through a network of distributors to smaller customers. Users of Tamura products are technologically savvy, and therefore have embraced the Internet as the medium they can count on for up-to-date product information. With its competitors turning fast to the Internet for disseminating technical specifications, Tamura knew that to keep customers from moving to the competition, it had to offer more than the printed product catalogs of the past—it needed a Web site to convey the very latest information on its products.

As a company of substantial size that had not yet established a presence on the Internet, Tamura was the target of a great many firms interested in helping it build its first Web site. "I didn't feel comfortable with a lot of the companies who came calling," said Bill Dull, Director of Sales and Marketing. "Would they be around next year? Would some key employee leave the company and leave us in a lurch? What if they had a server failure? We like to work with companies who have a substantial presence, who make us feel comfortable about continuity of service no matter what might happen, and that's what our selection, ZLand.com, offered. Furthermore, the price was right."

Tamura's foremost requirement was to publish online specifications for all its products and keep them up to date. "We used to rely on printed catalogs, but we used the ZLand.com e-marketing base package to build a comprehensive online catalog with detailed specifications on all of our products. Our customers are engineers, and they've come to expect a supplier to use the Internet to keep product information up to date. If we hadn't embraced the Web, we'd run the risk that they'd go to our competitors. Instead, our sales force is providing powerful feedback on the value of www. tamuracorp.com for retaining customers and building revenues."

Another highlight of the Web, according to Dull, is the intranet portion of the site. "The intranet is an emotional tool that allows us to keep our employees abreast of company developments, a place they can go that belongs just to them," he explained. "We use it to host the company newsletter, to post birth announcements, to highlight new employees, and a lot more. It's been a great unifying influence within Tamura."

"I'm very impressed with the new capabilities available and just recently introduced by our ASP, which will allow us to get into true electronic commerce," Dull said. "We're going to start with our distributor network because that's the biggest short-term win. Distributors deal with smaller customers. Therefore their orders tend to include a large number of product types, with low volumes of each. That makes for substantial paperwork for them and for us. By automating the process over the Web, we'll save everybody a lot of time."

"Next, we'll implement joint sites for us and each of our major OEMs, individual sites where they can place their orders for larger volumes of fewer product types," he continued. "Not only will it save time, but it will build loyalty because these customers will see that they're so important to us that we built a site just for them."

"There's a lot more in the new release that we're excited about, such as the new parameter search capabilities that customers can use to get to the data they need more quickly," Dull concluded. "We definitely made the right decision."

Getting to Know Early Adopters of the ASP Model

Tamura is just one example of hundreds of companies who are actively adopting the ASP model for their businesses. There is a common set of characteristics that these companies share. They are more forward-thinking and tend to have the capability to adopt and leverage technology for the benefits of their organizations with a minimal interruption to revenue and profitability growth.

The following sections describe the common characteristics of these early adopters.

Strong Focus on Their Core Business and Excellence at Serving a Vertical Marketplace

This is a market dynamic so strong with early adopters that even the venture capitalists are now looking for vertical market strength in application service providers they are considering funding to ensure the business models are sustainable over time.

Customer-Relationship Driven

Instead of being focused purely on the quickness and rapidity of completing a transaction, early adopters are focused on how to accentuate their relationships with customers through new and innovative approaches to keeping them informed. The priority is on responsiveness and keeping customers informed and involved. Customers become part of the development planning boards and councils to drive innovation and bring new, fresh perspectives into the company.

Four or More Distributed Locations

Many companies are adopting the ASP model because they need to communicate across time zones and even continents. Increasingly, small businesses that are based throughout several countries need intranets and coordinated information flows between key points. Often, ASPs provide both the Web site e-commerce and collaborative tools internally for both customers and employees with a separate intranet. The business models of companies with these distributed locations typically use information to their competitive advantage as well, hence the need for quickly having the latest sales, production, and development data online. This is particularly true with franchise-based sales environments.

Median Age of 14 Years or Less

From the surveys completed during the last year, it's apparent that the majority of companies adopting e-business partnerships with ASPs are also the younger companies that have less than 20 years of experience in their businesses overall. Although this metric in and of itself is not earth shattering, it does start to make an interesting profile of the early adopter in conjunction with the broad geographic distribution of the offices that make up the business itself. These younger, more geographically distributed companies have a corresponding high demand for information to continue to grow and keep the momentum of their businesses going forward. Apart from literal waves of hundreds of emails, the best solution is to have a centralized set of documents available over an intranet for handling internal communication and an e-operations–based site for customers and trading partners.

Revenue Growth of 20% or More Year-by-Year for the Last Five Years

Companies that are growing faster, therefore needing to automate and streamline applications, tend to be early adopters of technology. The relative growth rate of sales is one of the most telling statistics for a small business that is an early adopter of the ASP model. With high growth comes workloads with deadlines that are significant and can quickly tax even the most efficient of organizations. With revenue growth comes accountability to shareholders and the need for delivering ever-higher returns on their investments. That pressure creates the need for singularity of purpose and focus that is uncommon in other phases of a company's growth. Source procurement—the ability to automate purchasing and procurement functions and thereby free up the time of operations staff—is driving the widespread adoption of e-procurement throughout the world's mid-size and larger corporations.

Predominantly in the Services Businesses

The companies adopting the ASP model faster than anyone else are also predominantly in the B2B services sectors, and are using the Web to leverage their existing knowledge and expertise to serve their customers. Getting from concepts for a Web site to closure quickly is the main reason companies are looking to ASPs for their implementation expertise. Being competitive with the knowledge of the industry and customers is crucial for early adopters, and the capability to leverage the knowledge globally is one of the strongest reasons for getting an ASP included in an e-business strategy.

Successful Track Record Integrating Technology

This seems like common sense, yet there are companies who have the same profile as detailed previously, but stumble with technology and find it mysterious and even fearful. Early adopter companies, on the other hand, are selective about the technology they adopt, making sure a critical customer need is driving the decision. These companies typically have intranets and possibly e-marketing sites already, but need the further collaborative tools and a cohesive e-business strategy to fully leverage their in-house expertise to serve existing customers and find new ones.

Using Portals for Managing Projects

Increasingly, companies are creating entire portals behind their firewalls to enable collaboration on projects and make the process of sharing schedules and information more efficient. Forrester Research projected that U.S. trade online was expected to hit $2.7 trillion by 2004, and that 53% of the total was expected to flow through eMarketplaces, which are electronic exchanges serving as hubs of procurement. The early adopters in the ASP marketplace are driving the movement to exchanges, with the larger corporations leveraging outside expertise to get exchanges created.

Underlying the need for using portals to manage development projects is the increasingly important role partnerships play in Web-based development programs. In a recent survey for the eMarketplaces report, Forrester Research asked approximately 50 Fortune 1,000 executives responsible for product development how they collaborate internally and with partners. Of the interviewees, 96% said that three or more departments are intimately involved and 44% report working with five or more departments.

Also, 40% of execs expect to work frequently with partners in 2002—twice the number who already do so. The quotes from key executives who participated in the survey also show a bias toward having more people involved in the development cycle than ever before. Several of the comments from the participants in the survey showed that with a development portal, there exists the opportunity to get feedback from everyone who has experience to contribute. One of the comments came from an executive from an aerospace company:

> "The biggest difference with our latest project was the breadth of the people involved with design. We had customers, floor workers, and maintenance people in addition to the development regulars. It worked great. We had been planning to use a new part, but the maintenance guys told us it wears out quickly. Five minutes of dialogue saved major delays in production."

As the size of a project grows, handling communications becomes even more complex due to the total number of interactions that are possible. Most of the companies that are working with larger development teams say that the sheer size and number of the teams makes collaboration harder. Their greatest challenges? Thirty-six percent attribute difficulties to a lack of upfront planning, and 32% cite a misalignment of expectations. This is a common problem with larger Web and Internet projects as well; the need for making expectations very clear is a high priority in getting a project underway with multiple cross-functional teams involved.

Comparable to the model of providers delivering applications and Intranets, the use of portals is much less often used than many emails, teleconferences, and in-person meetings. In the work completed by Forrester Research and others, it's apparent that portals could greatly increase productivity within the development organizations that rely on extensive cross-functional work to make projects come together quickly. From the Forrester surveys, it was found that most of the teams still rely on phone calls, email, and in-person meetings for their communications. Although 26% have some electronic document sharing, only 12% have made information available via the Web. Of the respondents to the survey using the Web to collaborate, they report excellent results.

The dominant need being addressed by using the Web to provide the sharing mechanism is accentuated by the time-to-market required from each of these companies to stay competitive in their chosen markets. In the Forrester report, the pressure to condense the development cycle time is becoming more important to remain competitive, thereby making communication ever more important. Time-to-market was a serious concern for the interviewees in the Forrester study, with 72% expecting cycle time, or the time to complete projects, to decrease over the next two years.

"There is a lot of pressure from our business partners to reduce cycle time. It is critical to be first to market if you want to be a leader. With better communication and document routing, we could probably make an impact," said one member of the respondent groups interviewed for the study.

What Are the Lessons Learned from Using Portals?

Companies using portals for increasing the communications flow within their organizations see stronger results than companies that rely on traditional methods of collaboration. The ASP model provides the necessary technical expertise to create a portal, whether for use with partners outside the company or as part of an intranet within an organization. Many larger technology companies, Dell Computer for example, are extensively using intranets with portals and information exchanges for streamlining development, production, and support of their workstations, servers, and mainstream PCs. The following sections detail the key lessons learned from the companies that are now using portals for coordinating their development efforts.

Product Development Is Increasingly Cross-Departmental

Companies are relying more and more on partnerships to accomplish their shared objectives. These partnerships are crucial for companies in software-related industries, in which the shared development expertise of companies can greatly decrease time-to-market and provide the capability to create an entire series of products. A company becomes cross-enterprise when there is a real-time tool for handling the communications between departments.

The Internet Has the Capability to Scale for Multiple Project Coordination

Given the frustrations in coordinating cross-functionality and the need for obtaining closer and more accurate communication by members of cross-functional teams, the Internet is just being tapped for this information-sharing purpose through portals and exchanges. Clearly the companies using portals today are finding that the benefits far outweigh the costs associated with creating these cross-functional exchanges.

Time-to-Market Is Everything in Highly Competitive Industries

For companies such as HP, Sun Microsystems, Gateway, and others, having a product completed when the market window is ready is crucial and often has implications for the entire company's revenue and profitability picture. For example, in the cellular phone industry, missing or being late to a product generation can mean losing thousands of customers to a competitor. The issue of time-to-market in technology industries is directly related to the relative level of revenue and profitability success that a product or service has over its life. The extensive use of email, teleconferences, video conferencing, and now even the creation of enterprise development portals and exchanges further accentuate the fact that businesses are looking for ways to use technology to compete.

Product Development Must Never Stop

With the accelerating pace of product life cycles and the need for having products ready when market windows materialize, product development will never be "done" with a product but rather will be on a mission to continually modify products to align with the changing requirements of customers. Using portals for quickly communicating these shifts in customer demand and preference can be invaluable for keeping cross-functional teams focused on a single development objective.

ASPs Capable of an International Focus Will Become Development Portal Experts

With the programming talent in India generating more and more of the globally focused e-business applications and the focus in Japan on consensus decision making, the role of development portals and their capability to create value for all participants is becoming increasingly clear. The point is that these development exchanges or portals can assist in allowing a company to span time zones and cultures when creating a product or designing a service. There are ASPs today that are focusing on how to create exchanges for businesses around the world.

Lessons Learned from Early Adopters

Companies universally face the challenge of competing in a more accelerated, more time-sensitive marketplace in which time-to-market and development cycles are crucial for retaining customers. Many companies are adopting an e-business strategy based on the ASP model precisely for the time-to-market and efficiency reasons defined in the portal section of this chapter. These early adopters have also learned from their experiences, and their insights can assist you in defining your e-business strategy with the idea of potentially bringing an ASP into the plans you have. Presented here are the key lessons learned from the early adopters of the ASP model.

Looking at Service Level Agreements

The best place to start with an ASP is to check into their service level agreements, and what the minimum level of service is. The minimum level of service needs to be quantified in a service-level agreement as many early adopters tie these minimum performance guarantees into their leasing contracts. After going through a selection process with the ASP you want to use, get copies of its standard service level agreements and check into its terms for minimum service levels for your needs. One of the early adopters also found that having its specific customized applications also mentioned in the service-level agreements was useful because this made sure the company's applications were covered with a minimal performance-level guarantee.

Looking at Risk Management with ASPs

Risk elements are often overlooked during the outsourcing process, but they can dramatically affect the deal. Given the fact that the ASP industry is maturing very rapidly, there is the potential that market dynamics can greatly change its competitive land-scape, forcing companies out of business or driving mergers and consolidation in specific segments served.

Given the fact that ASPs are growing and many new ones are entering the market nearly every week, you should ensure that the ASP you choose can "go the distance" with your needs and ensure the delivery of the results you expect. You also can benefit from the lessons learned from early adopters in this area. Here are pointers from companies who have already adopted ASPs and their services into their businesses:

- Start with a project that is very similar to a previous project to benefit from the previous learning.
- Clearly define performance metrics and project scope, objectives, and deliver-ables. These metrics include the amount of resources available, the anticipated burn rate of both funds and other resources, timeframes for project reviews, and the product's performance as well.
- Assign a project manager within your organization to take ownership of the relationship and milestones associated with the project. Have the CEO select this person and actively voice support for the initiative and person handling the task. This brings credibility to the project and gives the project manager implied authority to get cooperation and time constraints removed when implementing the applications and services.
- Build contingency plans and have a fall-back plan in place for handling any delays or stoppages to the schedule.
- Have an extensive internal and customer preview center for beta testing the applications before they go live. This ensures both internal associates have a chance to get their insights shared on the project and also gives the eventual customers for the solution a chance to comment on the application/service offering before it goes live. This also instills a sense of ownership with everyone involved before the program formally launches.
- Insist the project manager and the team have a singularity of focus just on the project, excusing them from other responsibilities so they can complete the pro-grams with the ASP involved to ensure accuracy in the completion of the devel-opment.

The insights from the early adopters show that the ones who have been successful see that focusing a resource, in this case, a project manager, on the task of integrating the ASP applications and services to an organization provide the best results. Companies who have multiplexed people (those members of an organization who are in matrix-based organizations) into handling the ASP relationship while handling other responsi-bilities have had mediocre results at best, and even had projects stop half-way through due to time demands being placed on the person handling the relationship. Even for the most basic of Web sites for medium and larger organizations, the amount of con-tent needed for making a robust Web site is significant. Even for e-marketing sites in larger organizations, it is common to find teams of three and four individuals focused on making sure the content is accurate, timely, and has been checked by each functional area represented by the Web site's many sections.

The teams handling content on Gateway.com, for example, number 15–20 people, and they act as "traffic cops" for content, coming in from other functional areas of that corporation. With e-operations–based applications in which extensive and seamless collaboration is the goal, the teams have typically been 10–15 people, with a project manager handling the cross-functional communication and project schedule. It's imperative for even the most basic of Web sites to have a single point of accountability for handling project schedules and partnership relationships with ASPs and if needed, software companies providing utilities to complete the Web site.

Security in Hosting

You'll need to also determine how ready the company you're working with is to host your data in-house. There are many companies entering the ASP arena today, and the issue of security is foremost in everyone's mind, even the early adopters. Using the following series of questions, you can get a good understanding of how committed the ASPs you are working with are to the idea of client's data and application security. If your ASP has a "yes" answer to all of these, that is a signal they are very strong in security. Any single "no" answer requires more investigation and more evaluation of additional ASPs. Many early adopters have used these questions in the matrix format to evaluate ASP companies they are looking to work with:

Is the Network Operations Center supporting two-factor authentication (in which both the sender and receiver are authenticated) for administrative control of all routers and firewalls?

Are support for 128-bit encryption and two-factor authentication for the connection from the customer LAN to the ASP production backbone standard?

Are data redundancy and load-balancing services for firewalls and other security-critical elements available for all accounts the ASP has?

Does the ASP perform (or have an experienced consulting company perform) external penetration tests on at least a quarterly basis and internal network security audits at least annually?

Can the ASP show documented requirements (and ASP audit procedures) for customer network security to ensure that other ASP customers will not compromise the ASP backbone?

Can the ASP provide a documented policy for hardening the operating system under Web and other servers?

If the ASP collocates customer applications on physical servers, does it have a documented set of controls it uses to ensure separation of data and security information between customer applications?

Outbound Marketing and Search Engine Optimization

Before jumping in to a major project with an ASP to get an e-marketing, e-commerce, or e-operations site up and running, it's important to see what the ASP has in the way of ensuring that the hits to your site are going to increase. This area is called *search engine optimization*, and is invaluable for getting your Web site listed with the major search engines. Many of the ASPs today are looking at how to offer this service, as several companies are working on techniques for ensuring search engines can find your site. This is particularly important for companies providing B2C commerce, in which having a search engine recommend a site is critical for leveraging the investments in a Web site. Search engine optimization uses techniques for embedding metatags into Web pages so the search engines pick up the identity of the Web page and filter it to the top of searches on the topics applicable to the site itself.

An example of how this can work well for a small company focused on B2C e-commerce illustrates how search engine optimization can assist a company in getting its identity known. Many companies created their Web sites initially with a local developer and had mixed results. They were breaking even with their business and had disappointing results with getting new business over their Web sites. ToastMaster's International created another Web site with another ASP who had search engine optimization, and its site was found by a regional department store within a month. The result is that this organization who assists people with their speaking skills is much more in touch with potential customers.

The fact that the majority of people using the Web use search engines and portals such as Yahoo!, Excite, and Dogpile to find sites of interest makes being one of the top entries imperative. Forrester Research estimates that 8 out of every 10 Web users rely on a search engine to find sites they need for their jobs or for personal interest. Forrester also has found that Web users only look at the top thirty entries in a search engine. Clearly being able to optimize your site for ease of location by search engines is a service worth looking into. Be sure to ask your ASP if they offer this service; when evaluating potential companies to work with, see whether they offer this service.

Summary

The needs driving the ASP marketplace are the same ones driving outsourcing in other areas of B2B and B2C commerce today. With the growth of the Internet, the benefits of streamlining time-to-market and erasing geographic boundaries and time zones in product development and service delivery are accentuated. It's possible to meet business needs across geographic boundaries, delivering the same level of service and expertise as if the customer was located next door.

The characteristics of early adopters in this market show a pronounced focus on leveraging technology for the more efficient and timely use of company knowledge and service. The early adopters see the Internet as a bidirectional communications and commerce mechanism they can use for expanding their businesses and more responsively serving existing customers. The use of development portals is also accelerating as ASPs apply their expertise in creating Web sites to the needs of companies who have tight market windows and time-to-market pressures, which intensify with each product life cycle. The needs driving ASP adoption should be countered with the lessons learned from these early adopters, which include steps for minimizing risk and ensuring security of data located at the ASP's Network Operations Center. The ASP you choose for your e-business strategy needs to be able to go the distance and provide marketing and search engine optimization tools for driving traffic to your site. Clearly the role of the ASP as service partner overshadows the role of purely an applications-only provider. The ASP model is increasingly about service, and the early adopters are driving the industry in that direction as their needs for responsiveness, security, and proactive marketing support increase.

II

Fundamentals of e-Business

5

Communicating Online Using e-Marketing

As the first step toward an e-business strategy, many companies adopt e-marketing as the first tool in their Web initiatives to communicate what makes their organizations unique. Companies of all sizes quickly adopt an e-marketing strategy into their plans to continually keep customers informed of product enhancements and new products, to communicate with the press on significant news for the company, and to provide sales and product information for their distribution channels leads. The capability of e-marketing tools and techniques to interact and communicate with customers makes this area the fastest growing of all aspects of an e-business strategy. Transcending the typical unidirectional role of a site in its communication, the advances being made in e-marketing tools are emphasizing real-time conversations with customers.

e-Marketing is increasingly becoming interactive, and as a result, it is the fastest-growing area of e-business strategies. The days of taking brochures and putting them online, wrapping HTML around them or just taking them verbatim to the Web are quickly disappearing. The capability to interactively communicate with customers, gauge their level of interest in products and services, and bring them into the product definition process all are leading to the quick growth of e-marketing within e-business (see Figure 5.1).

Figure 5.1   Projecting the role of e-marketing in e-business strategies.

The focus in this chapter is the breadth of tools available today for handling e-marketing tasks throughout your e-business strategy. Being able to quantify the performance of an e-marketing strategy is also provided, as there have been advancements in how to track the number of visitors who become leads, the number of leads that turn into customers, and the number of repeat purchases customers make over time. There are also techniques described in this chapter for bringing your customers into the product development process, which is one of the best ways to first thank your customers for choosing you as a vendor, but also to ensure their voices and new ideas for products are included in the subsequent generations of products. Called *Customer Listening Systems*, this aspect of e-marketing focuses on building an interactive exchange with your customers.

Because e-marketing refers to the communication of your organization's core strengths, its unique selling points or value propositions, and its products, the term *e-marketing* has taken on a variety of meanings. It's more than taking corporate and product marketing brochures and sticking them into HTML for delivery on a Web site; it's about taking the message of your company and interleaving the message graphically with the broader branding efforts underway in other media as well. One of the best e-marketing companies is Ford Motor Company at www.ford.com. Taking on the task of guiding visitors to its site through the wide variety of product families it has, the Ford Motor Company team has created a configurator for quickly providing the site's visitors with the information they need. Ford's Web site is easily navigated and you can configure and price any vehicle in the e-marketing areas of their site.

Using online videos, Ford also provides site visitors with an opportunity to look at its latest Mercury, Lincoln, Jaguar, and Aston Martin cars from a technical and aesthetic standpoint. Ford's Web site is shown in Figure 5.2.

Figure 5.2   Ford's Web site uses configuration options for bringing Web site visitors into the process of defining their needs.

Taking the technologies that have traditionally been used for enabling collaboration within organizations and applying them to communication with customers is driving e-marketing to higher levels of performance than ever before. The capability to inter-actively communicate with customers and define their preferences to further personalize e-business strategies is the direction toward which e-marketing is growing.

Defining Your Differences

One of the most common questions customers, suppliers, and the press ask any company adopting an e-business strategy is what the differences will be compared to competitors and the industry in general. The major differences center on the role of a Web site and e-business strategy within the context of a broader strategy aimed at getting desired results. There are literally tens of thousands of companies that have built Web sites and had no additional traffic, no increased number of hits to their site, no customers mention the site during surveys or at trade shows—in short, the site was imperceptible to their efforts. The reason this happens is that the e-marketing strategy is often treated as a separate initiative, completely devoid of a tie-in to other branding and sales efforts. These companies needed to integrate their e-marketing strategy with all other branding, awareness, lead generation, and sales development processes under-way in the company.

Conversely, there are many companies that integrate their entire branding campaigns around their e-marketing efforts, making the Web site the centerpiece of their branding and messaging efforts. To ensure the site gets traffic, the companies doing this successfully use search engine optimization techniques for ensuring their sites are in the first twenty listed by search engines. Marketing efforts and awareness building can take the URL and its message just so far, and then you must take the site past the creation process and actively work on getting it listed on search engines. Forrester Research also has done studies of how companies find the sites they are interested in, and fully 6 out of 10 find sites through search engines. Clearly the need for getting your site into the top hits from a search engine is critical to your success. The ability to tie branding and awareness efforts around an entire Web site involves having the same graphical content and messaging consistently shown across all media vehicles as well.

The travel sites are an example of companies that are exemplary in their messaging for e-marketing. Expedia.com, the leading travel Web site in the world, is masterful at taking real-world experiences in their commercials and creating guidance online to show how to deliver yourself from travel surprises. One of the more memorable is the one in which the couple gets a reservation at Cliff Side Hotel in a beach community only to find the hotel on a cliff of other hotels inland a mile from the beach. Expedia's branding and value proposition communicates to present and potential customers that they will receive accurate, unbiased travel information from the Expedia.com site. The tie-in with other marketing vehicles is consistent and complementary of each other.

Another company that is integrating their branding strategies well on their e-business initiatives is Dell Computer Corporation. Their branding stresses their own unparalleled success at executing an e-business strategy and their commitment to bringing customers what they need to understand: Dell's hosting initiatives and their benefits. Dell doesn't stop there, however; they continue to bring all the advertisements and commercials online for the visitor to have a chance to check branding for the key points that brought them to Dell in the first place. Be sure to go to www.Dell.com and check out the Dell E Com initiatives. The use of content and the ability of a site visitor to find meaningful information are outstanding. The Dell commitment to content in e-marketing also takes site visitors quickly from being in "information accumulate" mode into purchasing one of their systems as the interface between e-marketing and e-commerce on their site is seamless. Dell wraps the entire Dell E Com initiative into a nice package by having product strategies that further reflect an e-business commitment. Dell's Web PC products are differentiated enough from the e-marketing efforts to retain credibility for the entire site as not trying to sell systems on hype alone, yet none of Dell's products are difficult to find. Figure 5.3 shows an example of how Dell has organized its key branding vehicles onto the Dell E Com portion of its site, providing an excellent tie-in to branding efforts taking place in other media the company is using.

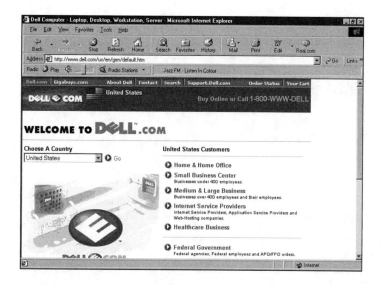

Figure 5.3   Dell's tie-in with e-marketing efforts shows its consistency of branding across media vehicles.

The quickly changing world of the business-to-business exchange or portal is another area in which e-marketing is quickly becoming more of a conversation with customers on what their needs are as opposed to simply blasting a message out to the world. Portals that are actively e-marketing for small business include Onvia.com, whose approach to bringing value to its site visitors via valuable and unique content is one example of a portal working toward collaboration with customers. Taking the needs of businesses and organizing them into separate areas of the site for ease of navigation and repeat access is going to be the hallmark of business-to-business exchanges going forward. Onvia.com's approach to marketing their site, even from within the site itself, is structured to make the value of the relationships with partners also participating on this site accessible and useful for a business. Onvia.com's approach to providing the steps for creating and maintaining a business also is part of their e-marketing strategy of being a central hub of information for visitors. Onvia.com's site is shown in Figure 5.4.

It's inevitable, when you look at one of these portal or exchange sites and see the depth of the content and checklists, documents, and insights into running a business, to wonder when these sites themselves will embark on a product strategy. Although many in the Web community argue that the content is the product for these exchanges, it's very clear from the direction of Yahoo! and others that there is eventually going to be a personalized ASP component entering these sites, just as calendar and reminder options exist today at Yahoo!

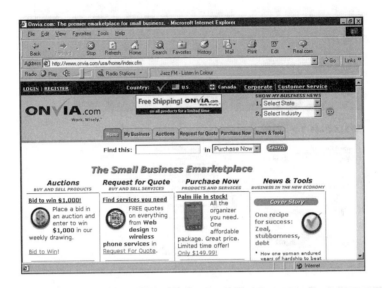

Figure 5.4   Onvia.com's e-marketing is in their content and navigational simplicity, in addition to partner relationships.

It's entirely feasible that the technology included in Agillion.com, for example, could serve as the basis of contact management and low-end customer relationship management applications leased to the portal companies. There is today a move by emerging ASPs that are grappling with channel issues and reseller mindshare issues to become original equipment manufacturers (OEMs) of applications for the leading exchanges. By 2001 there will definitely be low-end applications either developed by Yahoo! and other exchanges, or these emerging ASPs, looking to exchanges for revenue growth, will have supplied applications for use online. Far from being a competitive threat to exchanges and portals, ASPs will be the product enablers, bringing leased low-end applications for businesses through the exchanges gaining market share today.

Creating a Unique Identity Online with ASP-Driven Tools

The branding of your company and its products is the objective of having an e-marketing site at the beginning of a project and the integration of customer's opinions and needs into products is the objective at the more advanced levels. One of the quickest routes to completion of these objectives is to use application service providers (ASPs). In the scope of e-business tools and techniques, ASPs by far have the majority of their experience in the e-marketing arena.

One of the major reasons for this is that for an ASP to get up and running, they have many times had to compete with local, sometimes larger companies who are primarily interested in Web hosting and creating a series of pages that replicate content already created by its customers. Called Web site developers, these companies are increasingly competing with ASPs for the chance to provide e-marketing sites for customers. The typical role of the Web site developer is to create a site of multiple static HTML pages that reflect the key messaging for a client. Because the pages are static HTML, it takes significant effort to change text and branding, typically weeks.

Although providing Web sites is a valuable service, the very business model of a Web site developer does not scale well. Static HTML must be edited by hand, therefore taking a significant amount of time to get revisions up. Further, many Web site developers have multiple businesses, and many have abandoned their e-marketing efforts for more lucrative intranet development projects, custom networking programs, and the integration of their key strength—HTML programming and networking—with other companies that might provide e-operations tools. In summary, Web site developers might have a very attractive price for an e-marketing site, yet might not have the ability to scale across all the needs you have in the e-commerce and e-operations areas. Further, given the quickly changing marketplace, Web site developers might decrease their focus on e-marketing site development as other aspects of their business become more profitable. Clearly e-marketing and its pricing are very competitive today.

The role of the ASP in the e-marketing equation is one of building a foundation for further growth into other areas of a company's e-business strategy. For example, many companies that need just an e-marketing site today soon find that through search engine optimization they can ensure that they get noticed online. There are services that take your Web pages and embed terms and abbreviations within them so that search engines find them more efficiently. Many of these firms use a specific approach to getting the terms you most want mentioned into the frames of your Web pages, not viewable by people visiting your site. The company Meanduar, for example, provides this service.

Search engine optimization keys off the fact that most search engines do not understand the overall meaning of a given Web page. Instead, they look for clues included on the page and within the page structure itself to figure out how best to qualify the page's content for people searching the Web with the engine. These search engines all check the first two hundred words of the Web page for clues on how best to qualify the contents of the Web site. By taking advantage of the search engine's reliance on the contents of these tags, you can effectively boost your relevance scores for specific keywords.

The key tags you need to work with to ensure the highest level of search engine optimization are as follows:

- The title tag
- Header and text emphasis tags
- The image ALT tag

It's good to know these terms as you work with your ASP, so you can find out the extent to which its search engine optimization techniques use these tags. One of the best ways to learn about how your favorite sites use search engine optimization is to "view the source" for a given page in a browser window. You'll see how the specific keywords are listed and how the publisher of the site has worked to get his key messages across.

Branding Online

The Web provides the opportunity for any company to instantly create a brand identity literally overnight. With a substantial investment in advertising and forethought to ensure consistency between the Web site and other forms of media, it's possible to create an identity quickly, communicating it to the outside world. One of the goals of an e-marketing site is to provide branding for your company. With e-marketing focused on the communication of your key messages and your company's position, branding naturally follows as the overriding theme of your entire Web site.

The need for creating a unique voice is critical for the success of your company. Web sites can quickly create that awareness for you, provided you have used search engine techniques with your ASP to get traffic to your site to begin with, and have invested in advertising to drive potential partners and prospects to your site. Branding is the process of creating that identity online so that your company has name recognition throughout the industry. Just as the communication of the URL for your site needs to happen for customers to take advantage of the resources there, the broader message of your business needs to be broadcast and strengthened through consistent branding.

Doing branding well is more of an art than a science. When you start to work with an ASP to build your e-marketing site, be sure to think about branding as the most lasting impression you will make on your customers. The branding campaigns of companies can either make or break their identity in the marketplace, driving customers to them if their value proposition is solid. The following sections describe key aspects of branding to keep in mind when working with an ASP.

Make Your Branding Consistent Across All Media Vehicles

This is the cardinal rule of media usage and especially branding. This unifying voice of your company, whether it be the best service for air conditioners, or the most complete online store for pets (pets.com) needs to reverberate through all your messaging vehicles. The color and even the tone of the messaging need to be consistent as well. Many companies think that their Web site is separate and not viewed by the same customers who are visiting their showrooms, going to their brick-and-mortar stores, or talking with their sales representatives. From the extensive survey work done by Forrester Research, The Yankee Group, and others, it's clear that the Web site is the first place customers look to learn about you. Branding is the first chance to make a lasting impression, so be sure to have your key competitive strengths brought out and provided within the site during development.

Gateway Computer has done an excellent job of handling the task of creating a brand of PCs that are meant for both home and business. Gateway's Web site reflects the orientation toward both home and business in a balanced approach, along with a definition of their latest offerings, which is Web hosting for small business. Gateway has consistent messaging between its Web site and its television ads. Figure 5.5 shows the Gateway home page. Note the balanced approach to branding for both consumer and commercial PCs. Ask your ASP for examples of companies it has worked with that have initiated branding campaigns on their own, and see examples of how branding has been completed for a customer's company.

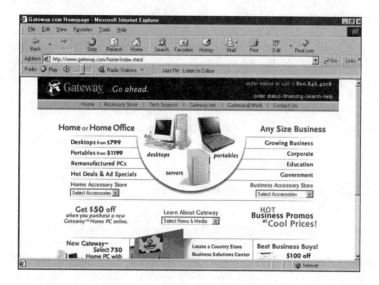

Figure 5.5   Gateway's Web page shows a balanced approach to branding its home and commercial PCs. The site also does a great job of introducing its Web hosting services.

Pick a Branding Strategy and Stick with It Over the Long Term

Nowhere is it more noticeable when a company is searching for an identity as when it is branding its Web site. The changes to Web sites are so instantaneous, so quick, that when companies do change the messaging on their sites without telling customers they can very often alienate future prospects by not providing a warning of the change. For example, Tiny Computers is relatively unknown in the United States, although it is well-known in the United Kingdom from its sponsorship of sporting events. Yet in the United States, Tiny Computers has brick-and-mortar stores in malls.

The consistency of messaging on a global level needs to be reinforced throughout the world. Whereas in the United Kingdom sporting events are the national pastime, the stores in the L.A. area, for example, are relatively unknown and not associated at all with sporting events. The result is that Tiny Computers in L.A. is seen as a clone manufacturer, yet in the United Kingdom, it's seen as a viable brand. Consistency of messaging would make Tiny Computers rise out of the many clone manufacturers throughout the Western United States and have an identity.

Mature Your Branding Strategy Inside First, and Then Promote It

Buy.com is a prime examples of a company that has changed their branding and messaging several times before focusing just on the simple message of being an e-tailer. Starting with the low-price messaging and then on to the outer space theme, to the relationship theme, to the simple Buy.com on black background, this company has matured in branding with the entire industry looking on. No doubt the outer space theme appealed to certain customers, and now the elegant approach to having "buy.com" in white letters against a black background says it all. The company recently went public, and coincident with that event, the branding strategy stabilized. The message of their experience is that branding is immediately noticeable and can get confusing when changed too often. Consistency is critical in branding overall.

Never Underestimate the Power of Branding on Your e-Marketing Site

When many companies first start a branding campaign and don't see initial sales results, they face the temptation to pull back funds from promoting their name for branding and choose to focus on lead generation or another aspect of the business. Although every business needs to grow its lead-generation pool to drive sales, the branding efforts, to be effective, need to be continually reinforced by active marketing. That's the powerful aspect of e-business—after a brand is accurately and consistently communicated on a Web site, it can continue to be leveraged throughout other marketing campaigns. Supplanting the messages with print, radio, and other forms of communication just furthers the key messaging for the company overall. It's an investment, and a tough one to continue with. Yet there is the need for creating that identity and also the need for generating leads.

As you'll see in Chapter 6, "Selling Online: How e-Commerce Works with ASPs," e-commerce strategies also have the potential of being lead-generation mechanisms. It's important in planning your e-business strategy to see the need for branding in the context of all the other sales generation programs also underway in your business.

Using Branding as a Differentiator

One of the key aspects of branding in the context of your e-business strategy is the role it plays in differentiating you from your competitors. You can use branding as a competitive tool, distancing yourself from your competitors and establishing your own identity. One of the first companies to do this in the highly competitive world of car sales is Ford Motor Company. Ford actively uses branding as a differentiator through extensive use of QuickTime movies, the capability to look at all the relevant aspects of a car with just four clicks of a mouse, and the navigational aspects of its site, which make the branding pervasive yet the products segmented for specific audiences. The other car sites do have a more product-focused approach, not providing the ease of navigation and ability to virtually get inside a vehicle and see how it looks. Branding in the car industry is everything; it's no surprise that Ford reinforced its brand on an e-marketing strategy with easy navigation that tells prospective customers about their cars.

On the subject of branding, it's very important to realize that any message conveyed on your Web site has an instant response from your customers. In creating a brand strategy for your site, think of what makes you unique; there is no need to create an entirely separate brand identity just for your online presence. Rather, your online brand needs to be in coordination with all other efforts in all other mediums. The essence of a strong e-marketing strategy is the consistency of the branding message and the efficient use of e-business tools to communicate the brand's uniqueness and key values.

Moving Beyond BrochureWare into Responsive, Personalized Content

Many businesses, when getting started with an e-business strategy, think that converting their brochures into HTML and having them on their Web page with little change to the original content is the most efficient approach to handling the task of getting a basic Web site up and running. It's as though a size 10 shoe is put in a size 7 box; it just doesn't fit, and it looks cramped. The integration of brochures into a Web site with no customization completed for the look and feel of the site is called "brochureware," in that the site is an exact replication of the company's brochures, with no additional information provided and little if any navigation. When companies take this route with an e-marketing strategy, they are shortchanging themselves of the inherent benefits a Web site provides. When creating your e-business strategy, resist the option of taking your brochures and quickly putting them onto your site. Technically it's easy to do, but from an effectiveness standpoint it doesn't work.

Trigon Electronics has taken the concept of communicating their core strengths in an e-marketing strategy, using an ASP to assist them (see Figure 5.6).

Figure 5.6   Trigon Electronics has taken its key messages and crafted a Web-centric message for its customers.

You can see from the Trigon Electronics site that the prominent pictures of their industrial security products and minimal amount of text along with the navigation bar across the left side of the screen make this site easy to navigate. Further, notice that even if you saw this site at 640×480 screen resolution on your system, you would still be able to see the entire message on the front page. Design aspects like these take a company's Web site away from being "brochureware" and one step closer to being a responsive Web site. The site is inviting to browse and easy to work with. This was a key requirement for Trigon Electronics because their distributors are locksmiths and specialists in industrial security products—they are not Internet and e-commerce experts. The need for making the site quick to load when viewed on a 28.8K and 56K modem was also a design consideration; hence the large amounts of whitespace, which also make the site easier to read.

One of the other key attributes of this site is that it is indicative of where e-marketing sites are going in the future. Many companies such as Trigon rely on their product literature and manuals to educate their distributors and salespeople. If you click through to the Product Literature section of Trigon's site and see the product definitions, notice the red and gray flashing PDF button on the lower right of the screens for products. Trigon, like so many other companies using an e-marketing strategy to promote their products, is using PDFs of their actual brochures in the context of a product section of their site. PDFs are now universally accepted worldwide as a document standard and are easily tagged for use on your site.

Instead of taking the entire brochure and turning it into HTML, Trigon and millions of other businesses are taking their brochures and turning them into PDF files. You can use Adobe Acrobat 4.0 (www.adobe.com) for accomplishing that task, or have your ASP do that for you. In either case, the integration of product information in the self-contained document is a powerful sales tool for your customers and selling partners. In the case of Trigon Electronics, for example, the distributors who resell the Trigon products have found the revamped product area easily navigated and very easy to use. One distributor actually remarked they were able to sell more products because they were able to download the PDFs and email them to prospective customers.

Figure 5.7 shows an example of how Trigon organized the product information areas to be the most effective in terms of communicating core strengths of its offerings, yet staying clear and simple enough to make it accessible and informative over its Web site.

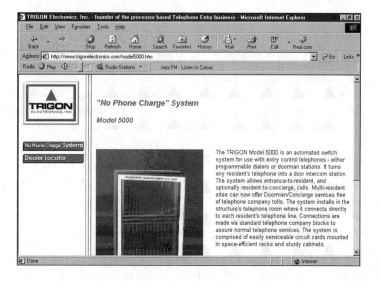

Figure 5.7   Trigon Electronics uses PDFs to distribute product information efficiently to its U.S. distribution channel members.

When creating your e-marketing strategy for your company, create a product area that provides PDF files of your brochures. You can take this approach to distributing documents for both product and service offerings, including the integration of pricing, packaging, and even presentations from your sales and marketing conferences. Adobe's Acrobat 4.0 is a great tool for document interchange, and should be part of any e-marketing effort, especially those using email for distribution of documents. With the tools available with the ASP partner you choose to work with, it's easy to see why the integration of the key concepts and selling points of your brochure can be cleanly and explicitly defined without having to copy the entire contents of a brochure online. You can take the PDF approach to distributing documents and be even more effective with an e-marketing site using that distribution mechanism for information.

Taking your e-marketing site from being only one-way focused in terms of communication and making the site a tool for actively communicating with customers is really the goal of creating an e-marketing site. Get away from the idea of your e-marketing site being an electronic billboard and focus on how to create an e-marketing site that invites everyone to participate and provide feedback. One technique for inviting feedback is to offer email alerts from the site as to when new information is available. There are several sites, such as www.internet.com and www.marketresearch.com, that are excellent at communicating with their customers, even though the majority of their sites are e-marketing or messaging based.

Internet.com is in the content generation business; thousands of articles are added to the site every day, including everything from the most technical articles on how ASPs are handling authentication and security to the most interesting aspects of the Internet. Using newsletters in which customers can "opt in" or choose to be on regular distribution of the email newsletters, Internet.com provides content on 120 different areas of the Internet industry. Many debates rage today on the subject of weekly email blasts; however, when customers have the choice (opt in) of selecting whether they want an email from you once a week, the netiquette rules favor the "opt in" as opposed to "spamming" approach to email newsletter distribution. *Spamming* is when thousands of emails are sent without prior approval of the recipient. **Do not ever use spamming tactics in e-marketing campaigns.** This will bring the wrath of many and is considered illegal as well. So the "opt in" approach works very well because the person receiving the email is one who asked for it.

Internet.com's approach to handling the opt-in process is well done and shown in Figure 5.8. Be sure to bring up this aspect of e-marketing with your ASP to make sure you get a chance to build contact points with your customer base. If you are a thinly staffed organization and do not have the bandwidth for a newsletter, take some other project off your list. Capturing potential customers' email address and information could lead to greater sales, so it's worth the time to complete the newsletter and have an opt-in marketing campaign.

At last count, Internet.com has over 7 million email addresses of companies it can work with and see how the content and promotional programs can best meet their needs. The opt-in email program is a great lead-generation device and should be aggressively pursued in your e-marketing programs.

Another site, which is creating responsive, personalized content for visitors, is www.marketresearch.com.

This site is actually a reseller of market research reports, and could have easily decided to go the "brochureware" route and create a static, boring site with literally mountains of information on the market studies and analyses being resold on the site. Instead, notice how in Figure 5.9 this site has an information-like appearance to it, which is both easy to navigate and understand. Also notice the "Update Me" link along the right navigation bar. This is an opt-in newsletter for those visitors to the site who are interested in getting information on new reports and analyses.

Figure 5.8   Using the opt-in approach to email distributions is considered good marketing and should be pursued in your e-marketing efforts, as Internet.com does with 120 newsletters today.

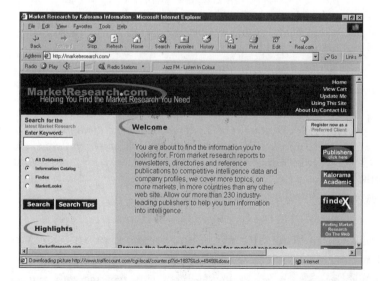

Figure 5.9   Creating an inviting, intuitive home page for its reports by industry, MarketResearch.com also invites visitors to get free information in Free Updates.

Finally, the search engine in the upper-left portion of the navigational bar is easy to find, even for the most novice Internet user. Overall, the site is designed so that it's easy to find the subject areas of interest. The lesson to be learned from this site is the proactive use of opt-in marketing. This site is going to be used more and more as a tool by visitors because it so quickly and simply meets a need. After using this site several times, it's apparent what the content is and that it's the best tool for the task of finding new information on markets. The site succeeds at e-marketing because it's easy to use, has opt-in email options, and provides the main headings of its content clearly and with a minimal amount of confusion.

It is imperative that your site embody the essence of e-marketing: communication. Communication takes a site beyond being simple brochureware to being a revenue generating machine. When working with the ASP partner you choose, be sure to make these issues a part of your discussions to ensure your e-marketing site and overall e-business strategy benefits from the lessons learned by others. The following sections present a checklist to make sure you have a site that is greater than brochureware and actually reaches out to communicate and actively serve your customers.

Remember, Less Is More

Instead of going for all the information you can possibly cram into your first page of the site, use the "less is more" approach and consider the MarketResearch.com site in which the key messages of reports by category are provided. Also consider the Trigon design, in which the whitespace and lack of rotating and flashing graphics makes this site accessible by distributors, many of which are dialing up with 56K modems or less to get information they need to sell with.

Create PDF Files from Your Brochures

Don't fall victim to the urgency of getting a Web site up by simply taking your Adobe Photoshop or Word files, creating HTML representations of them, and then putting them on your site. That makes your site look amateurish, and even if you are spending less than $1,000 on your e-marketing site with an ASP, strive for professionalism by making the effort to create content that is suitable for a Web site. Your customers will appreciate it and you will get more leads as a result.

Give Visitors to Your Site the Chance to "Opt In" for More Information

You definitely have a chance to capture leads online by working with your ASP partner to create an opt-in area of the Web site. You want to encourage your customer to speak with you and get additional information from you. The opt-in newsletter approach is accepted and provides the reader with information they might have not otherwise been able to get, in addition to providing you with valuable lead information. Taking this a step further, work with your ASP to get a database link from the opt-in area of your Web site to capture those names for further follow-up.

Don't Ever Spam or Send Unsolicited Emails

The entire idea of having an opt-in approach to handling the communication with your customers is that they have approved of the email being delivered. Never send messages to email addresses that have not requested information. Although there are companies who do provide email addresses, its best if you have the approval of the person receiving it. First, the message is relevant when they have asked for information, and second, you don't run the risk of alienating the potential customer with an unsolicited email.

Develop Reasons for Visitors to Come Back to Your e-Marketing Site

Gateway Computers is excellent at this, as they have segments of their front page dedicated exclusively to specials running on both the consumer and commercial sectors of their PC business. Gateway admittedly is one of the best e-commerce sites in the PC industry and has much more than e-marketing on their site, yet its e-marketing execution is worth studying to see how the weekly and even monthly specials are handled. Of particular interest is how Gateway handles product introductions on its Web site. The next time you see a Gateway ad on TV announcing a new system, you will also find an online purchasing special on their site. When working with an ASP to develop your e-marketing site constantly ask yourself, "What can I do to get visitors to come back?" Many companies are doing giveaways, such as the rival portal to Yahoo! Iwon.com, offering cash prizes. Work with your ASP to create a front page for your Web site that provides for "specials" areas to bring visitors back over time.

Provide Personalized Content in Email Newsletters

At its most fundamental, e-marketing is about communicating with customers. Work to bring the opt-in newsletter concept to reality by gathering content that matters and sending it out in a newsletter. Many companies are creating newsletters entirely in an email message, providing HTML links back to their home page.

Develop a Survey for Visitors to Your Site to Report Their Experiences

One of the best sayings inside Intel is that "what gets measured gets better," and developing metrics of performance for your company is one of the best approaches to understanding how people are using your site and what you can do to improve it.

Working with your ASP, develop an online survey you can use for gathering information on which parts of the site are the most successful, which are least, and what can be done to make the site more effective from an e-marketing standpoint in the future. Taking these surveys a step further, you can also gather feedback on future product direction by creating customer listening systems, the subject of the next section.

Creating Customer Listening Systems

Many companies develop and grow first based on the technological vision and innovation of the founder who creates the first generation of an entirely new device or service. One could argue that together, Steve Jobs, Bill Gates, Mike Dell, and Ted Waitt created the PC industry through their collective vision, which in fact they did. Their innovative insights into the needs of the man on the street took what large corporations saw as only a miniscule part of the market and turned it into an entirely new industry, ironically dwarfing the industry that was its starting point. What sets these companies and their founders apart from the millions of other companies that tried and failed is the fact that their sense of the market needs was more acute, therefore more passionate, than others. Although Steve Jobs and the others definitely have an innate sense of the needs of the people in terms of computing tools, many other companies have to work hard at understanding their customers more than ever before.

At the core of how e-business is transforming the global economy today there is a fundamental shift in how companies are being structured and how business gets done. e-Business is forcing businesses to focus on their customers more than ever before and be acutely aware of their needs first. In previous generations of business, the customer did have a voice, but businesses could be slow to listen to that voice. This fact is evidenced, for example, by the commitment of American car companies to continue creating gas guzzlers during the energy crisis of the 1970s while the operational excellence of the Japanese car manufacturers, which made smaller, much more fuel-efficient vehicles, took market share away in double-digit clumps every quarter for several years. Suddenly, American car companies woke up and realized it was the customer that needed to be in the driver's seat of their business, not the technology of "bigger is better" or the fact that operationally, GM, for example, had always made cars large and couldn't change operations easily.

The Internet is having just the same transformational effect on entire industries today, forcing them to be real about what their core values are to customers, and forcing them to be honest with customers as well. No longer can the claims of a company be hidden behind brochures, because the Internet has enabled even stronger communication between vendor and customer and also between customers. There is a new era of electronic accountability that needs to be embraced by companies, and an e-business strategy is the first step in accomplishing that.

For any relationship to be successful, there needs to be a commitment to listen and communicate. The idea of using an e-marketing site, which by definition is not actually selling anything yet is in contact with customers, to create an interchange with customers really typifies effective marketing. Creating a section on your site for a questionnaire is worth the effort and should be on your e-marketing site before it goes live. You can learn why customers came to your site, what they were looking for, why they left, and what products and services they thought you had compared to what you do have. You can also measure the branding aspects of your site as well, and gather information on what is going on with your competitors. The ability to listen to your customers is the most important task you can take on. Be passionate about driving your ASP to develop a questionnaire on your e-marketing site, and your efforts will pay dividends as your business grows from the knowledge you generate from your efforts.

A customer listening system is much more than just a survey; it's actually a commitment to create an ongoing exchange with visitors to your site in addition to customers. The following sections describe the key aspects of a customer listening system. This is included within the e-marketing efforts of a business because marketing at its most basic is about communicating with customers.

Provide an Incentive for Feedback

At the driveway.com site, where you can store files and materials online, there are surveys which when answered give you more storage space. The incentive is immediate and provided after a survey is completed, all automatically. This is by far the best approach to generating feedback on your site. When constructing your e-marketing site with your ASP, work to create incentives for customers to keep coming back and providing feedback. In the case of small businesses in the Las Vegas area, for example, coupons for free dinners are provided in addition to the chance to win a dinner show. Other companies have sponsored a drawing for a new Palm Pilot or even a laptop for visitors to the site who complete a survey.

Develop with Your ASP the Capability to Thank Respondents for Participating in Surveys

This is especially useful if you are providing an incentive and also if you are doing any special marketing campaigns. Keep these emails very short and in the tone of acknowledgment to respect the fact that the visitor must be getting many other emails as well.

Get Profile Information on Visitors to Your Site

Develop questions that provide insights into the speed at which the customer is connecting, her browser type, the type of system she has, and whether she is connecting at work or at home. These kinds of data points will assist you in further designing the site for the most efficient use possible by your customers. You need to get a picture of where your visitors are from an enablement perspective as well, because the size of the PDF files and the attachments you send out for them in the future need to be dictated in size by the speed of the connection they have to you.

Develop Survey Questions on Site Performance and Content

One of the best uses of a customer listening system is to see how your site's content is being perceived. Ask visitors to your site to rate it in terms of what they found compared to what they expected to find. It's also very important to see if the questions and issues the visitor first had experienced before coming to your site have been answered by the visit.

Define How Visitors Find Your Site

This is a critical question because it tells you which of your marketing efforts are the most effective at gaining new customers. The capability of a yellow pages ad, for example, to generate the majority of your business shows that the potential exists for getting a larger ad in the next edition and even branching into additional directories. Conversely, if direct mail is having little or no effect on driving visitors to your site, you can scale that activity back and put the money into more productive means of generating interest in your company.

Evaluate the Competitors and How They Appeal to Visitors

This is another key question because you might have an idea of who your competitors are, but ultimately it is the perception of your customers that defines who they truly are. For this reason, the customer needs to be involved and considered a key element in any of the e-commerce initiatives you undertake. Be open to listening to them and give your customers, in the context of the Web site, the chance to comment on just exactly who they see as the competitors and what these companies have in terms of value. One company, for example, that worked with an ASP to capture this information found it was really competing with much smaller and unknown firms than it had originally known. A PC clone company thought it was competing with Dell and found later it was competing with a Taiwanese company that was assembling PCs in a warehouse outside of Los Angeles. The company's pricing and branding was nearly identical to the other company, and it didn't know it until a customer provided the information. As a consequence, the company changed its approach to e-marketing, with its ASP developing more of a focus on the company's servers and successes in the ISP arena.

Focus on What Your Visitors Read, Watch, and Do

Your ASP partner can assist you in getting a questionnaire online that also captures what visitors to your site like to read, watch, and do on their days off. It's important to get a glimpse at these variables for your customers as well, in that they can assist you in making decisions about how to change your Web site to more closely align with your visitors' and hopefully customers' needs.

Work to Understand Your Customer's Purchasing Decision-Making Process

Another good example of how you can use a customer listening system is to find out how your customer makes a decision on your products and services. If you happen to be Krispy Kreme donuts, for example, you know the location and time listing is the most important part of your Web site, as is the case with many B2C focused e-marketing campaigns. Yet for many B2B companies, the need for understanding who is involved with the decision, for example, to purchase an entirely new information service or a new training service for novice Internet users can spell the difference between selling effectively into a company visiting your site for more information.

Working your ASP to create an easily navigating presentation of a new service that walks potential clients through the offering and then provides a quick screen for providing feedback is essential for most B2B companies' marketing efforts. Building product demonstration areas that invite the visitor to comment on which parts of the organization can meet his needs with the technology or service defined is essential to understanding the purchasing dynamics of customers. It's a critical step in getting to know how your customers make decisions in a B2B sale.

Invite Your Customers into the Product Development Process

The greatest benefit of creating a responsive customer listening system is the opportunity to get your customers involved in your product and service development efforts. As your installed base of customers grows, it becomes very important to have them give feedback on products and services as they are being created. Using the customer listening systems and the accumulated feedback from your customers, you can create a virtual team of contributing members defining future products. Many companies do this by rotating their engineering staff members into the roles of customer contact points for future development. Dell Computer Corporation continues to work on this aspect of its business by using internal Web sites and intranets to provide customers the opportunity to communicate their needs for future products. You can too, by working with your ASP to develop the tools necessary for creating these types of relationships with your customers. Remember, the Internet is driving businesses to be customer-centric, and the extent to which you can get your company focused on bringing customers into a dominant role in your product development efforts is the extent your company will have a chance of competing for their business in the future.

Commit to Quarterly Customer Councils to Discuss Product Strategy, and Get and Evaluate Customer Feedback

Moving from the very general aspect of getting feedback from your customers to the very specific aspect of creating councils for getting their feedback, a customer listening system has come full circle when it can get the customers into a council forum and drive product and e-business strategy with their needs in mind. Councils are best formed from a homogenous group of customers, being careful to screen for customers who have very negative attitudes about your company or the world in general. You are after a brainstorming and feedback session. Your customers need to be invited to these on a quarterly basis for the customer listening system commitments they see on your site to really have an effect on how you do business. You should also work to get your ASP in the room for the entire council session, because your ASP will need to implement many of the features. Your ASP should also present the background of the site and, especially if there are issues on performance of the site, have the ASP there to take accountability for its performance and speak to the changes that will happen to ensure higher performance in the future.

The customer listening systems of companies vary by their commitment to get their customers involved in their businesses. There are companies less than $10 million in size who have more active conversations with their customers than some $100 million corporations. The key virtue to this entire process is that your e-business strategy needs to be focused on your customers, and the e-marketing component, which is the subject of this chapter, needs to have the customer and even the visitor to your Web site as the centerpiece of all activities. It is the reason you have an e-marketing site: to serve the customers and visitors and provide them with information efficiently.

How ASPs Are Driving e-Marketing Innovation

The majority of ASPs take companies one step beyond the brochureware approach of merely taking content and pouring it into frames and completing customized work when the customer requests it. Take the top sites in your industry or profession and study how they are e-marketing effectively. Many times you'll find that ASPs have assisted customers in getting Web sites up and running that speak to both customers and visitors in a language they understand and entertain customers at the same time. ASPs, for example, have created sites that stress e-marketing and define the core values of a company very clearly. One of the most interesting examples of a company that used an ASP to create an innovative e-marketing site is Anderson Networks. Using a series of screens to define its business and training options, Anderson Networks has created a site that is both navigationally easy to work with and informative. Figure 5.10 shows how Anderson Network's site looks and how the site is designed as an e-marketing presence for the company. Anderson Networks worked with an ASP over a period of months to create the site.

Figure 5.10   An ASP created an e-marketing presence for a recruitment and training
company, Anderson Networks.

Marketing Online

Ultimately the goal of marketing online is to create a memorable experience for the
visitors to your site. Here are several topics to keep in mind when working with your
ASP to create your e-marketing site. These are critical for giving your ASP a definition
of the direction of your site. Keep the aspects of your value proposition, or what
makes you different, how you define content on your site, and the role of content
delivery options clear as they relate to your site's objective of bringing visitors and
customers to the forefront of your marketing efforts. In looking at each of these areas,
also keep in mind the visual appearance of these attributes and the fact that they need
to be communicated simply, clearly, and with the assistance of an ASP to make the
content easily updated and fresh for visitors.

Communicating Value Propositions

Answering the question of what makes you different is the most important message
you can convey with your Web site. Using the tools available from the ASP you are
working with can give you a sense of the options you have for conveying this message.
This is an area to spend a lot of time thinking about and being passionate about
because it relates to how your company is portrayed to the outside world. One of the
best exercises to do when it comes to this activity is to visualize a room full of the best
potential prospects, and pretend you have just a few minutes to tell them about your

business. The three key bullets you would tell them are what the value propositions and branding need to be for your Web site. Thinking in these terms is critical for giving the ASP you are working with direction on your project.

Defining Content

Instead of just taking the brochure copy from your previous documents and literature and then putting it into the formats your ASP has, think about the branding in its purest form and what you want to communicate to the person who happens to stumble onto your site for the first time. You need to answer the question of what's the greatest advantage of your company and its products, quickly and succinctly. Content is really a statement of what you have to offer the person stopping by your e-marketing site. The content needs to be sales-oriented, but not so much so that the site looks like an infomercial. Focus on the key problems you solve for your customers and tell the visitor to your site what those are.

Invite the Visitor to Participate and the Customer to Contribute

The ultimate compliment anyone can get is to be asked his or her opinion. Taking the time to ask for visitor and customer feedback is essential for you to develop your business. Work with your ASP to build systems that allow you to accomplish that goal.

Comparing Content Delivery Options

Many companies find that their sales force and distribution channel use their product literature extensively during cold calls and to introduce existing customers to new offerings. Instead of taking all that literature and creating HTML documents, opt for the approach many other companies are using today, which is the development of PDF files for ease of downloading and use. The PDF format is pervasive in many companies, including many of the world's research companies who distribute their reports in that format. Consider also the fact that many of the documents you are repeatedly using internally on your intranet could be more efficiently stored in a PDF file format instead of the more storage-intensive PowerPoint alternative, in the case of presentations, for example. Opt for the more concise storage alternative with PDF formatted files as well. If necessary, even get copies of Adobe Acrobat for each member of your distribution channel so they can concisely share information as well.

e-Marketing Site Development with an ASP

When embarking on your e-business strategy and direction, the first step is creating a sustainable competitive advantage through the aggressive use of e-marketing tools and techniques. Working with an ASP to create value for your customers is critical, and using the steps provided here will guide you toward having an e-marketing site that is adaptable for the needs of your organization as it grows. At the same time, the site will aim at best serving visitors and enabling customers to find the information they need as quickly as possible.

Defining Design and Site Objectives

Before beginning even the most fundamental of e-marketing sites, it's imperative that you focus on communicating what makes you different. You need to set metrics by which the success of the e-marketing site will be judged. Gather metrics from your e-marketing site and use them as a business driver.

Whatever gets measured must get better because people are held accountable for results, and quantified results are the best kind. So in creating your design and development objectives, think about how you can quantify performance and get the ASP you have hired to buy into them, thereby assuring accountability for a specific measure of performance over time. These are the steps recommended for defining design and site objectives:

1. **Develop a statement of the site's purpose.** If it's lead generation, define what mechanisms will be used for capturing leads, how many leads per month is acceptable, and which tools will be used for handling the generation of traffic to the site, including Web site optimization tools. If the site is aimed at generating greater levels of awareness and branding, then define the terms of a study for testing awareness levels. If the site is designed to do both, you must define the primary purpose to be successful. Focus on a singularity of purpose at this stage of your work with an ASP—that single purpose will bring focus at the ASP and will give you a higher chance of success.

2. **Define the key metrics for success of the site.** If this is a site on which you are going to eventually go into an e-commerce strategy, state that up front. It is recommended that you define a minimum number of email opt-in recipients over time as well, to see how the "stickiness" of your site compares over time. Lastly, you need to measure lead generation from the site, even if its primary purpose is brand building. In the world of e-business, the days of saying "We will earn $1 for every $1 invested" is gone. That's a myth. You need to be the champion of metrics in your company, especially if you are using an ASP, and drive for measured results from an e-marketing site in terms of lead generation. You can even develop systems that define how many sales were closed that originated as leads from the site. This is very much recommended so that as you want to expand the use of your site you can, by showing the return from the efforts expended.

3. **Develop a navigational flow diagram.** If you were walking someone through your store and wanted to explain to them the entry-level products all the way to the top of the line, you would use the appropriate aisles and walk

them through the product lines. It's the same basic idea with an e-marketing site. Define the navigation at a broad level and work to get the ASP to see your store in its physical state so they can understand how you want it electronically.

4. **Develop opt-in email newsletters.** Recall that from earlier in this chapter the opportunity to build interactive communication with your customer is key. Be sure from the beginning of the development of your Web site to define the opt-in opportunities and get them into the first release of your Web site. Be sure to check that the ASP you have chosen has the technical know-how to make this happen. If they do not, question the technical depth of the staff and possibly keep looking for another ASP. Building the communication link with your customers is what e-marketing is all about, and from those relationships the metrics of performance flow. Be focused on getting interactive communication with visitors and customers from the very first release of your site.

5. **Design the front page to invite specials and rotating messages.** Taking the hint from Gateway and its outstanding e-marketing efforts, check its home page to see how Gateway has built "boxes," or areas of the site for handling special promotions. Have these included in your first e-marketing site and tie back to them with other forms of media as well.

Integration with e-Commerce and e-Operations Tools

The message of this book is that e-business is the combination of e-marketing, e-commerce, and e-operations. When creating your e-marketing Web site, stay focused on the opportunities to move quickly into e-commerce by offering a catalog of your products and services, and also the opportunity to build collaborative environments with your customers and the divisions of your company using the e-operations tools many ASPs, including Zland.com, offer today. It's a good idea to create a "roadmap" of your e-business strategy (a topic touched on in later chapters) and then have the entire project of an e-business strategy in mind. When creating your e-marketing site, look for opportunities to create placeholders for e-marketing focus and talk with your ASP about creating operationally oriented areas of the site as well.

How e-Marketing Becomes Interactive

Taking e-marketing to state-of-the-art levels, several companies are now offering to place online tutorials in the form of Java applets and AVI and MPEG files on their sites for the benefit of their channel partners and their customers. The benefits of having interactive video and presentations for online training is considered by many research companies, International Data Corporation included, as one of the most innovative uses of e-marketing sites today. In creating an e-learning strategy for your company, possibly in conjunction with Human Resources, consider how to use your e-marketing oriented site to educate your visitors and customers about the benefits of your products through interactive forums and through the use of online broadcasting.

Case Study: How Razorfish Assisted National Westminster Bank UK

National Westminster Bank UK (NatWest UK for short, a part of the NatWest Group) was officially registered on March 18, 1968 following the merger of three of the United Kingdom's leading banks (National Provincial Bank, its subsidiary, District Bank, and the Westminster Bank) and was granted permission to begin trading on January 1, 1970. The company can, therefore, through the history of these constituent banks, trace its origins back as far as 1658. It is now a unified organization, focused mainly on UK and Irish financial services, which provides a broad spectrum of financial services to customers ranging from individuals and small businesses to multinational companies.

NatWest UK provides retail and corporate banking, credit card, mortgage, and insurance services. Operating income as per June 30, 1999 was £2,248 million (US$ 3,821 million) and profit before tax £665 million (US $1,130 million). NatWest UK has 46,200 employees, and worldwide the Group employs 64,400 people.

NatWest's Objectives

NatWest wanted to renew its brand identity to retain and reappraise its customers. It also wanted to show them it was keeping up with developments in electronic space and target those customers who wanted online access to its activities and services.

Selecting an Internet Services Company

The company engaged the TBWA agency (also part of the Omnicom Group) at the end of 1998 to overhaul its offline branding, advertising, and marketing, and integrate them with its online branding.

Razorfish's role was to implement customer-oriented Internet applications as part of the extended brand identity. The company advised NatWest on the branding strategy and development of a consistent electronic identity.

NatWest believed Razorfish, as a sister agency to TBWA through the connection to Omnicom, would improve the collaboration and provide an integrated solution. It would mean consistency in brand identity between the Internet and offline channels (for example, print campaigns).

Implementing a Solution

Razorfish started on the project in April 1999. The first part—called the E-dentity project—was concerned with bringing the established brand identity of NatWest into new digital channels. This involved building graphics, colors, and navigation tools, and creating a consistent and enticing, "fun to use" user experience. The aim of the second part—natwest.com—was to re-invent NatWest's main consumer banking Web site. NatWest wanted the site to present its users with a fresh, innovative, future-oriented organization with a specific interest in improving its customer services on a continuous basis. E-dentity and natwest.com were developed in parallel. Figure 5.11 shows the offline and online branding program.

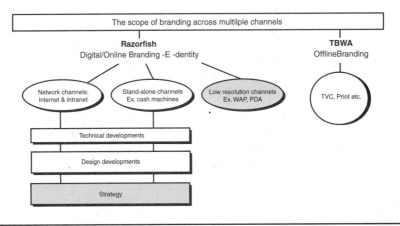

Figure 5.11   NatWest's branding strategy.

The NatWest e-Strategy

The E-dentity project took NatWest's strong brand and all experience factors (tone for example) and defined how they were to be extended across multiple digital channels, such as the Web, cash machines, mobile phones, PDA, and all online communications. Razorfish created a brand concept with interactive tools and an intranet, which integrate brand strategy and online style guidelines.

According to Razorfish, consistent branding across all new media channels is essential, but E-dentity goes much further. E-dentity is about developing a powerful, multiple digital channel strategy. Increasingly, companies are finding that getting the right mix of channels for their products is one of the biggest issues they face in the new digital marketplace; E-dentity combines both branding and channel strategy into one package.

NatWest already had over 2,000 pages online in the summer of 1999 as part of its existing site, but almost all needed enhancement to bring them in line with the new advertising style that NatWest had adopted earlier in the year. Additionally, new interactive features were needed to maximize the quality of the user experience. Razorfish had to re-create the online presence both technically and in terms of brand communication. This involved working closely with several NatWest departments including NatWest's own IT development staff, facilitating best practice and cooperation between agency and client, and ensuring the solution met all parties' requirements.

Razorfish undertook an analysis of the needs of personal and small-business, as well as corporate customers. This analysis, and the need to adapt quickly to new developments in financial services on the Internet, necessitated the introduction of online banking and other new site areas.

Razorfish designed the site to be simple to use and quicker to get from section to section. It also includes interactive features that, for example, help the customers budget for their vacation, save for the future, or work out how much they need to borrow for their mortgage. It also offers checklists for students, vacation planners, and home-buyers.

The first part took three months to develop and included the following three phases:

- **Clarify**—Agreeing with NatWest on the business objectives and creating a strategic plan.
- **Architect**—Defining the functional, technical, and creative requirements.
- **Design**—Completing information, interaction, and interface design. Also involved developing content and refining the technology architecture.

The second part, which was the building of the dotcom site, was done in six weeks and included the next two phases:

- **Implement**—Building the final product, as well as testing and performing quality assurance checks.
- **Enhance**—Monitoring and analyzing the solution's performance.

According to Ron Kalifa, Head of eCommerce Marketing, NatWest, the short development time was required because of the determination of all involved to get the service in front of NatWest customers as soon as possible. This meant Razorfish worked on the project 24 hours a day, pulling the appropriate resources from its network of offices around the world, including additional development support in parallel from New York.

Introducing Customers to the Internet

The strategy has been designed to introduce the new Internet services at a pace that gives NatWest's customers a chance to get used to the idea of using them. Customers can pick up a free NatWest OnLine CD-ROM from a NatWest branch, which gives access to the online services and free Internet access, which is available to non-NatWest customers also. Adding online services as an extra to other banking facilities gives customers more control over how, when, and where they use NatWest's products and services.

The solution will be promoted step by step. The first step is to introduce the services to its existing customers. In the United Kingdom, switching banks is rare, so NatWest is not afraid of losing existing customers to other competitors, such as pure Internet banks or supermarkets such as Tesco, which is also offering its customers a banking service. According to Kalifa, NatWest does not underestimate these new competitors, but is confident that with its existing knowledge of e-banking and its focus on Internet banking services, its services are competitive. Its aim is to remain so and give its customers the choice of accessing its services as easily through a branch or the Internet.

New customers are the next target segment. Young people and students in particular are a key target audience because the Internet is already a natural part of their lives.

Another segment is small- and medium-sized businesses in the United Kingdom. NatWest has introduced, as part of natwest.com, a service focused on advising small businesses on the different issues these companies face in their day-to-day business.

Organizational Issues

NatWest has an "e-team" that concentrates on e-commerce and functions as a think tank, consisting of a small team of people who have expert knowledge within IT, marketing, communication, and banking. This group can also draw people from different functions in the bank whenever needed. Razorfish's role is as an outside representative advising on the digital strategy, but not directly with organizational issues.

It is important to NatWest that its employees are aware of the e-business trend and new services. The online strategy outlined two ways to communicate new events to employees: via the intranet, developed by Razorfish, and through a focus on making the employees themselves use the Internet services offered.

NatWest continues to work with Razorfish as a partner and will continuously develop the site with new features and services. The management of the technical part is partly done internally and partly outsourced to Razorfish. The degree of the outsourcing is decided on a case-by-case basis, ranging from strategy, technology (front end and back end) design, online marketing, and so on.

Conclusion

The Internet is becoming a fundamental delivery channel for banks. Financial institutions are continuing to offer new products on the Internet, and customers are showing an increasing interest in them.

The surge in online banking will create several opportunities for banks to offer new services to customers, and in turn the banks' plans to offer new services will create a number of opportunities for providers of Internet banking applications and services.

Razorfish and NatWest have seen the opportunities in this trend and developed a partnership to ensure that NatWest will be perceived as a bank with a focus on bringing Internet banking services into the e-future.

With regards to new customers, NatWest is very concerned about promoting its services in the best possible way. NatWest has deliberately chosen a strategy that introduces the new services at a pace that gives existing customers a chance to get used to the idea of using the online services as a complement to the offline services. But at the same time, to attract new customers, especially young people and students who are already used to online activities, it has been vital to offer some new and exciting features.

Internally, it has been important that all employees grasp the idea step-by-step in relation to doing business online. There is a continuous flow of information on the intranet and all groups in the company are taken into account whenever changes or strategies related to the person's or groups' area is being discussed in connection with online activities. NatWest has decided not to split the company into an online company and a brick-and-mortar company, which gives customers consistency of brand experience across all channels.

According to NatWest, Razorfish will be involved in future online projects. The partnership has been a success, and according to Rassami Hök Ljungberg, marketing manager, Razorfish London, the importance of working closely with customers on an ongoing basis is part of Razorfish's strategy. Razorfish views client relationships as valuable partnerships and intends to leverage its relationships with its clients' senior management to expand the scope and length of current engagements and to enter into additional agreements.

Research companies believe this concept will bring Razorfish further advantages within the finance/banking sector. It is well suited to handling Internet projects focusing on design and branding strategies, and its track record within this sector shows that Razorfish is gaining a stronghold in the finance sector worldwide. Razorfish has succeeded in leveraging this knowledge into Europe, and research companies believe that during 2000 Razorfish will add several clients to its portfolio within the European banking and finance sector.

Summary

The essence of effective marketing is the enabling of communication. This chapter focused on how you can create an effective e-marketing strategy that services the needs of the visitors to your site and the customers and channel partners who rely on it for up-to-date information.

6

Selling Online: How e-Commerce Works with ASPs

WITH ALL THE LEADING INDICATORS of e-commerce growth pointing toward rapid adoption of technologies that make electronic catalogs more scalable, more robust at handling dynamic pricing strategies, and able to compensate for differences in currencies, selling online is growing at a robust rate. Forrester Research has projected the size of the total business-to-business e-commerce marketplace to be over $1.3 trillion in total sales worldwide by 2003. Many factors driving this level of economic growth are attributable to B2B commerce alone. These factors are explained in this chapter from the context of how ASPs are enabling companies of all sizes to compete in their chosen marketplaces using e-commerce as a revenue-generation tool and development of an entirely new distribution channel in many cases. The now-legendary success of Dell Computer Corporation, for example, is held up by many other industries as a case study of how to create an entirely new distribution channel. Even the *Wall Street Journal*, when describing the market dynamics of companies in industries relying on dual-tier distribution, describe the act of being disintermediated from a distribution channel as being "Delled."

The growth of e-commerce is affecting distribution channel and product strategy decisions within companies all over the world. With the successes of the direct marketers globally, including Dell, Gateway, Amazon.com, Buy.com, and Expedia.com (in the travel marketplace), e-commerce is accumulating credibility quickly in the eyes of small business owners, and respect from IT directors and CIOs of larger corporations.

Beyond the media hype around these companies, the hands-on challenges of bringing a site online efficiently and hitting a market window with the right solution at the right time is more of a challenge for companies entering into e-commerce strategies than coming up with the strategy itself.

Realizing that time-to-market is a competitive advantage for technology- and even non-technology–based companies, many ASPs are taking a vertical market focus with their services so they can provide valuable services to marketing departments at their customers' sites. ASPs, then, are only as valuable as the challenges they take on for their customers, bringing expertise in-house for handling the toughest problems.

This chapter provides you with an overview of e-commerce today and the future competitive landscape of e-commerce given current market dynamics. You'll also learn what an e-commerce strategy is, how to create one, and how ASPs can assist you in implementing your e-commerce efforts. This chapter describes the day-to-day running of an e-commerce Web site, comparing the time investment necessary to complete the site yourself versus outsourcing the e-commerce portions of your site to an ASP. Throughout this chapter there will also be definitions of acronyms and case studies of companies, some very well known, such as Amazon.com, and others relatively unknown to the level of the online bookstore, which have successfully implemented e-commerce sites.

Exploring e-Commerce from an ASP Perspective

To many, e-commerce connotes the idea of making an increasingly larger percentage of sales online compared to traditional selling channel methods. The success stories from companies by industry that are excelling at generating incrementally over 10% or more revenue from their e-commerce strategies is alluring to companies who have not seriously considered an e-business strategy before. In surveys completed by International Data Corporation, the median revenue increase from having an e-commerce strategy is 10%, according to the latest surveys of over 1,100 businesses across the United States. e-Commerce is seen as foundational by these companies for future revenue streams, so the amount of dollars in investments being made today in anticipation of future revenue has been steadily increasing. This amount is taking up larger proportions of the total revenue stream. These early adopters have been discussed in Chapter 4, and have been taking an aggressive stance on getting the most out of the technologies they invest in. Instead of being coaxed into e-commerce, these early adopter companies jump into initiatives and establish competitive strength in their markets before competing companies can. These early adopter companies are striving to develop their beachheads in respective online markets, and are initiating land grab strategies of their own.

This is one market dynamic in the ASP industry in which the customers are actually driving the behavior of the vendors. Just as early adopters strive for customer counts and market shares, so too are the ASPs focusing on the various sizes of organizations globally. As mentioned in other parts of this book, the entire ASP arena in the area of e-commerce is like a "land grab" from the gold rush years in San Francisco or land rushes when the American West opened for settlers. Many ASPs are so singularly focused on accumulating high customer counts that they sometimes neglect the total equation of bringing value to their customers. Ironically, the early adopter companies that are actually driving land grabs are the coveted accounts, and are driving ASPs to fulfill the entire equation of services that comprise a responsive and accountable business.

Instead of just launching into what e-commerce is, given the frame of reference of this book it's important to see the revenue generation capabilities as a service that an ASP brings to customers. Contracting with an ASP to generate revenue online for your company presents unique challenges that are the focus of this chapter. Given the market dynamics of selling on the Internet, there are continual refinements to e-commerce services as well. The ASPs in this context of e-commerce are the "buy" side of the make-or-buy equation when it comes to creating an online catalog or store for generating revenue. Figure 6.1 shows the results of a survey completed by Yankee Group on the relative level of interest in using an ASP to provide e-commerce solutions.

e-Commerce Defined

From the standpoint of companies considering outsourcing their e-commerce strategy to an ASP, *e-commerce* refers to the ability to dynamically price items, tie back customers' preferences for products and services, create a personalized shopping experience, and define customized sites that reflect the requirements of your largest customers (sometimes called *stealth sites* because they are visible only for the customers they are developed for). e-Commerce is much more than selling products or offering services online, it's the integration of the business model of a business with the manner in which transactions are completed.

International Data Corporation, a research company that is actively tracking the ASP marketplace, has defined e-commerce as follows:

> Electronic commerce is the integration of communication technologies and multi-enterprise based applications that accentuate buying and selling of goods and services between customers, regardless of the platform or operating system being used on respective networks. The integration of Internet technology and core competencies of a business (what a company does best) is the essence of electronic commerce. Technology is the enabler of efficiencies for the company's core business, often driving down costs and increasing customer satisfaction through more responsive support and communication. Departments that have the majority of contact with both customers and suppliers need to be enabled first to ensure a return on investment in electronic commerce.

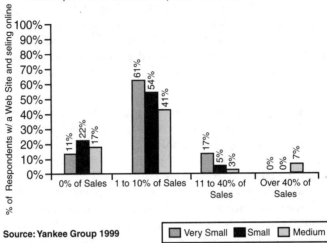

If They Sell Online, Then How Much?

- A small percent sell on-line
  And it represents an even smaller percent of revenue

Figure 6.1   How companies view e-commerce as a service looking to drive incremental revenue with an e-business strategy.

Take for example Harrods, one of the most upscale stores in the world, located in London. Catering to an international clientele who have needs as diverse as getting Vanilla tea to catering entire weddings and even renting the reception hall, Harrods has the breadth of offerings that makes them an end-to-end solution for both con-sumer-oriented and business-focused events. Its e-commerce strategy is oriented to the United States and Canada, and its branding welcomes U.K. residents. It's an inno-vative strategy of driving traffic into its store, yet also bringing the most popular mer-chandise with U.S. travelers to the Web for availability 24 hours a day, 7 days a week. The organization of the online store is also consistent with the needs of the interna-tional visitors the actual store itself attracts. The business gifts are located in an area of the site that is completely separate from the mainstream gifts. The overall structure of the site makes it possible for Harrods to target multiple online audiences with a single e-commerce presence. Figure 6.2 shows an example of the Harrods site.

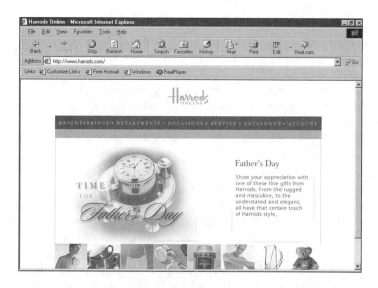

Figure 6.2 A great example of a site designed to appeal to multiple customer segments is Harrods Department Store, based in London. The breadth of services offered attracts customers from a variety of segments.

The Key Points of e-Commerce Execution

From the small business with a single product or service to sell, for example those companies who provide air conditioning in the desert Southwest, to the Harrods department stores of the world, e-commerce is the packaging for electronic sale of the goods and services a company offers. What separates the companies successful at e-commerce and those that struggle is their execution of the following key points:

- **Strengthen the direct sales model with effective pricing strategies**—For a company to be successful with an e-commerce strategy, the pricing of products needs to be flexible enough to change quickly in response to market needs. This area is one of the most paradoxical and challenging for many companies embarking on an e-commerce strategy, as the lower cost of sales should be applied directly to profit. In fact, the Web does bring price competition, especially on commodity-like items, forcing companies to drop their prices in response to market needs.

- **Keep product messages simple**—e-Commerce is excelling at selling the items that require little up front education. Books and travel are the most popular items being sold on the Web today. In creating an e-commerce strategy, think about which products and services you offer that are most easily understood and recognized by your customers.

- **Think fulfillment**—Before the first sale is made off of a Web site, it's important to think about how the orders will be fulfilled quickly, and how the customers who are purchasing from you will be tracked for future promotional efforts. The best lead for a new product is often a customer using the existing generation of a product or service. Although many companies think of themselves as having a marketing focus and strength, in fact, operations, the fulfillment of commitment to customers, is just as much if not more of a true marketing effort. Deliverables that are met and commitments that are seen through to the end are what keep customers coming back. Operations make that happen.

- **Reward customer loyalty with product strategies that serve them**— With the velocity of transactions that the Web is capable of producing, it's imperative that product strategies be developed that can be refined to support sales that are self-contained and require little outside support. One reason books are so successful on the Web is their self-contained nature, and the fact that brick and mortar stores have had varying levels of quality of service made the personalization aspects of Amazon.com very valuable in the context of the shopping experience. Books also are very amenable to frequent buyer programs in that they are easily categorized for sales analysis. Think about creating a frequent buyer program for the very beginning of your Web site to encourage repeat sales.

- **Encourage customer feedback**—It's very important to invite your customers into a dialog with you about their experiences. Think about how you can create multiple points of contact with your customers through a Web site. First, the option of opt-in emails can provide your customers with information pertinent to their personal or professional interests, giving them the opportunity to comment on how your company is doing. Be sure always to invite customer feedback after a sale to generate more knowledge of your customer base.

- **Ask your application service provider to create market metrics to gauge success**—One of the key benefits of working with a technology partner is the opportunity to learn from its accumulated experience. With the rapid adoption of e-commerce, companies of all sizes are increasingly looking at the ROI associated with it, starting with the Global 2,000 who are investing millions in their efforts to be online. The need for generating reliable metrics ties back to the fiscal responsibility of running an e-commerce site. Even if the e-commerce site is just for a single series of products, metrics give you a benchmark for planning on how to increase the overall profitability of the site itself. Be sure in your initial planning efforts with an application service provider to work toward a plan for getting the best possible metrics associated with your site as it is being built. You'll be able to measure its success much more efficiently and accurately that way.

- **Get your company known**—Many of the application service providers also provide services for getting your Web site known with search engines. You might have seen these sites that promise you will be listed in all search engines within six weeks of submitting your URL. These free services are somewhat limited in what they can accomplish for your site; Yahoo! for example, is turning away listings in many cases due to overwhelming demand. In response to the need for greater results from search engines, there are entire companies now offering these services. Using these services, you can have keywords embedded in your Web pages, causing them to be found more often than if just your URL was listed.

- **Build lead generation into your selling efforts**—One of the most challenging aspects of any business is the development of an ongoing stream of leads that will in turn feed revenue. When creating your e-commerce site, think in terms of how you will be able to leverage your selling efforts to create opportunities for lead generation. The ongoing development of leads is the lifeblood of any company, and you can develop yours much more efficiently through the use of tools that capture leads while you are selling.

- **Plan for personalization**—When structuring your e-commerce strategy and specifically your Web site, think about how you can customize your Web site for your customers' specific needs. You can do this with many of the server-based tools found in Microsoft and Sun-based server applications. When creating your Web site with an ASP, think about how you can add personalization to the shopping experience, thereby giving you a competitive advantage.

- **Verify payment gateway options first**—Instead of just relying on the payment provider your ASP might already have a relationship with, check out a series of payment gateways on your own first. This includes evaluating each in terms of its capability to scale on a global basis, to control fraud, and to verify credit card information from secondary Web sites in addition to your own. Increasingly, companies doing e-commerce sales are cascading them through multiple sites. Be sure the payment gateway can scale across multiple locations.

Don't let the list stop there. You can work with the ASP of your choice to get even more leverage out of its core strengths, and use this list for guiding the conversations with your ASP toward using e-commerce to the maximum extent possible. This list is a conversation starter for you to get an idea of how much depth the ASPs you are talking to have when it comes to getting an e-commerce site up and running.

Managing Rapid Changes in the Marketplace with ASPs

Further considerations when working with an ASP include the number of customers it has working in e-commerce applications and its capability to keep customers coming back for more functionality over time. When working with an ASP for your e-commerce solutions, be sure to think in terms of what it has done over time for other clients and get references. Get behind the success stories that ASPs provide, getting to the customers who have had challenges. There is a set of customers who has challenged the ASP to grow; it's important to find out about that group to see how the ASP is reacting to them, especially in the e-commerce arena.

Leveraging the experiences of ASPs when creating e-commerce Web sites is also critical given the rapidly changing nature of the market. Recent surveys by Forrester Research show that instead of the traditional early adopters purchasing over the Internet, there is a wider breadth than there ever has been before when it comes to purchasing behavior. According to Forrester Research, 11 million more consumers in the United States alone will try purchasing over the Internet for the first time in 2000, generating $38 billion in sales. The result of this quickening pace of growth is that the profile of the early adopter is changing dramatically.

Forrester's Christopher Kelley completed the analysis of the latest surveys on e-commerce adoption by U.S. consumers. "When we started surveying online consumers three years ago, Web buyers were a homogenous group consisting of affluent males who used the Net to purchase software," Kelley said. "As new Web shoppers—who increasingly resemble the offline population—become more comfortable shopping online, their Net spending habits will mirror those currently seen with experienced Web shoppers."

According to Forrester, two factors will promote the growth of the online retail market in the next year. First, Web buyers are confidently shopping across new product categories, with the most money being spent on researched products, including travel, computer hardware, and consumer electronics. Second, although the core of online shoppers are generally male, younger, and more affluent than the online population as a whole, the new Web buyer is more likely to be female, younger, and less affluent than more experienced online shoppers. In fact, for the first time, more than half of new buyers are female.

The fear of releasing credit card information remains the single most significant factor for online consumers who don't buy on the Net. Nearly half of online consumers in the United States and Canada have caught the e-commerce bug, but 52% of online households do not shop online due to fear of stolen credit card information and the distribution of personal information.

Another sign that online consumers are becoming more mainstream comes from the publications they read.

"Online shoppers are no longer just techies who sit around reading *Wired* all day long," Kelley said. "Instead, the top three magazines they subscribe to include *Reader's Digest*, *TV Guide*, and *Better Homes and Gardens*."

Forrester also found that although consumers embrace new shopping options, they expect a stream of innovations, reasonable prices, and promotions to keep coming. Experienced Web buyers embrace online auctions, drawn in by the fun of bidding and the possibility of acquiring a great deal. Of the surveyed online shoppers, 94% are also concerned with unreasonable shipping prices, with 44% having abandoned an online shopping cart due to shipping costs.

Online consumers have opened their inboxes to marketing, with 95% of Web buyers receiving offers or promotions via email, according to Forrester. Online coupon and promotion companies lead the email marketing race, filling the greatest number of inboxes of online shoppers and nonbuyers alike. Although consumers receive marketers' email, a full 32% of email targets delete most marketing messages before even reading them.

A survey done by Yanklovich Partners for Productopia found that 93% of online consumers have researched products online, and 85% have purchased a product online. According to the study, consumers say it is very important to find information across a broad range of product categories at a single site. For consumers who are searching for product information online, 88% say that it is somewhat to very important to have all the information available from a single source. Among users who have researched online for product information, 86% are somewhat to very likely to purchase that product online.

But the Web is also changing the way consumers shop offline. In 2005, U.S. online consumers will spend in excess of $632 billion in offline channels as a direct result of research that they conduct on the Web, according to Jupiter Communications. That amount dwarfs the $199 billion that consumers will spend on the Internet. Web-impacted spending, which includes both online purchases and Web-influenced offline purchases, will exceed $235 billion this year and reach more than $831 billion in 2005. Consumers who are online represent a large and growing portion of U.S. consumer spending: all told, U.S. online users will account for 75% of all expected U.S. retail spending (both online and offline) in 2005, up from 43% in 1999.

The NRF/Forrester Online Retail Index, created in conjunction with Greenfield Online and the National Retail Federation, found online sales patterns for the month of April 2000 following a pattern similar to what would be expected by traditional offline sales, further proof that online shopping is being used by mainstream consumers for mainstream products. The arrival of spring saw increases in online sales among sporting goods, tools, gardening products, apparel, and footwear.

"The same cold weather in April that contributed to the soft retail sales as reported by the U.S. Department of Commerce might have helped fuel the increase in online sales, as consumers opted to avoid the weather outside and shop from the comfort of their own homes," said David Cooperstein, research director at Forrester. "Consumers are also cleaning out their closets and replacing last year's spring and summer fashions by shopping online. Our data shows that spending on apparel and footwear grew from $175 million in March to $223 million in April."

Although the growth of business-to-consumer (B2C) continues to gather the majority of the press coverage of e-commerce today, the majority of sales over time will be between companies, typically called business-to-business (B2B) commerce. The nature of B2B commerce is also rapidly changing, being driven by the advent of small businesses purchasing online. In fact, small businesses and their purchasing online is driving the B2B sales trends today.

The Access Markets International (AMI) research company completed a survey in May, 2000 for *Inc. Magazine* that focused on the spending by U.S. small businesses for online transactions. The study confirmed that sales in fact are growing very quickly, from $2 billion in 1998 to $25 billion in 1999, a 1,000% jump. The number of small businesses transacting business on the Internet drove this significant jump in revenue. Growing from 1.8 million in 1998 to 2.8 million in 1999, the study concluded that there was a 55% jump in the number of companies transacting business over the Web. Given the fact that the number of small businesses projected to be using the Web for transactions will jump to over 3.5 million in the next year, many research companies, such as Access Markets International, are projecting the total B2B marketplace will grow to $118 billion by 2001. The majority of these small businesses have e-marketing oriented sites, where the primary message of their companies is presented on the Internet. There is also an increasing focus on the companies using the Web most often to create portals or exchanges, in fact intranets, to streamline the development cycle on projects.

An essential part of the B2B commerce is the disproportionately high growth of larger corporations that are actively making investments in the development of their e-commerce capabilities, and the increasing role Razorfish and others are having in the definition of this market. The continued growth of e-commerce is also being driven by small businesses as well, who are expected to drive the first adoption of B2B auctions for their services. In looking at B2B auction sites and the possibility of implementing one for your company, ask the ASP provider you are working with for references of auction sites it has created in the past. This is a relatively new area, and the field of ASPs varies in terms of their experience working with auctions.

The promise of B2B auctions is a strong market driver into the future and is one of the aspects of B2B commerce that has attracted 670,000 small businesses onto online B2B auctions to date, with an additional 1 million expected by 2001. Armed with this information, it's clear that you need auctions and dynamic pricing as part of your e-commerce strategy. Online auctions will become eventually a major part of online catalogs, as the level of differentiation that is provided by auctions diminishes within the same timeframe that catalogs need to create value by differentiating themselves. The result: Catalog morph auctions into their baseline offerings. ASPs that have strong e-commerce packages will either create catalogs that include auction-like features or work with their technology suppliers to create auction-friendly additions to existing catalogs. In embarking with an ASP on an e-commerce strategy, make a point of having a discussion about online auctions and their role in the ASP's service strategy. Admittedly, only the most forward-thinking e-commerce ASPs have adopted a plan for providing auction capabilities in their catalogs.

Despite the limitations of catalogs today and the fact that the range of offerings varies widely between ASPs, there are an estimated 600,000 small businesses alone selling their products and services via e-commerce sites in 1999 up from 400,000 small businesses in 1998. The value of such transactions rose from $14 billion (1998) to $25 billion (1999), representing an increase of 79 percent. Forrester Research has been instrumental in quantifying this marketplace, as has The Yankee Group.

These small businesses are finding that the Internet offers a wide variety of opportunities to sell their services to larger IT organizations that have established Web presences and IT organizations staffing e-business initiatives. The small businesses that have adopted the Internet have done so to serve their largest customers, who have e-commerce strategies and requirements for vendors to be online. Otherwise, small businesses are finding the Internet tough to work with due to the trust factor. When working with your ASP, find out how many small businesses (under 1,000 employees) it is working with, because this will give you a gauge of how strong the ASP strength is in the area of customer education and retention. What's ironic is that many of these small businesses are driving overall Internet growth and are the true early adopters of e-commerce.

Among the 7.4 million U.S. small businesses, 4.2 million access the Net, representing a penetration of 57%. Almost 17 million, or one-quarter of small business employees, use the Internet, according to reports from AMI-Inc. research. Because 80% of small businesses have fewer than 10 employees and they're relatively split between metropolitan and outlying areas, e-commerce offers tremendous efficiencies and economies of scale and the capability to compete on a global scale. More than half of the small businesses responding to the AMI-Inc. survey noted that a constant, high-speed connection to the Internet would be useful, and 40% were interested in receiving and providing customer service and support via the Internet.

In looking at the technology adoption curve in Figure 6.3, it's important to think in terms of the underlying drivers causing such a rapid adoption of e-commerce throughout the world. These key drivers include increased quantification of trust, development of secure trading systems, continued education of businesses on the benefits and expectations for e-commerce tools, and the industry-specific successes of companies as they revolutionize their own areas of the economy.

The true message of the chart in Figure 6.3 is that the application service provider industry is actually a change agent in e-commerce growth. When you partner with an ASP, it's important to recognize just what it can do and what it has the bandwidth to provide from the aspect of customized services, if you choose to take your e-commerce strategy in that direction. Here are issues to think about when selecting an ASP for your e-commerce strategy:

- **Flexibility of choosing payment gateway providers**—First and foremost, check into the payment gateway and credit card verification services that are offered by the ASP you are considering. Ask the ASP whether the payment gateway being used is compatible with all countries your business works with and has plans to work with in the futre.

  You also want to find out about plans for expansion for the payment gateway you are working with, including the ASP's plans for handling the Euro currency (Euro currency is getting increased attention in Europe as the British pound is very strong relative to it today), and the ability of the payment gateway to deal with VAT tax requirements by country. Of course the payment gateway needs to be able to handle the various currencies across the countries you plan on marketing to.

At first glance you look at a payment gateway and think it is global; be careful and probe into the tough questions on currency and VAT compatibility because this area can cost you if you change providers midstream. CyberSource is one of the best companies in this area, and CyberCash is a close second. Ideally, your ASP should have relationships with both of these companies, or at least be able to tell you the strengths and weaknesses of each.

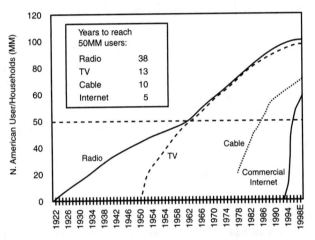

Source: Morgan Stanley Dean Witter Technology Research. E = Morgan Stanley Dean Witter Research Estimate.
Notes: (1)   We use the launch of HBO in 1976 as our estimate for the begining of cable as an
entertainment/advertising medium. Though cable technology was developed in the late 1940s, its initial use was
promarily for the improvement of reception in remote areas. It was not until HBO began to distribute its pay-TV
movie service via satelllite in 1976 that the medium became a distinct content and advertising alternative to
broadcast television. (2) Morgan Stanley Dean Witter Research Estimate.

MORGAN STANLEY DEAN WITTER

Figure 6.3   The technology adoption curve for the Internet is outpacing television and is comparable to cable television's ramp-up.

- **Average time to clear a transaction through a payment processor—**
  Card Service International is one of the better companies at handling credit card verification and authentication of credit card and electronic check transactions; however, it is very slow on the fulfillment side of the transaction. This translates into a very slow payment cycle back into your merchant account; it can take as long as a week before the transaction closes and the funds from a credit card transaction appear in your account. Be sure to probe other providers as well; don't just settle for Card Service International. Get a payment processor that can get a transaction completed in 24 hours or less and get the funds into your merchant account. It's a disappointing experience to wait over a week for

payment on transactions from your Web site. Ask your ASP for references of companies who have successfully used the payment processor they are recommending to you, because the actual performance of these companies has direct bearing on how quickly you are paid for your transactions.

- **Security of transactions and transaction data**—This is the biggest hurdle that e-commerce needs to overcome in order to capture its full potential in the world of e-business today. With regard to your ASP, you need to make sure they can successfully handle the following issues:

  - **Security of where transaction data is stored**—This is a big issue and is the primary reason the ASP approach to hosting applications is gaining market share steadily and not in a torrent of customers. The need for having the security of transaction data is tantamount to many companies. Knowing that the data is safe is a tough concept for many information systems managers to contend with as the health of the data and its security has a direct bearing on their jobs. It's a tough leap of faith for many companies to let someone else have their transaction data and report back on the transactions completed. That's where the issue of quantified trust comes into the picture and why Microsoft and others who initially sold software over the Web needed to have an independent third party verify the transactions. You need to think about how you can verify transactions and what levels of control on transactions your ASP includes.

  - **Web site security and firewalls**—You should determine the capability of your potential ASP to keep the hosted Web site secure from intruders. You'll need to also find out about the internal firewalls to the ASP: how separate the sites are, and how likely another customer for your ASP would be able to hack into your site from the same server. Check to see what safeguards are in place that ensure the security of your site from others on the server as well.

  - **Support for 128-bit encryption**—This is essential especially if you plan to jump into global commerce quickly. Encryption refers to the capability of your site to protect the servers it is hosted on from browsers that try to intercept or compromise the security of servers. 128-bit encryption is included in the latest browsers and is a requirement for trading electronically with many of the third-world countries and countries that are a security risk. Make sure you find out your ASP's position on encryption and security of transactions originated at locations outside the United States, and in areas of the world that pose a security risk as well.

  - **Authentication and verification**—This includes the technologies that Web hosting and server tools use to ensure that the persons using your site are actually who they say they are. Authentication is the process of authenticating that people are actually who they say they are. Check to make sure your ASP is working on these technologies. Also, find out their level of commitment to the concept of authentication and verification of visitors.

- **ASP stress testing**—Check to see if your ASP has sponsored an Internet security company to see if they could break into your ASP's hosting facilities. Many of the CIOs of companies looking to outsource global operations require the larger ASPs to complete these tests to ensure hackers cannot get to credit card and transaction information. Ask the ASPs you are working with if they have undertaken this level of testing and what the results were. If none of this testing has been done, continue shopping for an ASP that tests itself using security firms.

- **Catalog scalability**—Before you sign with an ASP, check the relative level of scalability that its catalogs provide. For many, the maximum number of items is 50,000. Check to see also whether the catalog can provide for easily upgraded pricing, number of hits by item, and uploading image files of products featured. Make sure the catalog can be upgraded to localization standards throughout Europe as well. Many of the ASPs based in the United States are actively developing partnerships and programs to share their technologies with strategic partners in the countries of Western Europe, for example. Scandinavia is one of the most wired nations on the planet, and so is Germany. Check to see the global reach of your ASP as it relates to the scalability of its products and services across international boundaries. This will give you an accurate gauge of how adept the engineering and marketing organizations are at handling the diverse needs of an international audience.

- **Percentage of business from outside the United States**—Although the ASP early adopters are predominantly based in the United States, it's important to find out how much of the ASP's business has revenue generation outside the United States. An international revenue stream has the potential of offsetting downturns in other areas of the world as well. Think about the investment in your ASP as if you were buying stock in the company, which in fact you are, and you will be in the right mindset to make the best possible decision for your Web site and e-business strategy.

- **Dynamic pricing and B2B auction support**—The option of taking your e-business strategy into an auction role is a viable alternative because auctions are the beginnings of the supply chain dynamics affecting the larger corporations of the world today. Auctions and their integration into catalogs will be the change agents that will drive supply chain integration into small businesses.

- **Must have a shopping cart in the catalog**—Given the rapid changes to catalogs, there is no excuse for an ASP not having a shopping cart in its catalog. It is a must-have and you need to make your requirements of this clear to your ASP.

- **Order Status is the application superstar**—In research completed by Ingram Micro, Tech Data, and Inacom to find what their resellers and customers wanted first in terms of a Web-based application, Order Status was the clear winner. Giving your customers the opportunity to get the status of their orders is a strong value-add and is essential for the growth of ongoing traffic to your site. Be sure to get this into your first e-commerce site as well. It is a must have just as a shopping cart is. Together these two components are essential, and given the fact that even free Web sites are offering this, there is really no excuse for an ASP not to offer these features.

- **Digital wallets and personalization**—Made famous by Amazon.com as a technology that greets the visitor to the site and informs them of recent additions to the bookstore, CD store, and even Z-Shops, which have items of interest to you given your previous history. The latest generation of catalogs has the capability to provide this functionality. In conjunction with this personalization aspect of catalogs is the capability to keep track of credit cards and passwords for authentication and account management, and the capability to query on shipping address. All these features are essential for an online catalog. Your ASP should already have these personalization technologies engrained into several sites. It's a technology that has been around for several years and is readily available in several different catalogs already. This personalization aspect is critical to the success of your site and e-commerce efforts. It streamlines the customers' experience with your site as well.

- **Flexibility of catalog formats and appearance**—In the first generation of e-commerce tools including catalogs, they all resembled each other and to a large extent seemed to be figuratively sitting on the sidelines to see which graphical approach to navigation worked best. Today the appearance of the catalog is morphing into a tool that can be blended directly and seamlessly into an e-marketing site. InterShop is a catalog vendor that has jumped to the forefront of technology innovation. InterShop started out in Germany and has since set up U.S. headquarters in the San Jose, California area for the ease of recruiting world class talent and creating partnerships with other e-commerce companies in that region of the country. Check out InterShop at `www.intershop.com` to see the standard you should use for getting the catalog you need for an ASP.

- **Searching capability**—In the same league as the features of wallets and order status, making sure your ASP provides a search feature is essential for the success of your site. You will be competing online with companies building their own sites and spending maybe 15X as much as you are with an ASP, so the need to be competitive with them on features is critical. In the same survey completed by the three companies mentioned in the Order Status area of this chapter, the need for an easy-to-use and powerful search engine capability was brought up as the second-most requested feature by resellers working with Ingram, Tech Data, and Inacom. Make sure the ASPs you are considering have both primary and advanced search capabilities.

- **Promotional program and product features**—Ask potential ASPs if their catalogs are able to define featured products, on-sale promotions, and customer discounts. Also, find out if the ASP's catalog feature can develop affiliate programs for those customers and other businesses that want to create links to your site.

- **Support for order notification and routing**—Order notification and routing is handled presently through email distributions and event email alerts. Be sure to get this as a feature in the first catalog you use to ensure you have the ability to communicate responsively with your customers.

- **Comparison shopping**—This is one of the best features on CarPoint.com, for example, because it gives you the chance to compare one vehicle with another. Just as this is very useful for choosing a car, it's also great for comparing your products to each other and to competitors' products. This is a feature that your ASP might just be working with, so check into any references they have for completing this with other companies. It's a great sales tool.

What the Experts Are Saying About e-Commerce Growth

In May, 2000, International Data Corporation released the results of its comprehensive market modeling exercise, which is called the Internet Commerce Market Model. It's one of the most often-quoted sources of information on the Internet marketplace, and it provides interesting insights into the development of the e-commerce marketplace today. Keep in mind as you read over these findings that the role of the ASP is driving the learning curve of the Internet in general and of online commerce because the biggest challenge to sales growth for an ASP is education. Here are the key findings from version 6.1 of IDC's Internet Commerce Market Model:

- The application service provider marketplace will grow to $7 billion by 2003, with primary growth from personal productivity and applications that enable the use of legacy data. Personal productivity applications are enabled through Web browsers for common office automation applications including word processing, spreadsheets, and creating presentations. One of the key market drivers in making the marketplace grow to $7 billion is the role e-commerce applications will play in driving new e-businesses to the Internet for revenue generation.
- In 1999, 237 million devices were used to access the World Wide Web; in 2003, that number will increase to more than 750 million. Growth in the number of Web users will follow a similar pattern.
- Some 29% of Web users will buy something over the Web by the end of the year 2000, and 38% of Web users will be buying over the Web in 2003. The increase in buying will be driven by the greater availability of products, improved buyer confidence in security, and the move toward local-language sites.
- As a result of the increase in the number of buyers on the Web, the size of the average transaction, and the adoption of the Web as a viable vehicle for business procurement, the amount of commerce conducted over the Web is expected to grow dramatically—to more than $1.6 trillion in 2003.
- The United States continues to dominate Web commerce, but not for long. As the number of international buyers increases and international B2B transactions conducted over the Web become more commonplace, the U.S. share of Web commerce will drop to less than half.
- Web commerce will undergo tremendous growth in Western Europe: from $24 billion in 1999 to $150 billion in 2001 and to more than $500 billion in 2003.
- The Asia/Pacific region (including Japan) is experiencing very fast Internet growth despite its economic woes. This growth is partly driven by governments,

which continue to encourage Web adoption in homes, businesses, and education establishments. Devices used to access the Web in Asia/Pacific (including Japan) reached 40 million in 1999 and will increase to 163 million in 2003.

Despite the challenges facing e-commerce and the development of online transactions, the growth trend is aggressively optimistic, as defined by one of the leading industry research firms. Figure 6.4 shows the ramp of B2B commerce relative to B2C, where the existing levels of the latter are dwarfed by the growth potential of B2B trade by 2003. The number of users who buy and sell goods and services over the World Wide Web increased to 240 million in 1999. The number of users is forecast to reach 327 million by yearend 2000 and to surpass 600 million in 2003. The increase in use will drive commerce on the Internet to more than $1.6 trillion in 2003, reflecting a 1999–2003 compound annual growth rate (CAGR) of 88% as shown in Figure 6.4.

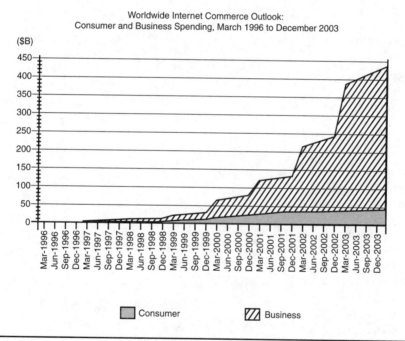

Figure 6.4 Worldwide Internet Commerce Outlook: Consumer and Business Spending, March 1996 to December 2003.

How ASPs Enable Selling Products Online

With many ASPs working to provide the necessary tools for creating an online presence for companies interested in fulfilling their e-business strategy, it's important to see how these objectives are being accomplished from a technology standpoint. Table 6.1 presents a definition of how a variety of ASPs are enabling e-commerce sites online.

Table 6.1   **Comparing delivery technologies by application service provider**

ASP	Through a Local Browser on a PC	Through a Browser PC Device PC Device	Using the Citrix Metaframe /ICA Protocol	Via Client Applications Resident on Customer Desktop	Using Microsoft WTS/RDP Protocol
Applicast	X	X	XXXX	X	
AristaSoft	X	XXXX	X		
BrightStar	X	XXXX	XXXX	X	
Corio	X	XXXX	X		
CyLex	X	X	X	X	
eALITY	X	X			
ebaseOne	X	X	XXXX	X	X
EDS	X	X	X	X	X
Eggrock	X	XXXX	X	X	X
eOnline	X	XXXX	XXXX	X	
FutureLink	X	X	X		
IBM Global Services	X	XXXX	X	X	
Interliant	X	XXXX	X	X	X
Interpath	X	X	XXXX	X	
LearningStation .com	X	X	X		
NaviSite	X				
Oracle Business Online	X	X			
QSP	X	X	XXXX	X	
Qwest CyberSolutions	X	XXXX	X		X
Telecomputing	X	X	X	X	
TriZetto Group	X	X	X	X	
Usinter networking	X	XXXX	X	X	
World Technology Services	X	XXXX	X		
Zland.com	X				

Source: International Data Corporation

When comparing each of these companies, it's also important to compare their relative market orientations. Table 6.2 shows the market orientation and level of organization each ASP targets. There are more ASPs around than those in this matrix; however, these are the major ones in the industry.

Table 6.2 **Target market profiles by application service provider**

ASP	Target Customer by Revenue	Target Customer by Number of Employees
Applicast	$0–200 million	50–400
AristaSoft	$0–250 million	50–1,000
BrightStar	$250 million–10 billion	500–10,000
Corio	$0–250 million	Any
CyLex	$5 million–500 million	50–2,000
EALITY	NA	20–500
EbaseOne	$0.5 million–200 million	50–500
EDS	$50 million–600 million	NA
Eggrock	$5 million–50 million	NA
EOnline	$0–1 billion	NA
FutureLink	NA	10–1,000
IBM Global Services	NA	50–1,000
Interliant	$50 million–1 billion	50–5,000
Interpath Communications	$100 million–1 billion	100–1,000
LearningStation .com	NA	NA
NaviSite	$5 million or more	NA
Oracle Business Online	NA	NA
QSP	$20 million–100 million	50 or more
Qwest CyberSolutions	Up to $1.5 billion–2.0 billion	Up to several thousand
Telecomputing	NA	20–500 per site
TriZetto Group	NA	NA
Usinternetworking	$50 million–1 billion	NA
World Technology Services	$50 million–500 million	50–10,000
ZLand.com	$0–200 million	1–1,000

Source: International Data Corporation

Exploring e-Commerce Partnership Strategies

One of the most intriguing aspects of the ASP model is the role of software companies relative to the development efforts within the companies themselves. It's an issue that raises the question of how the ASP you are partnering with is handling its dependence on independent software vendors (ISVs). For many ASPs, they are strongly independent and do not want to let go of the control of their own destinies on the one hand, yet also realize to grow they need to partner with ISVs to deliver applications. As a company or organization looking to partner with an ASP, it's important to look at the relationship your ASP has with the software companies it needs but at the same time doesn't want to be too dependent on. International Data Corporation has done extensive research on these relationships, and the findings on partnerships are briefly defined here.

The first model as defined by IDC is called *mass market*, and focused on low-complexity applications that are easily hosted to a broad range of users. This is the volume market model in which the essential nature of the hosted application is that of providing a key functionality at a very low price.

The second model is that of a *hybrid* ASP, in which more complex applications, including e-commerce applications, are enabled for small businesses. The value of this approach is the development of consulting and integration partners to provide responsiveness to customers. The real value of the hybrid model is the capability to deliver a stable hosting base.

The third model IDC has defined in the context of ASP relationships is the development of *domain expertise*. This is the type of partnership between a software company and an ASP in which high levels of service are provided and the most complex of applications are hosted, typically for larger organizations. Called domain expertise because it implies mastery of the basics of the ASP model, this approach is at the highest levels of delivery and is emanating out of the service-intensive industries that have a legacy of providing the world's largest corporations with tools and software development. Serving the largest customers and yielding the highest margins, this business model is attracting the least number of customers as the entrenched I.S. competition from other areas of the industry make breaking into this marketplace more difficult.

The fourth model focuses on the specific needs of a small set of customers. Called the *niche* market model by IDC, this model focuses on developing superior customer service and support, and includes the capability to provide enhanced services at higher margins due to the vertical market nature of the niche business model adopters. ASPs taking this approach are focused on a specific vertical market need and are targeting their resources exclusively for the needs of the targeted niche segments.

Table 6.3 provides a comparison of the various business models discussed here.

Table 6.3   Comparing partnership strategies

	Mass Market (Personal Applications/ ASP Provides No or Low Service)	Hybrid (Enterprise-Level Applications/ ASP Partners Service)	Niche (Personal/ Collaborative Applications/ ASPs Provide High Level of Service)	Domain Expertise (Enterprise Applications/ ASPs Provide High Level of Service)
Market focus	Individual users	Small and medium-sized businesses and large organization departments; technology decision makers	Focused user communities	Small and medium-sized businesses and large organization departments; business decision makers
Value proposition	Easy access to fully functional applications at a reasonable cost; no need to worry about upgrades	Application hosting services; Capability to leverage robust infrastructure of the provider to host applications; Capability to provide customers with a "low service" alternative	Capability to provide firms with personal applications tailored to their needs (industry and job function) at a reasonable price, along with requisite services and support	Capability to provide customers with a single source for the complete application solution and support
Critical success factors	Price; ease of doing business (billing, access, and so on); speed of application/ access	Infra-structure/ service levels; billing systems;	Feature/ function applicability; value-add services available capability to personalize/ specify	Application breadth/ expertise; price; service levels

Table 6.3 Continued

	Mass Market (Personal Applications/ ASP Provides No or Low Service)	Hybrid (Enterprise- Level Applications/ ASP Partners Service)	Niche (Personal/ Collaborative Applications/ ASPs Provide High Level of Service)	Domain Expertise (Enterprise Applications/ ASPs Provide High Level of Service)
Partnering focus/needs	Marketing partners; channel partners to reach end-user community (such as ISPs)	Consulting and integration partners; complementary product vendors; channel partners	Software product vendors; marketing partners; content partners; channel partners	Application software vendors; other software product vendors
Size of deal margin	Low	Low	High	High
Source of margins	Advertising, user fees, value-added services	Hosting services	Community: value-added services and revenue to provide access to the community	Multiple: hosting services, implementation/ integration services, customization, software, and potentially hardware margin
Relative volume of customers	High	Medium	Medium	Low
Relative business complexity	Low	Medium	Medium	High
Length/ complexity of sales cycle	Low	Medium	Medium	High

Source: International Data Corporation

Creating an e-Commerce Strategy

When creating your e-commerce strategy, many considerations must be kept in mind. One of the best approaches to communicating your expectations is to create an e-commerce strategy in the form of a planning document. The intent of this section is to provide you with the framework needed for creating an e-commerce plan.

An e-Commerce Strategy Needs a Sense of Urgency

The Internet is changing the pace at which business plans for the Internet are being written. John Cristos, the CEO of E★Trade, recently told a class at Pepperdine University that every 2–6 months the business plan for E★Trade is completely rewritten from the bottom up. This is to ensure that E★Trade is on the forefront of the latest changes to Internet technology, affecting the capability of the company to handle transactions interactively. E★Trade is one of the more forward-thinking companies that has focused on electronic commerce as the main component of its online business model. There are other companies that have set an initial direction via a business plan used for generating funding, and then moved so quickly from one initiative to another that a business plan would have been written in the past tense. The Internet is changing the pace of competition, yet is still being evaluated from the same metrics as any other communications vehicle that requires investment over time.

Step-by-Step Guide to Creating an e-Commerce Plan

Before you create a business plan for an Internet-enabled business, which has an electronic commerce component as a main source of revenue, begin with the following key information items. Having these key components will assist you in clarifying the direction of your e-business:

- **Define key differentiators for your business relative to others, outside of e-commerce**—It's important to get a grasp of your organization's key strengths before integrating e-commerce into its overall structure.

- **Define your distribution strategy relative to the direct nature of the e-commerce model**—Dell was able to use the Internet to further its reach into its client base, leveraging off of the existing distribution strategies used for going after large corporate accounts. Dell was able to quickly take the advantages of the Internet and create Premier Pages, which has in turn been developed into Premier Commerce, an approach Dell now uses for electronically enabling its clients to order internally. You can read more about the Premier Commerce offerings of Dell at www.dell.com.

- **Develop a suite of products that are easily sold over the Internet**—The essence of any strong business plan is the integration of Return on Investment (ROI), Return on Sales (ROS), and other metrics of financial performance to a product strategy that is driven by the needs of clients. Successful business plans, especially for the Internet, include combining innovative products, which are based on clients' needs, with a large potential client base. Taken together, these two attributes can drive the return on investment to levels in which public funding can be generated. The Apple iMAC, and the many Gateway portables, consumer desktops, workstations are specifically designed to be ready-to-run the minute they are unpacked. From product concept through delivery, more and more products are specifically being designed to be sold over the Internet.

- **Know your clients better than anyone else**—e-Commerce is predicated on the idea of the Internet being available 7 days a week, 24 hours a day. This translates into sales occurring virtually all over the world at every hour of the day, or sales occurring within a specific geographic/economic segment at a specific time of the day. The alluring nature of the Internet is the idea of frictionless transactions, yet for your organization to achieve this efficiency there needs to be in-depth knowledge of your client base. Who are they? What are their preferences? When do they surf the Web for product information? Who are your competitors? Are there options available for you to partner with a complementary product or service, making your product more competitive in the process? You need to really understand how to reach, motivate, and retain your customers when you embark on an e-commerce–based business. Spend time during the phases of getting a site up and running to fully understand your existing client's product needs, preferences for Internet access, times of shopping online, and the needs of potential clients your product offerings might not be fully providing yet.

- **Pricing and marketing strategies for the Internet**—Many resellers that purchase from Ingram Micro, the world's largest distributor of computing hardware, insist that Ingram Micro lower its prices for products purchased over the company's Web site. Ingram operates at less than 5% gross margin corporate-wide, and with the squeezing of margins from resellers who themselves are selling products over the Internet, margins continue to fall sometimes to 1%. At the same time, however, Lands End sells its clothes at margins in the high teens or even in the 20% range. This discrepancy is explained because Lands End is first the manufacturer, and second, has developed a more direct model of distribution, which can sustain order rates from end users who need a customized item of clothing quickly. The differences between an Ingram Micro and a Lands End are many, yet the comparison brings the point of pricing and margin on the Internet into focus. If your organization is migrating from a dual-tier distribution strategy to the Internet, expect to hear from your distribution partners and their needs for you to lower your margin on products they in turn will sell electronically.

Transitioning from one distribution model to another in the context of e-commerce has pricing implications. If your organization has continually had a direct model, the pricing strategies you have had in the past will continue to hold true into the future, and can actually be revamped for the cost efficiencies of the

Internet. Savings from selling, general and administrative (SGA) expenses, distribution and warehousing incentives, and even market development funds paid to a distributor can in turn be re-allocated to benefit the pricing structure of your products, yielding a higher margin. In a recent speech, Michael Dell mentioned that there has been a 9X reduction in selling and support costs for Dell, along with an 11X increase in sales since the inception of the Dell Web site over three years ago. Clearly, pricing and margin strategies favor the direct model in the context of electronic commerce.

■ **Product strategies for personalization**—The Internet has created an impact on many industries much faster than those industries had expected. Take for example online trading. Just three years ago Charles Schwab would show you their best and brightest brokers assisting clients with trades; the concept of an investment team of Schwab and you, the client. Consider now the commercials and ads you see for online trading today. Schwab now shows you individual investors—some are working mothers, others are men and women near retirement—and each speaks about using eSchwab to handle their own trading and accounts. The difference is clear. We are now entering an era in products and services of complete personalization. Gateway's YourWare Programs for Business and Education bring the benefits of leasing directly to the end user or client, in addition to giving clients the opportunity to define the product configurations they need for their businesses or universities.

Example of an e-Commerce Strategy

Here's an example of a table of contents for a business plan in which e-commerce is the primary focus:

Executive Summary

Business Model Definition. Defines how the business being proposed has both a value proposition for clients and a high return on invested capital for the investors, whether they are members of your organization or venture capitalists.

Marketing Plan. Includes a definition of the company's mission statement in the context of the clients served, a definition of the marketing objectives as defined in both gross margin and unit sales results, and a definition of profitability targets for 3–5 years. This section also includes a profile of the products, the extent these products have been personalized for segments of clients, and a definition of the market potential for the products being introduced. There is also a risk/reward segment defined and a Gantt chart showing when specific actions will be taken for the product introduction. There are also pricing, advertising, and promotion strategies included within the section.

Technology Plan and Roadmap. Defines the roadmap for the products being introduced, and includes a definition of the technologies that will be used for handling the Web site's transactions. This section also includes transition plans for moving legacy data from previous generation systems to the Web server for handling client transactions efficiently. Goals and objectives for system uptime and response to clients' orders and requests are also defined here, along with a Gantt chart, that defines system implementation schedules and costs.

Operations Plan. Defines the implementation plan for the Web site and the costs of operating it for the year. Also defines the costs of service and the level of support that will be provided for clients.

Financial Plan. Includes the pro-forma financial statements, including the balance sheet, income statement, and cash flow statements. Also includes costing and margin data by product. This section provides financial projections for the electronic commerce initiatives, and includes a statement showing P & L Projections for five years out.

How ASPs Can Assist in Selling Online

By now you have seen how ASPs have the potential to transform your business and make it more productive through the use of the ASP model. The role of e-commerce continues to expand in businesses as the metrics measuring success are becoming easier to gather and use in making informed decisions about the direction of an e-commerce site. Of all the approaches to handling e-commerce, the following areas are showing the most promise for companies developing their own e-business strategies.

Catalogs and Auctions

The continual development and growth of catalog technology is already revolutionizing the role of companies selling online. As more and more companies get online, the role of catalogs will become crucial. Even though the free sites that pervade the low-end of the market offer catalogs, their implementations do not have the key features defined in this chapter as must-haves for an industrial-strength e-commerce solution.

Customized Selections by Customer

The ability to personalize the experience your customer has when visiting your site is invaluable from a personalization perspective and also from a repeat business standpoint. It's essential to consider how you will market your site with an ASP by stressing the customization aspect. Your competitive strength in a local market against competitors could very well be the ability to personalize the shopping and visiting experience for your customers. In working with an ASP and also in creating your e-commerce strategy, always look for opportunities to add personalization for your visitor and customer.

Cross-Linking with Products from Other Sites

Building affiliate programs and working to create partnership levels is critical for the long-term growth of your site. Consider the affiliate programs for your industry and also consider creating one of your own to reward frequent visitors to your site. Be sure to ask about the limitations and capability of your potential ASP creating an affiliate program to promote your company.

Day-to-Day Running of an e-Commerce Site with an ASP

Because you are working with your ASP, running an e-commerce site day to day is much like checking a stock price online. It's a matter of checking on the configuration screens accessible over a browser to see statistics on Web page creation and overall performance statistics. Having your ASP provide search engine optimization techniques to your Web site will also be measurable from companies who can track the level your site accomplishes in terms of queries to specific search engines. Using products such as WebTrends, you can get an accurate measure of the level of traffic to your Web site as well. Chapter 12 of this book focuses on the aspects of metrics for measuring your Web site's performance. You can use the metrics provided for better managing the relationship with your ASP as well, getting a specific level of service.

Defining the Future Direction of Your e-Commerce Strategy

The one constant is change, and in the area of an e-business strategy this is certainly the case. You can see that the need for staying current on technology is the basis of your future e-business strategy. Often companies find themselves taking the technology that the market offers and meeting the latest customer needs within their organizations with it. You can find the latest information on the ASP industry from the Web sites listed in Chapter 1, "Meeting the Challenge of e-Business with Application Service Providers," and the industry site WebHarbor.com is an excellent source of information as well. For industry-specific information and the direction of technologies, consider attending an IDC conference once or twice a year on the ASP industry to keep current with the latest technology.

Summary

e-Commerce is changing the business models of companies every day. What's critical about embarking on an e-commerce strategy is the development of a robust series of functions you can quickly turn into revenue streams for your company. This chapter has focused on the necessary key points you need to know to make an informed decision with an ASP about defining an e-business strategy. This chapter also included key terms and concepts you can use to both guide and initiate discussions with e-business experts to get your strategic goals accomplished.

7

Automating Your Business and Information with e-Operations

T HE CAPABILITIES TO COLLABORATIVELY share information throughout companies, streamline the procurement and purchasing functions, and address the continual need for sharing information are just a few benefits of integrating e-operations into an e-business strategy. e-Operations is the area of e-business that generates the greatest benefits and quantifiable gains in financial returns. Taking the immediacy of information made possible by the Internet and the constant need for information in companies, e-operations is clearly going to dominate the direction of e-business for years to come.

What Is e-Operations?

The area of e-operations encompasses the processes of how products and services within companies fulfill customer commitments. This includes the procurement of products, the arrangement of shipping and transport, and handling production—in short the development of fulfillment systems—for handling the business that e-marketing and e-commerce generate. The capability to fulfill orders and having the e-operations tools in place to handle them can spell the difference between success or failure for online initiatives. Inherent in all these approaches to streamlining tasks using e-operations tools is the automation of workflow processes. The study of processes and minimization of steps to streamline them is the direct payback for adopting a comprehensive e-business strategy. One example of taking the e-operations approach first, and then having the e-marketing and e-commerce areas reflect the fulfillment capabilities of a company, is exemplified in the evolution of Amazon.com.

How Fulfillment Makes Book Orders Happen at Amazon.com

In 1995 Jeff Bezos read a forecast that electronic commerce over the next five years would have a 2300% compound annual growth rate. He started brainstorming ideas about how he could build a business that would grow at a correspondingly rapid rate. He settled on books because as a product category there are more unique and marketable products (books) than any other area of commerce, and because order fulfillment can be done very efficiently with books. He and his wife set out for Seattle to start their company—originally called Cadabra.com. When venture capitalists either mispronounced it or even mistook it for another name, Bezos realized that he wanted a name that would appear at the top of lists, so a name starting with an "A" was a consideration, along with a name easy to identify and spell. With these considerations in mind, Bezos decided to take name of the world's largest river and apply it to what he wanted to be the world's largest bookstore. Amazon.com was then born. From the speeches Mr. Bezos has made at industry conferences, it's clear that his vision for the company started with fulfillment in mind first. The conferences for Industry Standard Magazine have been particularly useful for gaining insights into the Amazon.com strategy.

Bezos chose Seattle as a base of operations due to the strength of technical talent in the area and the fact that there was a major book distribution center to the south, in Oregon. These two factors, Bezos reasoned, would allow the fledgling company to get the necessary talent to build the fulfillment systems and also the ability to be responsive with orders. The first priority that Amazon.com focused on was building a scalable, robust fulfillment system that would not only work with the ordering needs of book distributors but also attentively deal with a single customer's order. The fulfillment system would need to aggregate orders of comparable books and place orders in minimum blocks of ten to the distributors. It has often been said that book distributors can deliver any book you want virtually overnight as long as you order a pallet of the same title. It's the internal fulfillment systems of the distributors that capitalize on volume requirements. The same holds true in many other industries as well, especially in the computer industry. Amazon.com's fulfillment systems act as an aggregation point where individual orders are grouped into orders that book distributor's fulfillment systems can work with.

As the fulfillment systems continued through development, the Amazon team worked with book distributors to test and refine ordering, returns, and queries of inventory position. Because the book distribution companies could only work with minimum orders of ten, Bezos and Amazon.com even offered to pay a fee per transaction for having an individual book provided. The distributors couldn't provide the service as their systems deal with entire blocks of books as a single unit; there was no way to split them up. Bezos and his team solved the problem by finding on obscure book on lichens, which was hardly ever in stock. For testing the fulfillment systems at Amazon.com, the lichens book was ordered to round out orders to get to the minimum order levels required. The testing of the fulfillment systems then continued.

The Amazon team developed and tested Electronic Data Interchange (EDI for short) links back to the book distributors. These links gave Amazon.com the chance to take all the orders from their site, group them into batches, and send them overnight to book distributors. EDI is a commonly used technology for communicating orders between companies who do a high volume of business with each other. The EDI links initially set up by Amazon.com could handle more than 100 times the amount of orders initially taken.

With Amazon.com being singularly focused on building a scalable fulfillment system, another aspect of their e-operations strategy was to develop relationships with UPS and Federal Express. Jeff Bezos, his house now full of orange cables and programmers building the Amazon.com fulfillment systems, would meet in a local Barnes & Noble café with vendors his company would need as part of its overall fulfillment efforts.

After the fulfillment systems had been built and tested, online transactions from friends and family were next sent through the system. The credit card verification processing tasks were tested for several months, with Bezos at one point dedicating a credit card to the single task of testing and retesting the ordering systems. As the site was completed, actual book orders started streaming in from friends, family, and people in Seattle curious about how the new online bookstore would work. Bezos recalls the first order from a customer that no one knew. Everyone kept asking each other if they knew this customer—when they realized it was someone new, the team realized they had their first true customer.

With Amazon.com open for business, word spread quickly that the new online store had a great selection and could ship overnight if necessary. Soon Jerry Yang of Yahoo! heard about Amazon.com and called Jeff Bezos to see if he would be interested in having Amazon.com on the What's Cool area of Yahoo!. In 1995, Yahoo! was (and is) the portal of choice for millions using the Internet for both business and pleasure. The result for Amazon.com was a steady yet unmistakable rise in traffic, with orders following. Soon the industry press was picking up Amazon.com, and within months, orders had grown so fast that developers and programmers would work until 2 or 3 a.m. packing books from orders placed during the previous day's sales.

The sales volume was greater than Bezos and his team had predicted. With the rapid sales growth and industry coverage, soon the *Wall Street Journal* had heard of Amazon.com and featured them in the front-page news story. The result was even more orders and the need for creating fulfillment systems that could deal with the manual processes of getting books out the door for customers. The fulfillment systems worked and provided the books necessary to fulfill orders. With the manual aspects of fulfillment being the next challenge, Bezos opted for creating warehouses to hold the most popular books to ensure responsiveness to customers.

As the history of Amazon.com shows, getting the fulfillment systems in place makes growth possible. Instead of focusing on e-marketing, the Amazon.com team took the most critical links—those with their suppliers and partners—and worked to make sure they were as scalable as possible.

e-Procurement in Business

The aspects of e-operations that lend themselves to measurement the best are those that make an immediate impact on the costs of doing business. The area of e-procurement is one of the hottest areas of e-business as it directly affects the costs of procuring products and very often contributes to the profitability of a company quickly. With immediate gains possible and the returns so quantifiable, e-procurement is attracting new companies into the industry every month. Companies that already have a presence in the enterprise-wide applications area are quickly building applications to address the need for e-procurement in companies of all sizes.

e-Procurement is the application market that covers applications written to allow an entity to conduct business-to-business transactions over the Internet. Applications typically include the capability to interact with another entity to obtain information, create a request that can be routed for approval, issue a purchase order to the supplier and fulfill the request with a receipt, receive delivery notification, and order updates as well as providing an electronic means to settle the payment.

When considering an e-procurement solution, realize that these applications are delivered through the use of a portal or exchange, trading community, or even through online licensing, with the day-to-day functioning of the application possible only over a browser.

Starting in 1998, the e-procurement marketplace started with applications that have been used for processing orders for indirect materials under maintenance, repair, and operations category (MRO). Typically, these MRO goods and services include computers, safety and janitorial equipment, and office furniture and supplies. Increasingly, these applications are processing orders for services such as airline tickets and hotel reservations, and intercompany orders of manufacturing services. These Internet commerce procurement applications have also started to cover orders for direct materials that usually go into a company's finished product, such as an automobile or aircraft engine, or a transmission tower for the telecommunications industry.

Previously, legacy applications or enterprise resource management (ERM) software handled the data processing of orders for direct materials. Companies that had previously been providing these ERM applications are now in the process of creating Internet-enabled versions of the programs. Baan, PeopleSoft, and SAP now have extensive programs for developing Internet-enabled applications. These three companies have the strongest customer bases in the legacy and ERM markets and have significant influence on the ERM to e-procurement transition now underway in the applications arena. After the applications of these companies are completed and Internet-enabled, the worldwide market size of e-procurement applications will grow significantly. This will in turn translate into a wider and more diverse series of applications, tools, and techniques for companies looking to adopt e-procurement into their operations.

In defining e-procurement, there are four major segments:

- Buy-side applications
- Sell-side applications
- Catalog-conversion applications
- Trading community applications

Buy-Side Applications

This is the area of e-procurement that is getting the most attention today as the benefits of companies trading electronically with each other show significant cost savings for both companies involved. This application area covers software applications written to allow an entity to conduct business-to-business transactions over the Internet with another company, where both information and transactions can be shared. Companies adopting this type of application are those that are in the procurement business itself, including distributors and service industries such as rental cars businesses and hotels.

Sell-Side Procurement Applications

Although sell-side procurement applications have functions similar to those of buy-side applications, they are primarily marketed to sellers that want to automate the process of connecting to their business buyers. For example, a number of computer distributors installed applications that allow their corporate customers to use the Internet to look up items, place orders, and settle payments under pre-negotiated contract prices. The capability to deliver the inventory position on a specific product or part is one of the benefits of employing applications in this market area.

Catalog Conversion Procurement Applications

One of the most challenging aspects for larger corporations is to take their catalogs and create electronic catalogs that reflect all the features, functions, and benefits of the products listed. There is an entire industry devoted to assisting companies with taking larger catalogs and creating online representations of them. In response to this need in organizations, companies including Aspect and Requisite Technology are building catalog conversion applications.

Trading Community Procurement Applications

Applications that are designed to build either vertical or horizontal market portals are called trading community procurement applications. Think of this as infrastructure software, providing tools to build a trading community. Examples of this are Plastics.com and Metals.com.

With many applications becoming available in these four segments, the market for e-procurement software is expected to grow more than 300% per year. Strong user demand is fueling the growth of the Internet commerce procurement application market. With the compliance issues related to the year 2000 largely behind CIOs and CFOs, Internet procurement represents a golden opportunity for businesses to lower costs, improve productivity, and maximize efficiency.

In a recent survey completed by International Data Corporation, the majority of users cited several strong benefits for taking on e-procurement applications. These early adopters of e-procurement applications report that processing a requisition order over an Internet procurement system takes just a fraction of the time a manual system takes. These early adopters also mentioned that the e-procurement applications that offer reporting capabilities also make it easier for users to consolidate suppliers, curb maverick buying, and finally, secure steeper global discounts.

e-Procurement Vendors

With the immediate benefits being measurable from buy-side and sell-side applications, the majority of companies in e-procurement are focusing initially on these two areas. The following sections briefly profile early entrants into the e-procurement marketplace.

Ariba

Ariba was formed in September 1996 and shipped its first e-procurement application in June 1997. Over the next two years, Ariba established itself as a pioneer in the burgeoning business-to-business e-procurement market with an e-procurement solution it called Ariba ORMS (operating resource management system). Ariba is now the leading application vendor in the e-procurement buy-side marketplace.

Ariba has attempted to differentiate itself from its competitors by building a robust buy-side application. Although it recognizes the future potential for large transaction revenues associated with trading communities, Ariba remains committed to ensuring its buy-side application is the best in the market. For example, Ariba offers industry-specific solutions to the financial services, high technology, pharmaceutical, manufacturing, telecommunications, and government sectors. Both Ariba and Clarus share the same vision for their applications, although the Ariba e-procurement solution is geared toward the high-end of the market.

Over time, an increasing percentage of its revenue will come from transaction and subscription fees generated by Ariba.com, its e-procurement portal. The difference between CommerceOne and Ariba in their portal strategies is that Ariba is being more cautious in terms of relying too heavily at this point on the viability of the transaction-based portal model.

Baan

In April 1999 Baan entered the online procurement software market by announcing its e-procurement application, which delivers self-service requisitioning capabilities. The application went into beta test in the third quarter of 1999 at a price of $150,000 for 150 named users. Over the next year, Baan estimates that the application could win between 50 and 100 customers.

Baan is having significant difficulties penetrating this marketplace, and has suffered through several channel initiatives. Baan's e-procurement solution is not positioned as a standalone point solution, but rather as an enhancement to Baan ERM.

Clarus

Founded in 1991, Suwanee, GA based Clarus Corporation started out as a developer of financial and human resources management software. After going public in May 1998, Clarus entered the e-procurement area through its acquisition of ELEKOM Corporation in November 1998. Based on the ELEKOM solution, Clarus' e-procurement application is built on a Windows NT platform. Clarus has seen a significant slowdown in the growth of its financial and human resources management software over the past 12 months, while its e-procurement business has blossomed. The company just announced it is selling its financial and HR applications business to Markham, Ontario, Canada based Geac Computer Systems, Inc., allowing it to focus entirely on business-to-business e-commerce.

That means Clarus is putting its entire focus on business-to-business e-commerce, and specifically its e-procurement solution. Internally, Clarus had already gone through a process of reorganizing its business into two distinct business units: ERM and e-procurement. Its decision to completely focus on e-procurement is a good sign for potential alliance partners looking to exploit B2B e-commerce opportunities.

Clarus' e-procurement strategy has been directly focused on the buy-side market. Unlike Ariba and CommerceOne, who are scrambling to build trading communities, Clarus would rather generate momentum for its buy-side application called Clarus E-Procurement. A byproduct of this approach is Clarus' intention to make its e-procurement solution compliant with prevailing Internet standards, whether the standard is OBI or an iteration of XML, such as the schemas being proposed by the BizTalk initiative. The Clarus strategy rests on its capability to develop an application that is adaptable to any Internet standard.

CommerceOne

Mark Hoffman and Thomas Gonzales originally established Walnut Creek, CA based CommerceOne in 1994 (although the company was originally called DistriVision Development Corporation). Prior to co-founding CommerceOne, Hoffman was CEO of Sybase, Inc., a company he co-founded in 1984. The company name was changed in 1997 to better reflect the company's business-to-business e-commerce focus.

CommerceOne has based its strategy on the transaction revenues from e-commerce portals or trading communities around the globe. Its goal is to establish a marketsite in each major geographic region. Marketsite.net is the marketsite for the U.S. and will be operated directly by CommerceOne. The remaining marketsites will be licensed like franchises to large telecommunications companies in each major geographic region. CommerceOne has already sold franchises to British Telecom in the UK, NTT in Japan, and SingTel in Singapore.

CommerceOne's e-procurement strategy is also characterized by its open architecture. Unlike Ariba ORMS, the BuySite application has the capability to interface with any trading community that supports open Internet standards such as OBI and XML. Rather than limiting itself to one trading community, buyers can use BuySite to interact with multiple communities over the Internet.

Each marketsite will generate revenue based on the number of transactions being driven through these portals. CommerceOne believes that most of their future revenue will be generated in this manner. Supporting this strategy is an aggressive pricing model for their applications. BuySite's buy-side application software is being priced well below the competition to maximize the number of potential buyers and therefore drive higher levels of traffic through marketsites. This strategy largely accounts for the increasing losses being posted, especially over the last five quarters, as the company pushes to reach critical mass.

Intelisys

Intelisys Electronic Commerce, LLC ("Intelisys") was a spin-off from the Business Development Group at New York, NY based Chase Manhattan Bank. With an initial venture capital infusion of between $20 and $30 million (Chase Manhattan Bank and Summit Capital were the principal investors), Intelisys was formed to develop the e-procurement technology that was the initial vision of the Business Development Group at Chase Manhattan.

Intelisys is very focused on deploying its buy-side application, called IEC Enterprise. Its strategy is to sell the buy-side application and then aggregate 100% of the suppliers with which their customers want to do business. This aggregation of suppliers makes up Intelisys' supplier e-commerce portal, called B2Bonramp. Unlike some vendors, such as Ariba, this portal is accessible by any buy-side application that supports open Internet standards such as OBI and XML.

A key element of the Intelisys strategy around e-procurement is to keep catalog content outside a user's firewall and its maintenance and updates in the hands of suppliers.

iPlanet

Netscape, now part of America Online, formed an alliance with Sun Microsystems to further develop its e-commerce software applications, which include BuyerXpert, the e-procurement component. In 1998, Netscape secured 12 customers for BuyerXpert. That represented just a small fraction of the deals Netscape won in business-to-business e-commerce last year. As a result of the Sun-Netscape Alliance, the companies will launch a revamped marketing strategy this year as the alliance begins to market its combined solutions under the iPlanet banner.

The Sun-Netscape Alliance is undergoing a major rebranding campaign to promote the iPlanet moniker. The e-procurement solution will fall under the iPlanet banner and is considered one of the key applications that will drive its e-business solution set forward. Despite significant enhancements to its buy-side application, called BuyerXpert, iPlanet is keener on providing the platform for e-business using Sun Server and Netscape technology (in direct competition with Microsoft).

J.D. Edwards

Like PeopleSoft, J.D. Edwards has opted to partner rather than build an e-procurement solution. In this case the agreement is with Ariba. The J.D. Edwards-Ariba alliance has not been engineered to the same level of commitment as the PeopleSoft-CommerceOne partnership. J.D. Edwards will integrate Ariba ORMS into its OneWorld ERM solution, effectively acting as a reseller for Ariba. (J.D. Edwards has a similar arrangement with CRM vendor Siebel Systems.)

Although Ariba is the market leader in the e-procurement buy-side application space, there is a disconnect between the two companies. Ariba is squarely focused on selling its solution into Global 2000 companies while J.D. Edwards has always viewed the mid-market as its sweet spot. J.D. Edwards might be looking to move up-market using Ariba's customer base; however, it appears to be an unusual combination.

Mro.com

Bedford, MA based PSDI provides maintenance management software for large process manufacturing, transportation, and heavy manufacturing companies. The company's flagship product, MAXIMO, is used to plan and manage ongoing maintenance and repair operations. The client/server version was released in 1991. In April 1999, PSDI branched out into indirect procurement with the creation of its MRO.com subsidiary. PSDI is a public company trading on the NASDAQ market under the symbol PSDI.

PSDI has been very successful in the maintenance and repair markets with its MAXIMO product. The creation of MRO.com is a natural extension of its expertise in this area, and the company is focused on cross selling its buy-side application, mroBuyer, to its existing MAXIMO customer base. Like Ariba and CommerceOne, PSDI has developed both buy-side and sell-side solutions in addition to an e-business portal (www.mro.com). Its business strategy revolves around leveraging its existing customer base to sell mroBuyer. The company admits that it will be difficult to penetrate new accounts with its e-procurement solution because of the intense competition from Ariba and CommerceOne. Where PSDI has an advantage is in being able to seamlessly integrate MAXIMO with mroBuyer to manage a company's entire maintenance, repair, and operation processes.

Oracle

Recognizing the threat posed by upstarts such as Ariba and CommerceOne, enterprise software giant Oracle is accelerating its push into the e-procurement space. In May 1999, Oracle rolled out a series of programs designed to jumpstart its e-business offerings. Among them is the Fast Forward program, which promises to help organizations implement an Internet procurement application in less than 60 days. The price of this type of implementation ranges from $175,000 to $750,000 depending on the number of users and the number of transactions. The prices do not include the cost of converting the catalog content from the suppliers, which is likely to be handled by Requisite or TPN Register, Oracle's primary partners in content conversion.

Oracle promises swift and substantial payback on its Web procurement application. It estimates that the application will allow savings of more than 50% in processing time and at least 10% in procurement costs.

Oracle will also be promoting its Business Online application outsourcing service to enable users to outsource its Internet procurement application.

PeopleSoft

Unlike rivals Oracle and SAP, PeopleSoft will deliver its e-procurement buy-side solution using CommerceOne's BuySite application. The partnership between PeopleSoft and CommerceOne is far-reaching and goes well beyond most application vendor partnerships.

PeopleSoft has provided CommerceOne with a one-time payment of $15 million for the right to integrate, enhance, and resell BuySite to its base of 3,000 enterprise application customers. Prior to making this royalty payment, PeopleSoft has already invested $8 million in CommerceOne that makes the company a major equity investor. PeopleSoft and CommerceOne have formed a joint development team to enhance the capabilities of the PeopleSoft e-procurement application. CommerceOne will then have the option of bringing these enhancements to their own BuySite application. CommerceOne has agreed to not sell its BuySite application directly to PeopleSoft accounts. The companies have identified 3,000 named accounts to which PeopleSoft has the exclusive right to sell its e-procurement application. PeopleSoft will take a share of transaction revenue generated by the business flowing through Marketsite.net. This agreement between the two companies is typical of the partnerships occurring in the industry today, where PeopleSoft is providing the technology expertise while CommerceOne provides the access to new customers.

SAP

SAP's e-procurement solution, called SAP BTOB Procurement, was rolled out in early 1999. The SAP solution includes a robust set of tools including a workflow and business rules engine, and of course fully integrates with R/3. In May 1999, SAP launched a number of initiatives to help its customers pursue its business-to-business e-commerce strategies (what SAP is branding as mySAP.com). By working with content conversion vendors Aspect Development and Requisite Technology, SAP is able to deliver a complete online procurement solution.

Under the alliance between SAP and Aspect, which specialize in component management systems for the electronics industry, SAP will bundle Aspect's MRO Express Catalog into its Business-to-Business Procurement application. This will allow users to access more than 2 million MRO items in the catalog over the Internet. In addition, SAP signed a deal with Requisite to offer its catalog engine as an option within the Business-to-Business Procurement application.

Trad'ex

Although Trad'ex dabbled in providing buy-side solutions to the e-procurement market, its strategy going forward is to concentrate on providing the infrastructure required to build e-commerce portals. The fact that Trad'ex has in the past offered a buy-side solution has more to do with its need for short-term revenue. However, the company does not plan on delivering a buy-side application.

Clearly the e-procurement aspects of e-operations is growing rapidly, with the best-known companies in the enterprise software arena driving the innovation in this marketplace. With the quantifiable gains of using e-procurement, the pace of change, which will be seen in these applications, will quicken over time. In looking at e-procurement as a potential application to be enabled in conjunction with an ASP, check to see the extent of partnerships in place with the companies mentioned here. These companies are the market leaders, driving the partnerships that today deliver value to mid-sized and larger corporations. It is much anticipated that these companies would work toward a small business application suite enabled through their portal and exchange strategies aimed at companies with fewer than 250 employees.

Sales Force Automation

At the basis of all e-business efforts is the need to compete more effectively in serving customers. The area of e-operations, which focuses on customer acquisition and retention, is Customer Relationship Management, or CRM for short. One of the main aspects of holding onto customers is getting the right information to your sales force at the right time. The entire area of Sales Force Automation, or SFA, is one of the major growth areas of the CRM arena. With the speed of competition, the need for keeping the sales force in the loop concerning new developments on the one hand and giving them the tools for communicating with customers on the other is critical for the growth of a company.

Given the increasingly competitive nature of more and more industries, industry analysts are predicting the Sales Force Automation marketplace is going to be marked by significant growth. International Data Corporation, for example, predicts that the worldwide SFA packaged software market climbed to $581.8 million in 1997 and $887.6 million in 1998. Both of these figures represent a significant increase from IDC's previous forecast, which predicted revenues of $732.0 million and $541.0 million, respectively.

Businesses of all sizes are realizing the benefits of leveraging the speed of the Internet in serving their customers via strong sales force automation tools. With the increased capability to collaborate and share information globally, quickly uncover new leads with integrated database marketing, and standardize the selling process and manage the selling cycle, salespeople are better able to manage their activities and spend more time on actual selling. Demand also continues to increase for selling tools that help salespeople configure complex products to meet a customer's specific needs and analyze sales and customer information. This is very apparent in the PC industry, where Trilogy first spun off PCOrder.com, and has also courted the world's largest distributors for the configuration technology. The integration of e-procurement applications, daily task management and calendaring tools, and the development of permission email programs all are driving the Sales Force Automation suite of applications to new levels of functionality and performance. The integration of these technologies is driving several key trends in the Sales Force Automation marketplace, which are defined in the next several sections. Both International Data Corporation and Forrester Research have done extensive analysis of these markets, and their conferences and reports have been invaluable in learning about market dynamics.

CRM Applications Now Include Tools for Integrating with Customer Relationship Management Systems

Increasingly companies are seeking to integrate as many functions as possible that contain customer information, to accentuate the speed of competing for their business. Many companies seek to integrate all facets of their interactions with customers across all channels (the Web, email, fax, call centers, and mail), from lead generation and prospecting to customer service and support. As a result, vendors have embraced the idea of CRM, which integrates SFA, marketing automation, and customer service and support. The new segment in this equation is marketing automation, which focuses on activities that involve finding and keeping customers, such as campaign management and execution, customer segmentation, database marketing, telemarketing, and personalization. SFA, by contrast, seeks to manage sales functions and serve the sales force and sales management. The CRM market is growing in excess of 40% per year through 2003, attracting new entrants, especially traditional ERP players whose core market shows signs of slowdown or even stagnation. At the high end and, to some extent, the midrange, of CRM, companies are linking to back-office systems such as inventory, shipping, and manufacturing, providing a seamless link across the enterprise. Some vendors are calling this category of complete end-to-end solutions enterprise relationship management, or ERM.

Speed of Competition

Just three years ago, the Internet was seen as having strong potential for making communication between customers and suppliers faster, more accurate, and much more candid. The most powerful change the Internet has brought about is a new singular focus on the customer—no longer are processes at center stage in industries—the needs of the customer and their fulfillment are. As a result, the Internet is causing entire businesses and industries to go through remorphing and change as the needs of the customer are redefining value chains. Sometimes called *dis-intermediation*, this is very apparent in the PC industry where the direct model introduced by Dell and Gateway are driving distributors to redefine their businesses from simply being product aggregators to being electronic enablers.

As the need for competing in Internet time becomes more and more apparent, the need for having instantaneous access to central, real-time corporate and customer information through thin clients with browser access is transforming the nature of business. All SFA vendors have Internet-enabled their applications or rearchitected them using Web technology. New vendors, such as Octane Software, have been built on the Internet platform from the beginning. Austin-based HotData announced a service that delivers business and consumer intelligence directly into applications via the Internet. HotData has enabled Symantec's ACT! product with its business intelligence offering, and recently announced additional partnerships with MultiActive Software and Pivotal.

Increased Product Functionality and Scalability Continues

Traditional distinctions between contact managers, organizers, and personal information managers (PIMs) on the one hand (traditionally called the low tier) and full-featured, enterprisewide solutions for large, global companies on the other (the high tier) continue to erode. In addition, many vendors offer a range of products, some of which might appeal to the enterprise, others to the single user. The trend of vendors adding functionality to their products and scaling upward continues, but I believe that there will continue to be a place in the market for standalone products that serve small businesses and solo users. However, even these products will need to have Web capabilities.

Siebel Has Emerged as the Dominant SFA Vendor

The only company to have achieved a double-digit market share in 1998 was Siebel, which had revenues of $190.6 million, representing 21.5% of the market. This revenue figure represented a significant growth of 242.9% from 1997. Although the company has focused on the high end of the market, with comprehensive solutions for Fortune 1000 companies, it is moving into the midrange via partnerships with J.D. Edwards, Great Plains Software, and others. Siebel also gives away a standalone version of its product, called Siebel Sales, which it explicitly compares to ACT! and GoldMine. Siebel Sales includes contact management and opportunity management, as well as travel expense management. At the low end, the company hopes that users will eventually upgrade to its Siebel for Workgroup product. Siebel has also introduced a portal for salespeople (www.sales.com), which it hopes will eventually generate product sales. Other SFA vendors, such as Clarify and Vantive, have also prospered, but to a much lesser extent.

Sales Force Automation Is Now Globally Focused

As the Internet itself has made it possible for companies of all sizes to compete on a global level literally within weeks, the need for tracking customers globally through Sales Force Automation and CRM applications is growing. Major companies who are positioning themselves as enterprise-wide ASPs are making inroads into global markets due to their scalability and capability to execute on a global level relatively quickly. Companies in this group include Siebel, Oracle, Onyx, and Pivotal. Their ability to be global competitors is to a large extent attributable to design objectives for products including this as a key criteria during the development phase of applications. International Data Corporation predicts that 71% of the total usage of sales force automation applications are in the U.S., with significant gains in the European marketplace in the years ahead.

Customer Resource Management Is Driving the Need to Consider Application Service Providers

The level of performance and scope of functionality delivered in CRM applications today is distancing the comparable level of application value that can be built inside even the largest corporations today. Increasingly companies are looking to outsource their SFA and CRM initiatives, partially due to Siebel Systems legitimizing this market through their rapid success at the mid-tier and larger Fortune 1,000 companies.

Internet Access Via Wireless Devices Is Fueling Both Sales Force Automation and Customer Relationship Management

The rise of cellular technology in the Scandinavian countries, evidenced by the integration of e-commerce capabilities with Nokia phones for example, is just a foreshadowing of things to come. The capability to communicate instantly with customers as to the status of their orders, providing feedback on when a problem will be solved, and most importantly, the creation of expectations with accurate information is going to be crucial for companies to grow. Accuracy of expectations becomes more attainable than ever before, using the tools defined within sales force automation, and with it, customer relationship management.

e-Logistics

Logistics *business process outsourcing (BPO)* involves the outsourcing of a company's logistics process to a third-party service provider. Logistics BPO is an integrated function that stretches from the vendor to the end customer. This set of activities comprises much more than delivery- and warehousing-related functional activities. Many analysts echo this definition of logistics. Logistics actually goes beyond merely the physical flow of the products to encompass the process and information necessary to optimize a customer's logistics activities. These activities, taken together, will drive the growth of the logistics BPO industry and will be the effective integrating and bundling of traditional third-party logistics services with today's information technology-based solutions.

Who's Who in e-Logistics?

The legacy of the logistics starts with the first companies that provided freight services for businesses. In an industry where service is everything the speed of execution often spells the difference between holding onto a new customer or losing them to a competitor who can deliver quicker and at diverse locations at the same time. The founders of the logistics industry have driven offerings into four different segments:

- Order fulfillment
- Transportation management
- Warehousing management
- Reverse logistics

These companies have also embarked on significant e-logistics strategies as the competition in the industry itself has always strived to improve the ability to deliver to customers quickly. The expectations of customers are being driven every day by the pervasive branding of United Parcel Service and Federal Express. Both companies are actively pursuing logistics strategies entirely on the instantaneous nature of the Internet. In this section there is a profile of the competitive nature of United Parcel Service and Federal Express.

The e-logistics marketplace is also being driven by many factors, including a rapidly changing industry, expanding categories of services, divergent backgrounds of players, the growth of information technology as an enabler, and offerings with a vertical industry focus. The next three sections describe major industry trends in e-logistics.

e-Logistics Is Now a Mainstream e-Operations Application

The immediacy of the Internet is now driving entirely new business models for logistics companies. Today the fulfillment systems of these companies are increasingly Internet-based to optimize the availability and distribution of the highly complex information and data that drive the growth and development of the logistics BPO world. One of the prime examples of a company that is taking e-logistics to an entirely new level in their business model is Ingram Micro. A long-time partner with Federal Express, Ingram Micro now has the capability to drop-ship on behalf of their VARs to any end user. Ingram's constant redefinition of their business model to a more e-logistics focus is paying dividends as the company maintains a $20 billion sales run rate.

Strategic Partnerships Are Driving Innovation

As logistics companies extend their reach into a broader scope of market opportunities, they are finding the need to refine the attributes of their services and to seek a range of partners to help them deliver different elements of total or whole service solutions. By measuring success in terms of incremental revenue, companies can gauge the health and strategic importance of their partnerships, and they can avoid spending unnecessary time with partners that do not significantly expand either the vendor's solution set or the market opportunity.

Global Reach Will Be Everything in e-Logistics

The challenge of being globally strong as a provider of e-logistics is one that is now starting to divide the various companies in this market into segments of performance. In looking at an e-Logistics provider for your business, the need is very apparent for having a company capable of spanning several continents, complete with knowledge of local laws, customs, and being able to handle the language differences and expectations associated with each country's customers.

e-Logistics is the necessary component of any e-business strategy that takes the expectations of customers and meets or even exceeds them through execution. In considering your e-business strategy and its implications on your customers, meeting their expectations by having the product arrive on time is really what your customers want and what e-logistics is all about. In evaluating an ASP to work with, check to see the level of experience they have working with the major e-logistics providers, and the depth of their experience integrating with these leading provider's systems.

Case Study: UPS e-Strategy Initiatives and Competitive Position Relative to Federal Express

United Parcel Service (UPS) provides express carrier and package delivery services to 200 countries and territories around the world through a network of more than 1,700 distribution centers. The company, founded in 1907, is based in Atlanta and employs more than 331,000 people worldwide. Their revenue was $24.8 billion in 1998. Most recently, the company sold a 10% stake of the company to the public.

On February 7, 2000, United Parcel Service (UPS) announced the launch of its e-Ventures and e-Logistics (e-commerce logistics) services, both focused on the opportunity to provide back-end services to emerging online sellers. Due to its track record in transportation management, package delivery, and supply chain management, UPS today enjoys significant brand recognition between the existing and emerging online retailers. However, despite this head start, as it moves forward in developing and offering services to the marketplace, UPS will need to adapt its culture and operations to the challenge of serving a new breed of .com players. At the same time, to preserve its brand identity, UPS will need to send a strong and well-articulated positioning message to the market to compete with a growing set of traditional and e-commerce—based logistics service competitors.

A wholly owned subsidiary of UPS, UPS e-Ventures will be the research, development, and incubation arm of UPS's e-commerce practice. UPS e-Ventures is designed to identify and rapidly develop entirely new businesses specifically related to supply chain management and e-commerce. The first company that UPS e-Ventures is developing is UPS e-Logistics. UPS states that UPS e-Logistics plans to provide complete end-to-end business solutions for the rapid, low-cost launch of e-commerce start-ups. The group plans to create a service bundle for small and medium-sized Web businesses to provide solutions for everything from warehousing to order fulfillment to customer service.

UPS not only has the physical infrastructure, but understands the importance of information management and a forward-looking business model as well. To date, UPS has invested $11 billion in acquiring up-to-date technologies and has established partnerships with top-tier companies, including CommerceOne, PeopleSoft, Oracle, Hewlett-Packard, Compaq, Harbinger, Open Market, IBM, Harvey Software, AT&T, and Cambridge Technology Partners.

As it addresses the burgeoning e-commerce opportunity, UPS is moving from a position of strength in its launch of its e-Ventures and e-Logistics services. UPS enjoys a strong brand presence in package delivery and has made significant investments in new tools and technologies. However, the competitive landscape is fierce and getting fiercer.

Business-to-Business e-Commerce Strategy: Enabling Global Commerce

The company's overall e-strategy, as articulated by a UPS executive, is "to weave UPS into the infrastructure of e-commerce." UPS believes that it is directly affecting the e-commerce landscape by

- Extending its technology portfolio to facilitate easy collection of and quick access to package information
- Creating seamless interfaces between the buyer and seller by integrating UPS functionality into its customers' business processes
- Promoting this approach has a direct impact on the company's business-to-business strategy, because 80% of UPS's deliveries are to business customers.

UPS Organizational Structure

The UPS eCommerce Team (eTeam) is a cross-functional group reporting to the company's Corporate Marketing division. e-Commerce technical development and deployment groups also support the company's eTeam. UPS's account managers are a key component of the company's e-strategy. This specialized sales force works with UPS customers to integrate transportation tools into their e-business processes. There are currently 35 e-commerce account managers. The company plans to increase that number to 133 managers by early 2000.

History of UPS e-Commerce Efforts

The company traces the inception of its e-commerce strategy to the 1980s, when it invested $1.5 billion on technology improvements to expand and enhance customer service. This initial outlay was followed by additional investments of more than $1 billion per year throughout the 1990s.

As UPS looked for growth opportunities, it realized that it needed to find a way to integrate its customers' network systems with its own to provide a much quicker, more efficient, and reliable service. Technology became the tool to achieve this goal.

Mission

UPS's mission is "to move at the speed of business" and be the enabler of global commerce. Particularly, the company has identified five fundamental concepts that are basic to global e-commerce:

- Integrating the physical and virtual world
- Creating new value-chain models
- Working directly with customers on solutions
- Collaborating with alliance partners
- Extending the enterprise

Key Requirements for a Successful Business-to-Business Strategy According to UPS

The company attributes its current success in the Internet marketplace to several factors:

- A strong global brand
- The capability to leverage existing infrastructure (physical and technological)
- The capability to provide multiple transportation service levels (digital, air, and ground)
- Crucial buy-in from the top and bottom
- A strong presence in the three flows of commerce: information, goods, and funds

Business-to-Business e-Commerce Execution at UPS

UPS has developed a diversified portfolio of products and services, as well as engaged in strategic alliances with technology suppliers, to ensure customer satisfaction and continue to expand its global reach. UPS.com was launched in 1994. Since then, the company has continuously improved its site. For instance, in 1997 UPS introduced multilanguage tracking, which allows customers to access tracking information in 19 languages or variations of languages.

The company offers the following Internet-based interactive services via its home page at www.ups.com. These services allow customers to do the following:

- Obtain detailed information about where a package is during shipment
- Calculate shipping costs
- Print shipping labels
- Maintain an address book
- View shipping history
- Order supplies
- Determine transit times and view service maps
- Request a package pick-up
- Find package drop-off locations, 50,000 with detailed maps
- Send questions and suggestions
- Download UPS Internet Tools, integratable Web tools that provide package tracking and UPS Quick Cost Calculator for Web sites
- Download UPS Document Exchange, an electronic delivery and management service for shipping anything over the Internet that can be contained in a digital file, including document, audio, and digital files

Other UPS e-commerce applications solutions include:

- UPS World OnLine World Link, a service deployed to customers to provide free fenced Internet access to UPS Web sites. OnLine World Link will be available in the United States in the first quarter of 2000.
- UPS OnLine tools, transportation tools that can be embedded directly into e-commerce applications and reapplied into business processes across the enterprise.
- API modules are integrated to provide enhanced tracking, rating, and service selection, shipping and handling, address validation, electronic manifesting, U.S. delivery time-in-transit, and service mapping.

UPS Partnerships Show Commitment to e-Logistics

In addition, UPS has established partnerships with numerous technology suppliers to incorporate UPS software into its own offerings, including

- AT&T, to provide hosting and transaction services. Merchants can build Web sites, set up an electronic store, and integrate a Web site and call center.
- Commerce One, to integrate UPS tracking, time-in-transit, and address validation into MarketSite.net, its MRO procurement portal.
- Harbinger, to create inexpensive, commerce-enabled Web sites containing up to 100 pages. The service includes a searchable catalog, unlimited updates and site changes, and automatic tax and shipping charge calculations.

- IBM, to offer two levels of service: an entry-level solution hosted on IBM servers and an advanced offering for large enterprises, which includes Web authoring, administration, email, discussion groups, and order fulfillment to the buyer. This service is available in 10 languages.
- iCat, to provide, in addition to the basic features, database capabilities, customizable payments, and tax and shipping options.
- Lotus, to provide integration with workflow applications, which includes UPS tracking, through Lotus's Domino.Merchant.
- Open Market, to develop an integrated logistics and fulfillment module called the UPS Logistics Gateway, whereby users can prepare packages for shipment through an interface with UPS OnLine Professional shipping software and can track packages with a standard UPS tracking number or a reference number assigned when an order is placed.
- Oracle, to embed UPS transportation functionality (reference number tracking, address validation, service selection and rating, time-in-transit calculator, and integration with UPS OnLine WorldShip) into Oracle for seamless integration of supply-chain management, customer service, and fulfillment.
- Pandesic, to support all the business processes required for financial management, credit card validation, electronic payment and settlement, catalog creation and management, and order processing and returns as well as inventory management, merchandising, shipping, and customer service.
- PeopleSoft, to integrate shipping and logistics within enterprise planning for supply chain management.

Most recently, UPS partnered with and made an equity investment in TanData Corp., a privately held developer of logistics software. TanData's Transportation Application Programming Interface (API) allows businesses to collect and share shipment data from multiple carriers with a single seamless system. In addition, UPS has made an investment in TRADEX through its Strategic Investment Fund.

UPS Success Metrics

Some of the key metrics that have resulted from UPS's e-strategy are

- 80% increase in Web traffic in the last three years
- Nearly 20,000 Web sites connected to UPS tracking
- 12.5 million packages delivered per day
- 13 million hits per day
- 1.5 million tracking requests
- 600,000 e-commerce solutions deployed

Lessons Learned by UPS

UPS considers its e-commerce experience an evolutionary process. The company mentioned the following key areas:

- Be proactive about telling your success story; it will help strengthen your brand.
- Don't be afraid to make mistakes, errors will happen. A UPS executive expressed it best: "If you think e-commerce is scary, drop the 'e' and get to work. e-Commerce is commerce first; it has been the same fundamentals since the dawn of time—we just have some new tools at our disposal."
- Surround your company with superior talent. Technology does not create sustainable competitive advantage, people do.
- Align your company to deliver new e-commerce solutions at Internet speed. e-Commerce is a horizontal issue in a vertical world.

UPS Future Initiatives

UPS is very enthusiastic about the opportunities presented by global business-to-business and business-to-consumer Internet commerce. The company plans to continue expansion of its international presence as well as its investments in new technology solutions. Future initiatives will focus on these themes and leverage UPS's position within the three flows of commerce: goods, information, and funds.

Competitive Position Relative to Federal Express

The critical question of competition between UPS and Federal Express is if the latter can ever catch the former in the high-volume home-delivery marketplace. Clearly today UPS is the market arena leader.

Its recent announcement of an expanded home delivery strategy is a bold move on the part of FedEx to compete head-to-head with UPS in the *business-to-consumer (B2C)* logistics services market. B2C home delivery presents a tremendous opportunity for increased logistics revenue as e-commerce continues to expand. FedEx has already established a competitive position in *business-to-business (B2B)* logistics services; its new strategy to launch e-tailing home delivery is a necessary step to remain competitive in the delivery business. However, FedEx's new venture will face serious competition from established home-delivery players, such as UPS and the U.S. Postal Service (USPS), as well as from newer ".com" start-ups, including Webvan, Peapod, Streamline.com, Kozmo, and Urbanfetch. FedEx's success depends on its capability to wring efficiencies out of its decentralized delivery network and to expand geographic coverage and specialized services.

Background on Federal Express

With annual revenue exceeding $17 billion, Federal Express Corp. (NYSE: FDX) is a global provider of transportation, logistics, e-commerce, and supply chain management services. The company offers integrated business solutions through a network of subsidiaries operating independently, including FedEx Express, the world's largest express transportation company; FedEx Ground (also known as RPS), North America's second largest provider of small package ground delivery service; FedEx Custom Critical, the world's largest provider of expedited time-critical shipments; FedEx Global Logistics, an integrated logistics, technology, and transportation-solution company; and Viking Freight, a less-than-truckload carrier operating principally in the western United States. More than a million customers are connected electronically through the FedEx information network, and approximately two-thirds of FedEx's domestic transactions are now handled online.

FedEx has viewed the low-cost, residential ground-delivery market as a gap in its service portfolio. Low-cost ground delivery is how many consumer goods bought on the Internet are delivered. Earlier last year, FedEx Ground, primarily a B2B delivery division, began testing residential delivery in Pittsburgh. The test centered on the implementation of process and technology in support of a residential delivery service. Test results convinced FedEx to launch the residential service nationwide.

On January 19, 2000, FedEx announced its new initiatives for providing expanded home delivery services. Beginning in March, FedEx Ground will provide FedEx Home Delivery in 38 U.S. cities via 67 delivery terminals and cover 50% of the U.S. population. In four years, the company's home delivery network will expand to 98% of the U.S. population via 380 delivery terminals. FedEx will spend $150 million in initial cash outflow and expects to break even within three years. This delivery-only service will be dedicated to the needs of businesses specializing in B2C e-commerce.

FedEx states that its new services will offer the following value propositions to these customers:

- Convenient and customized service. FedEx Home Delivery will provide customized delivery options, including delivery by appointment, day or evening, with a money-back guarantee.

- Unique and efficient service. FedEx Home Delivery will take advantage of the FedEx Ground operational network for pick-up and package sorting to maintain a low-cost structure.

- Dedication to deliveries. FedEx Home Delivery will be different than the competition because it will be dedicated to the delivery side of the equation. Hence, it will be able to focus on and excel at meeting the distinct customer interface requirements of residential customers.

- An effective e-commerce solution. This service will complement FedEx's leadership position in the B2B e-commerce market—by far the largest and fastest growing segment of e-commerce. FedEx Home Delivery will give electronic retailers, or *e-tailers*, an option that combines reliability with cost-effective ground transportation.

What does this mean for UPS, B2C, and B2B Commerce?

While FedEx Ground and its main competitor in home delivery, UPS, both maintain three different operations—air, ground, and home delivery—UPS integrates these three systems into one network. Specifically, the same UPS truck picks up the package for all types of deliveries. UPS customers do not need to separate their requirements for air versus ground; all they need to determine is how many days they want the parcel to take and how much they are willing to spend, and UPS selects the optimum delivery method for its clients. With UPS, the customer has one single point of contact, which is a significant competitive advantage over other carriers.

In contrast, FedEx is taking a decentralized approach to its home delivery operations. FedEx separates its air delivery from FedEx Ground's ground services. FedEx Ground intends to leverage its existing pick-up operation and automated hub and linehaul network while initiating a separate delivery network composed of distinct terminals and a separate team of independent contractors to handle its home delivery service.

FedEx Ground's operational model poses potential challenges for the company's launch of its residential service. The use of nonintegrated facilities and systems for home delivery, ground delivery, and air express dilutes delivery stops and reduces the volume of packages handled in each segment of the network. UPS's integrated system maximizes the capacities of its delivery trucks. In addition, having different trucks and different drivers reduces the level of intimacy that the company can develop with its customers. Although FedEx contractors are paid based on the number of stops made and packages delivered, the number of stops a contractor can make in a day is a function of density. If there are only a few stops and packages in a particular area, it will be very difficult for a contractor to make money—ultimately there has to be some level of efficiency to make a delivery network a "win-win" situation.

Forecasts of Market Sizing by Research Firms

IDC and Forrester both estimate that the rapidly increasing number of businesses and individuals buying and selling goods and services over the World Wide Web will drive commerce on the Internet to more than $1 trillion by 2003. The demand for faster, cheaper delivery is rising daily and represents one of fastest-growing e-commerce segments. Online buyers expect goods to be delivered from the click of mouse to the knock at the house. To meet this expectation, B2C e-tailers must build effective relationships with delivery service providers to streamline the customer's entire experience, from ordering to delivery and beyond. Delivery services will become an increasingly important link in the chain.

Currently, air delivery is expensive, and two well-known providers dominate ground delivery: UPS and USPS. The 93-year-old heavyweight delivery giant UPS delivers 3 million packages to homes everyday. UPS maintains 1,700 facilities with 150,000 delivery vehicles in place. UPS has become a household brand name for home delivery, a position further evidenced by its recent successful IPO.

New Entrants from the B2C Arena

New entrants in this space are also gearing up to roll out their own niche delivery models. These players include online grocery stores such as Webvan, Peapod, Streamline.com, and HomeGrocers. Grocery (perishable goods) delivery is a thin-margin business, and the way for these players to succeed is through building an efficient distribution network, including highly efficient home delivery. Another small but growing category of start-ups—examples are Kozmo and Urbanfetch—plan to sell CDs, videos, and books to residential customers with a promise to deliver merchandise ordered online within an hour.

Compared with these start-ups, FedEx enjoys advantages in its mastery of sophisticated logistical networks and systems through 27 years of experience in pioneering express delivery service. FedEx has the opportunity to bring this experience to bear in meeting the needs of B2C e-tailers. Specifically, service features that enable e-tailers to offer enhanced services, accurately track deliveries, and expedite merchandise returns will be important to e-tailers. In addition, FedEx's advanced systems should enable it to measure the impact of its services on the e-tailers' business performance and to potentially highlight the resulting business benefits. However, FedEx should continue to push the service technology envelope to demonstrate its contribution to customer satisfaction and repeat business.

Despite the flood of new types of players, there are plenty of opportunities in the B2C e-commerce logistics (e-logistics) services space. For B2C e-commerce to prosper, home delivery needs to catch up and deliver at Internet speed with lower costs. FedEx will be going head-to-head with two market leaders that are also technology savvy. At the same time, newcomers must travel a steep and probably treacherous learning curve in their efforts to reengineer the home delivery business. In the short term, FedEx has the opportunity to capitalize on its strengths to gain quickly in this rapidly changing delivery segment.

To make home delivery a profitable business, FedEx will face some substantial challenges in competing with established players such as UPS and USPS in terms of geographic coverage, cost structure, and the operational efficiencies associated with its nonintegrated operating systems.

The strength of the Internet's ability to reach customers on a global level is central to the strategy of each of these companies. The initial offerings by FedEx to reach 50% of the U.S. market might place constraints on the ecumenical geographic coverage for which e-tailers are looking. To speed its service coverage and increase operational efficiencies, it's reasonable to anticipate that FedEx might have to consider a more aggressive strategy (such as acquisitions of delivery in specific markets).

FedEx wants to differentiate itself from UPS and USPS by providing money-back guarantees, extended service hours (including Saturday delivery), and custom-scheduled delivery. Delivery by appointment and guaranteed delivery on Saturday and evenings will inevitably result in some add-on fees passed on to the customer. Whether demand can generate enough revenue and provide economies of scale (in the short and the long run) to justify the additional operational costs associated with extended services will remain one of the most serious questions that FedEx faces. At the same time, if the demand for Saturday delivery and custom scheduling continues to grow, there is no reason why UPS or USPS could not expand their service lines and potentially provide the same offerings with a lower cost structure, while at the same time covering 99% of U.S. homes through their established infrastructure.

Although FedEx states that it will differentiate itself by focusing on delivery, its competition is taking the similar approach, just without the specialization of parcel delivery. Competition by eager .com delivery start-ups is right next door. At this point, they are not as experienced as FedEx in logistics operations, but they are extremely well-funded by Wall Street and venture capital firms and benefit from high market capitalization and a steady cash flow. Some of the start-ups, such as Webvan, have even built their own sophisticated package-delivery systems in a manner similar to FedEx, which uses a hub-and-spoke system. Shipper.com, another start-up, recently announced that it was offering same-day delivery service on weekends and holidays to cover 40% of U.S. households by the end of 2000.

Final Analysis and Conclusions

FedEx Express was originally created as an express service to deliver office documents. As fax, email, and other types of electronic document exchange systems became common, FedEx's initial business model needed to be adjusted. FedEx deserves credit for its courageous move to catch the opportunity in the B2C e-logistics services space, which is still an open playing field when it comes to last-mile, low-cost delivery. FedEx could not afford to miss out on the booming opportunity represented by B2C e-commerce. Now it must leverage its strengths to rapidly position itself in the home delivery space.

FedEx's move adds to the competitive mixture in the space. Overall, it will be a positive thing for e-tailers and consumers to have more choices in shipping, and FedEx's track record and experience make it a logical choice. It remains to be seen whether FedEx will gain sufficient momentum to break even in three years. If FedEx cannot leverage its technology lead to compete with the large economies of scale that UPS currently enjoys, FedEx might need to rethink what its next move will be as it tries to replicate its past success in the new millennium.

Exploring ASPs Providing e-Operations Solutions

With the breadth of applications in e-operations being driven by the need for communicating both with customers and between companies that combine efforts in the support of customers, the need is definite for getting a strong e-operations strategy in place.

In embarking on a strategy of working with an ASP in the development of an e-operations strategy, there are many factors to consider. Here's a series of issues to consider when getting an e-operations strategy put together with the application service providers you choose to work with.

Level of Experience with Collaborative Projects Including Intranets

The capability to solve problems quickly during the completion of more complex intranets is the skill set most desired in a potential ASP partner, especially on initiatives that affect everyone in your company. With an idea of how many intranets have been developed over time, you'll get a good idea of how resilient the technical staff is at the companies you are considering working with on your projects.

Extent of Application's Breadth and Depth in e-Operations

With many ASPs that are just seeing the opportunity to enter the e-operations marketplace, today there is only a small but rapidly growing set of proven applications available. Be sure to check out the length of time and roughly the number of customers by application your ASP is offering in the e-operations arena. This provides you with a relative level of performance sustainability by application, and is also prudent from the standpoint of the accumulated hours of support time spent on the application.

Programming Expertise

The extent of integration with third-party logistics systems and domain expertise with programming languages is an essential element that your e-operations implementation plan must have. Being able to link back to Federal Express, UPOS, DHL, and other carriers is absolutely essential for the development of your fulfillment systems. Your company might already have relationships in place with these companies. Having the electronic integration in place for being able to fulfill orders is crucial for the growth of any e-business strategy. Federal Express clearly has the edge on the business side of e-Logistics, UPS is by far stronger on a global level, in addition to the home delivery challenges both face. It is anticipated either or both of these companies will acquire a dot com in the coming years, bringing a strong front-end e-commerce engine to their core strength of fulfilling orders.

As has been seen from the case studies in this book and throughout the entire industry, the need for a strong e-operations structure is critical to being able to fulfill the commitments made by e-marketing and e-commerce strategies.

Capability to Provide Assistance with e-Procurement Application Tailoring for Your Company

Taking the procurement aspects of a company and bringing them to the point of capitalizing on the speed of the Internet is the challenge of every company considering an e-business strategy today. Companies mentioned in this chapter have consistently delivered results on their solutions at the midrange of the marketplace, and have had strong success in the Fortune 1,000 marketplace. The continual need for an e-procurement solution for small business will force these companies to develop VAR programs that can affect the needs of companies with 250 employees or fewer.

Ongoing Development of Strategic Relationships with Key Companies in the Industry

This is another "must have" that any ASP being considered for projects has to illustrate. Competing with one another on the relative level of functionality they deliver to their customers, ASPs are often looking to partnerships to extend the reach of their applications. Partnerships are providing ASPs with the capability to extend the value of their offerings. Without partnerships, an ASP has to make it completely on its own— a daunting task that not even IBM or Oracle is taking. In evaluating an ASP for an e-operations strategy implementation, be sure to check that partnerships exist and are in good standing.

Ongoing Security and Authentication Testing with Regard to Intranet Development

The need for ensuring that once an intranet is developed that it is very difficult to hack into is critical for the long-term success of any ASP. Holding an ASP accountable for random security tests is always a good idea, as a lax attitude on this area could jeopardize not only the ASP's business but yours as well. Hold an ASP to high security standards and insist that periodic, even spontaneous tests are done by security consultants to determine how resilient the security measures actually are. With e-operations the life blood of a company is circulating through an intranet. Having the assurance that your data is securely transmitted and stored is worth the due diligence at the beginning of an ASP relationship.

Experience Working with BackOffice Integration in Conjunction with e-Procurement Applications

With many organizations there are extensive legacy systems and data that need to be integrated into an e-operations strategy. The capability of an ASP to address these integration needs is crucial to the overall success of your plans for outsourcing intranet and e-procurement plans for example. Building on the legacy data and systems and yet also being able to deliver on the speed of the Internet for expediting purchasing and therefore driving costs down is the challenge for the ASP you choose to work with. Probe into the success stories an ASP has in this area of integration. If your ASP tells you that they cannot provide references due to the confidential nature of the work done, keep looking. Satisfied customers are the best assurance of expertise in BackOffice integration. Of all tasks an ASP takes on, this is the most difficult to do well.

Creating an e-Operations Integration Plan

Bringing together all the components of an e-operations plan involves looking at the key objectives your company is trying to accomplish. In terms of an overall e-business strategy, many companies drive first for increased revenues, yet the biggest payoffs are often in reducing costs through innovative ways of taking the speed of the Internet and applying it to solving operations issues. Take for example the speed at which companies can now solve customer satisfaction issues by heading them off in the first place with Sales Force Automation and Customer Relationship Management applications. Taking the steps toward being a resource for customers using these tools to supplant that direction will yield stronger returns than using the Internet to shield your company from direct contact. If any strong lesson continues to be learned by companies working with SFA and CRM it is that spending to get closer to customers, and making the Web just one of many vehicles for accomplishing that goal, is rewarded. The growth of CRM is really seen by many analysts as a backlash to the email only option companies offered in the beginning days of the Internet.

The following section describes the key attributes or foundational elements you need to keep in mind as you develop an e-operations strategy.

Use Your Roadmap to Manage Expectations

As was discussed earlier in this book, the roadmap is an essential deliverable your company needs to use in driving the ASPs you choose to work with in fulfilling your strategic direction. Check to make sure your ASP has the technical capability to integrate with the industry's leading logistics systems from Federal Express, UPS, and others. The roadmap provides a frame of reference for the e-operations plans you have.

Technology Exists to Serve Your Internal and External Customers More Efficiently; It Is Not an End Unto Itself

Many companies get completely wrapped up in their information systems plans and, falling in love with the technology, forsake the reason the technology is there in the first place—to serve customers! Keeping a focus on the customer is possible even in the most complex of projects by having periodic review sessions on progress to ensure that the original needs of the project are still guiding the project today.

Leverage ASP Expedites Both CRM and Sales Force Automation

With the majority of e-operations being focused on the tasks associated with minimizing costs, the CRM and sales force automation areas are focused on driving the costs down of prospecting and further revenue generation. Leverage fully the expertise and applications of ASPs in creating Web-enabled customized tools and solutions that give your company the capability to drive new business is where e-operations fulfills the commitments made by e-marketing and e-commerce. Many ASPs are verticalizing their own businesses, with CRM attracting more ASPs every day. You could architect a CRM system that would give your sales force the ability to query on orders immediately from their cellular phones, for example. That would be state-of-the-art, yet if your business is closely tied to logistics, it is the future of your business anyway, so why not beat the competitors to that level of performance? It's a rhetorical question with a solid answer. Creating value using e-operations tools for maximum responsiveness is worth more in the long run for your business than any incremental cost reduction or revenue program—responsiveness drives repeat business.

Build in the Capability to Scale and Exceed Customer Expectations

The lesson learned from studying Amazon.com from an operational standpoint is simple: scalability gave them the capability to execute when their business growth exceeded even their expectations. Build scalability and with it the capability to exceed your customers' expectations into any metrics in an e-operations strategy. Look at it this way: The Internet is all about time to value for you and your customers. Being forward-thinking and driving innovation will distance you from competitors and also give you the ability to exceed customer expectations in execution.

Summary

Taking the most time—and cost-intensive tasks—in an organization and creating Web-enabled approaches to providing their functionality is at the core of an e-operations strategy. Unifying this area of an e-business strategy is the need for having collaborative efforts organized between groups within and among companies. At their most quantifiable level, e-procurement, Customer Relationship Management, Sales Force Automation and e-logistics all are delivering on the promise of cost reduction, with appreciable contributions to the bottom lines of companies using them. The incremental revenue gains from companies taking CRM into their mainstream businesses practices is where an e-operations strategy grows companies from just thinking of the next customer to thinking about the entirely new segments and classes of customers for existing and new products.

8

Understanding Acquisitions and Alliances in the ASP Marketplace

IN THE BUSINESS PLANS OF MANY APPLICATION SERVICE PROVIDERS today there is a strong focus on leveraging partnerships to create differentiation. Many ASPs today are partnering for access to technology, while many others with strong technical expertise are partnering to get access to distribution channels. There are also ASPs that are singularly focused on bringing a unique solution to a vertical market, and need access to the targeted markets through alliances. As the market moves very quickly and the dynamics of competition are driving the advent of the click and build Web site providers, who from their sites enable small businesses to build entire Web sites at the low end of the market and the migration of the most sophisticated of larger competitors from the high ends of the market, the mid-market is getting squeezed with competitive offerings. In addition, both the click and build companies and the ASPs currently serving the Fortune 1,000 marketplace are all interested in converging on the small and medium-sized business needs of the global marketplace. The implications of these competitive strategies is going to be seen in the value provided to mid-size and larger businesses everywhere as the breadth of applications becomes increasingly wider to compensate for these larger markets.

In striving to expand their customer base and either migrate up into serving larger customers as the click and build companies are intent on doing, or migrating to the mid-range and smaller businesses as many of the enterprise providers want to do, ASPs are now completing acquisitions and partnerships at a fever pace. Take for example BigStep.com and their partnership strategy, which is taking their already formidable strength as an e-marketing and e-commerce provider and extending it, with partnerships aimed at bringing e-operations functionality into their service offerings.

BigStep.com has more than fifty partnerships at last count, placing them in the role of being able to start attracting customers in the mid-range of the market.

Partnerships are necessary for extending the reach of ASPs into market areas they do not have the resources to address on their own. Companies that include Gartner Group, Zona Research, International Data Corporation, and the Yankee Group have all brought their respective analysis to the partnership arena. Gartner Group's work specifically is focused on defining overall ASP market dynamics from the standpoint of partnerships. The ongoing partnering of companies is even hastening the generations of applications themselves. Earlier in this book the point was made that you, the early adopter, can and will impact the product strategy of companies growing forward just by voting with your dollars for various solutions. In being able to meet present and potential demands of customers, ASPs are first anticipating needs and then looking for all forms of partnerships—mergers, acquisitions, strategic alliances—to assist in strengthening service offerings and building entirely new services altogether.

Looking at the implications of these alliances to you, the early adopter, is the intent of this chapter. Any ASPs you are considering need to have a partnership strategy in place and progressing if they are going to be able to meet your needs and other customers' future needs. The implication of a consolidation of the industry from the concerted approach at building partnerships is overstated. As the industry itself grows, so does the number of customers. Clearly this industry is so young and growing that what will appear to be a shakeout is actually the fact that companies calling themselves ASPs will need to deliver hosted applications, because more and more companies will be expecting performance over promises. That's the reason for all the partnerships—ensuring the highest level of performance possible through a team approach makes the most sense in delivering superior value to customers.

Alliances to Watch for in the ASP Arena

One of the most visible trends of alliances occurring today is that of telephone companies, sometimes called *telcos*, and Application Service Providers. Both The Yankee Group and Cahner's In-Stat contend that the future of service providers serving small business will rely on the telcos for the bandwidth for delivering applications in a responsive manner. The recent announcement of Verio, an ASP focused on the mid-markets, being acquired by Nippon Telephone & Telegraph is just the first evidence of global telcos sensing an opportunity with the ASP model. The implications for companies partnering with Verio can be a double-edged sword. On one hand there are far greater resources now for application development, yet as with many acquisitions, the focus of the company can easily be shifted to the needs of making both companies work in conjunction with each other. The need for staying focused on the customer needs to pervade the acquisitions, and given the size of the acquiring company, this is something the acquired companies need to stay passionate about. Presented here are several of the more visible alliances now pervading the ASP model.

SMBs Are the Focus of Telcos Worldwide

As reported by the Yankee Group's Small Business Service, NTT Communications Corp., a subsidiary of Nippon Telegraph and Telephone (NTT), announced in May 2000 that it would acquire Verio, a leading provider of Internet access, Web hosting, and enhanced services to American small- and medium-sized businesses (SMBs) for $5.5 billion in cash. The deal is an extension of NTT's $100 million equity investment in Verio at the time of its IPO in 1998. The acquisition of Verio gives NTT the capability to become a global communications provider of voice/data network services and Web-based enhanced solutions. This acquisition also provides Verio with the capability to tap into a significant Asia-Pacific presence. And the torrent of cash from NTT also enables Verio, as a subsidiary, to deepen its current international footprints in 130 countries (via reseller relationships with established local companies). With NTT's backing, Verio will expedite its data center buildout to support mission-critical applications across a global network. This buy-versus-build strategy is an increasingly common approach for companies to quickly capture technology assets (such as human capital and expertise) as well as customers, according to The Yankee Group Small Business market research analysis.

IBM's Many e-Business Initiatives

Almost acting as if they as an organization want to dispel with a vengeance any thought of this generation's IBM being out of touch with the needs of customers, today's IBM is a lean, mean e-business machine. The IBM of today is aggressively pursuing e-business strategies in many areas of the Internet. Starting with their very successful e-business branding and marketing efforts, IBM is now staking out territory in every aspect of e-business, from their low-end IBM NetConnections Servers to the Service Providers. IBM's many strategies show a commitment to being in a leadership position in the e-business markets aimed at.

IBM formed an Enterprise Web Management unit to lead IBM's efforts toward building the company into an e-business. The task of the unit was to create a single Web presence for the company and determine standards and technologies to support that Web presence. IBM outsources its entire Web infrastructure through IBM Global Services, including Web servers, data centers, networks, and workstations. This provides IBM Global Services with solid e-business experience, capability, and offerings.

When building an internal e-business, the Enterprise Web Management unit focused on the following areas:

- **Procurement**—Through this initiative, IBM interacts with more than 800 key suppliers online. Another e-procurement initiative is the creation of a central in-house requisition catalog on the Web. In 1999, IBM procured $13 billion in goods and services, saving more than $270 million worldwide. This is according to their annual report.

- **Commerce**—IBM has built-in e-commerce transaction capabilities. The company's e-commerce revenue totaled $14.8 billion in 1999. Business-to-business (B2B) extranets with IBM's Business Partners, original equipment manufacturers (OEMs), and enterprise customers are generating the majority of this revenue.

- **Customers**—IBM supported more than 42 million self-service Internet transactions last year. The primary focus in this area is responsiveness to customers, although cost savings of $750 million are an added bonus.

- **Employees**—The activities in this area revolve around distance learning and knowledge management. With respect to knowledge management, the site includes personalized news feeds from internal and external sources as well as creation of communities. IBM also provides the usual self-service offerings for human resources aspects, such as enabling employees to check on benefits and medical programs.

- **Business partners**—IBM applications allow 14,000 worldwide partners to access product and marketing information in 10 languages. Another application provides users with the ability to check supply status, purchase products, and track orders.

Making Partnerships Part of a Branding Approach

Starting in mid-1997, IBM embarked on what would be one of the landmark branding campaigns in the world of electronic commerce. IBM's primary goal in creating these ads and the resulting branding image was to make the entire series of ads resonate with reality. What was so creative about the campaign is that it relied on bringing in partnerships and customers to show the true benefits of the e-business products being offered.

IBM believes that the campaign has been well received by its customers, because customers and partners both identify with the way that the campaign is presented to them. Customers can also identify with the IBM people in the ads because they emphasize a more personal face of IBM. Although the links between increased advertising and increased sales are difficult to measure directly, the company has had a definite uptake in more complex, detailed e-business-oriented projects since the launch of the branding.

What is unequivocal is that IBM was able to take their extensive partnerships and emerging e-business customers and then create a very definite message that reinforced IBM no longer being a stodgy, old-line hardware manufacturer but a company looking to embrace and even define the future of e-business.

IBM's Focus on the Small Business Marketplace

As well as promoting e-business solutions to its traditional large enterprise customers, IBM has been aggressively targeting the e-business market for small businesses. The company is one of the few e-business networking vendors aggressively addressing this market, and it believes that SMBs are very active in adopting e-business. IBM feels that SMBs have quickly realized that building an e-business infrastructure enables them to compete anywhere across the world.

The company views SMBs as having the same generic requirements for an e-business network infrastructure as large companies. It needs to be secure, scalable, and available; however, the offerings to SMBs need to be packaged slightly differently. IBM is addressing this market through three sales channels: direct sales, Web sales, and partners.

In 1999 IBM introduced the IBM Small Business Program, which brings together IBM's small-business solutions under the e-business banner. Small businesses are encouraged to get online and are offered a variety of products and solutions to help them do e-business, including hardware, software, and services.

For example, IBM announced an e-business solution for small businesses in which the companies pay a one-time activation fee and thereafter a monthly subscription fee for all their Internet hardware, software, and services. Essentially, the solution enables small businesses to lease rather than buy an Internet solution, with prices starting at $99 per month.

Other thrusts from IBM in the small-business market include tools such as the IBM Home Page creator, which enables SMBs to build and maintain their own Web sites. IBM also offers services including Internet marketplaces for businesses, free secure file storage, banner ads, and back-up and recovery services.

Exploring the Many IBM Strategic Alliances

IBM's rejuvenation as a company focused on the e-business needs of businesses is also visible from the strategic alliance partners they are working with. Table 8.1 illustrates the breadth of the e-business alliances they are involved in. Notice the alliances include software, network applications, and wireless technology expertise. International Data Corporation's analysis of this area is one of the best known in the industry, and excerpts are provided here.

Table 8.1   IBM's many strategic alliances show a broadening of the company's priority at building a wide foundation of technology for future growth

Company	Scope of Alliance
Cisco	IBM and Cisco are partnering in two main areas: deploying networking applications (allowing businesses to migrate to an Internet infrastructure) and jointly creating and delivering end-to-end e-business solutions. Together, they will work on areas such as Internet infrastructure, e-business systems, and e-business services to deliver end-to-end Internet business solutions.
Novell	Novell and IBM are covering technology areas including caching, systems management, and integrating Web applications into the enterprise. They have brought together IBM's Web application servers and Web development tools with Novell's directory-based operating system.
Ariba and i2	IBM, Ariba, and i2 technologies will bring their software products into one portfolio and provide customers with a range of products that can build and operate business-to-business exchanges and automate interaction between business partners.

Table 8.1   **Continued**

Company	Scope of Alliance
Nokia, Motorola, Cisco, Ericsson, Intel, Symbian, Palm	IBM is cooperating with various vendors on aspects of wireless technology to enable the IBM vision of *pervasive computing*. The company is working with Nokia, Motorola, and Cisco to address the needs of wireless service providers. For example, IBM and Motorola intend to create a voice-and data-engine for businesses to develop and access wireless applications and services. Nokia and IBM are concentrating on application-enabling technologies such as WAP. On the wireless side, Cisco and IBM are developing wireless networks for service providers and businesses. Furthermore, IBM is partnering with Ericsson, Palm, Symbian, and Intel to develop solutions for mobile e-business on their handheld devices.

IBM's e-Business Alliance Objectives

IBM and Cisco had been traditional competitors in the networking market with their specific network connectivity products. Yet in the true sense of making partnerships work better than the competition, both of these companies have become partners, with significant numbers of each company's staffs devoted to making the partnership work. For example in mid-1999, IBM and Cisco announced initial details of their alliance, which also involved IBM selling the patents for its networking products to Cisco and effectively withdrawing from the networking hardware market. Cisco has taken IBM's technology on board and is now in the process of converting IBM's customer base over to Cisco products and focusing on IBM's top accounts. These customers can now use a combination of Cisco's network hardware and IBM's Global Services. This alliance has definite implications for the future development of the ASP model, as the costs of hosting and infrastructure as it relates to being an ASP will drop based on this alliance between Cisco and IBM.

The two companies have an ongoing technology alliance, and together they plan to deliver highly available, high-performance, and scalable technology foundations for e-business solutions. The aim is to produce solutions that will reduce the complexity of an e-business infrastructure and speed deployment. The alliance has announced two solutions, one that combines IBM's servers and software with Cisco's networking products, enabling the system to distribute the workload and increase availability and scalability. The second solution enables the server and the router to time priority transactions for e-business.

Novell

Novell and IBM announced a strategic alliance in Europe during 1999 aimed at providing networking and software solutions for e-business customers. The two companies have identified various business opportunities and plan to align their sales forces and marketing strategies as well as build technology solutions.

Novell and IBM are covering technology areas including caching, systems management, and integrating Web applications into the enterprise. The companies have brought together IBM's Web application servers and Web development tools with Novell's directory-based operating system.

The e-business alliance seems to run deeply through both companies—the sales organizations and marketing are cooperating, IBM's engineers are being trained as Certified Directory engineers, and the channel and business partners are being trained to sell and implement the new solutions.

Ariba and i2 Technologies

IBM announced a broad strategic alliance with Ariba and i2 Technologies within the B2B e-commerce marketplace. IBM has also taken a minority stake in both companies. Together, the three companies will bring their software products to market, providing customers with a range of products that can build and operate B2B exchanges and automate interaction between business partners. The combined portfolio of software products will be sold by merged sales teams and by IBM's Global Sales operations. Support, hosting, and integration services will be provided by IBM's Global Services division.

KPNQwest

IBM and KPNQwest also have an e-business alliance in which the two companies will build an extensive network of Web hosting centers across Europe. The KPNQwest Cyber Centers will deliver e-business services and applications throughout Europe and will be located in up to 18 cities.

The centers will deliver a wide range of hosting services including operating customer servers, hosting complex Web sites and providing colocation facilities. Network services such as Internet access, IP transit, and managed bandwidth will also be presented. The e-business customers that IBM and KPNQwest will target with their Cyber Centers include ASPs, ISPs, dot-com companies, SMBs, and large enterprises.

Wireless Technologies

IBM is cooperating with various vendors on aspects of wireless technology to enable the IBM vision of pervasive computing. IBM has distinct partnerships with Nokia, Motorola, and Cisco, and together with these three vendors, IBM plans to address the technology needs of wireless service providers.

For example, IBM and Motorola intend to create a voice-and-data engine for businesses to develop and access wireless applications and services. Nokia and IBM are concentrating on application-enabling technologies, such as WAP, to enable operators to deliver wireless e-business services to their customers. On the network side, Cisco and IBM are developing wireless networks for service providers and businesses, combining their expertise to develop mobile e-business solutions.

In the name of pervasive computing, IBM has also partnered with the leading hand-held device makers, Ericsson, Palm, and Symbian, to develop solutions for mobile e-business on their handheld platforms. The final major wireless partner is Intel, and the two companies are working together to further the development of wireless Internet technology.

The Oracle Technology Network

Oracle, with headquarters in Redwood Shores, California, is one of the largest suppli-ers of software for information management in the world. The company's portfolio includes database applications, database tools, and enterprise application products, along with related consulting, education, and support services. Oracle operates in more than 140 countries, employing 36,000 people worldwide.

Oracle derives its revenue from two principal streams: license fees and services. Services revenue is divided into support, consulting, and education components. Oracle Services are a large and rapidly expanding part of Oracle's business (growing at 42% in fiscal 1998). Consulting and education services grew 47% in 1998 as the com-pany continued to expand its services to assist customers in the use and implementa-tion of applications based on Oracle products. This information comes from Oracle's annual reports, which are invaluable in learning about key metrics of this dynamic organization.

Oracle Services has introduced several initiatives intended to strengthen its remote capabilities. These initiatives include applications management products and applica-tions administration services. In September 1998, Oracle announced that it had begun a pilot program for its Oracle Business OnLine hosting service for enterprise business applications. The ASP program will provide the full complement of Oracle applica-tions for financials, manufacturing, distribution, and human resources. The target mar-ket is small to medium-sized companies. HP and Sun are providing hardware infrastructure and technical services for the Oracle Data Center. In the future, Business OnLine data centers will be operated by Oracle and by select Oracle partners. Oracle applications will be available through select partners that will provide additional value-added services such as business processes, systems integration, and network-based services.

From its foundation, Oracle's strategy has been to provide full solutions to its users. Its services are seen as vital to the effective use of its products. It refers to its services divi-sions as being all about creating and sustaining customer success. Oracle also under-stands that the transfer of knowledge and therefore the perceived ownership of the technology is a way to create future demand.

One of the key issues that affects the strategy for Oracle's continued expansion of its services provision is that it derives more than half of its revenue from the delivery of services. Services are also the most rapidly growing portion of its business. Oracle has not been known for its use of the channel for the sales, marketing, and delivery of services.

Exploring the Oracle Technology Network

One of the major initiatives that Oracle has undertaken is the development of their Developer Portal, which will make all Oracle products available to developers for free, including its flagship Oracle 8i database, JDeveloper, Developer, Designer and a host of other tools, white papers, help materials, and conferences. Developers register via the portal and can either download point products, sign up for early adopter releases, or subscribe to product lines. The portal is designed as a career path facilitator, with peer-to-peer forums and an array of how-to threads.

All these features come with the promise that developers' privacy will be respected and their registration information will not be turned over to the notoriously aggressive Oracle sales force. When projects are deployed, developers sign up for deployment licenses and money changes hands. To date, more than 70,000 Oracle 8i CDs and tens of thousands of tools copies have been shipped. These figures were released in recent industry articles on the success Oracle is achieving in the database arena.

CommerceOne's Alliance Programs

CommerceOne provides business-to-business electronic procurement solutions. The CommerceOne Chain Solution links buying and supplying organizations into trading communities. Automating the buying and selling cycle increases efficiencies and reduces operational costs. The company is privately held and has had a total of $51 million in venture capital infusions. Investing companies include GE Capital, SAP, and Morgan Stanley. The company claims that the combined buying power of its customer base is $161 billion, which is the potential amount that could flow through its installed systems. Internal ROI analysis states that the cost of a purchase order has been reduced from $79 through a manual system to $6 through an automated CommerceOne system.

The CommerceOne products, BuySite and MarketSite, automate the entire procurement process of nonproduction goods by providing application software, catalog content, and interoperability between an enterprise and its suppliers. BuySite automates the internal procurement process from requisition to order, and MarketSite automates supplier interactions from order to payment.

CommerceOne targets a number of large companies across a variety of industries, including PG&E Corp., the County of Los Angeles, and those companies profiled previously.

CommerceOne has forged integration and technical partnerships with the Sabre Group, Ernst & Young, SAP, PeopleSoft, PriceWaterhouseCoopers, Microsoft, and MCISystemhouse, to name a few.

CommerceOne not only boasts a number of high-profile clients but suppliers as well, including Office Depot, NECX.com, Wareforce, BoiseCascade, and Staples. With its MarketSite strategy, CommerceOne hopes to build an open trading community. With this strategy, the company becomes a service provider and will recruit whatever supplier its clients need. The company is also building a global network of suppliers with its announcement that British Telecom will set up a MarketSite in Europe and NTT will set one up in Japan.

Consensus Achieved in the CommerceOne Global Trading Web

Taking the initiative of creating partnerships with companies through the expertise they now have in enterprise portal and exchange technology, CommerceOne recently held a summit of their key partners. One of the CommerceOne partners, Siwsscom, sponsored the event and hosted it in Switzerland.

The three-day council meeting was one of a series of meetings being held around the globe to discuss group bylaws and strategies. The consensus of the group was to move forward on incorporating the Global Trading Web partnership. Moreover, substantial progress was made in developing a set of bylaws to govern the organization. Additionally, committees were created to develop policies, technical standards and infrastructure.

The regular GTW meetings are intended to define the policies and processes that will make international Internet commerce effective. By establishing guidelines for trade agreements, including service level agreements, interoperability agreements, revenue sharing agreements and content syndication agreements, and e-commerce services such as directories, trading partner profiles and master catalogs, it is anticipated that the Global Trading Web will help revolutionize world trade by eliminating the cost and time of today's paper, telephone, and fax-based trading processes.

"We believe that the CommerceOne Global Trading Web represents a first-of-its kind plan to truly develop guidelines and processes for seamless global e-commerce," said Carl Falk, senior vice president of CommerceOne's Global Trading Web. "This meeting was another step toward achieving our goal to be the world's most open, dynamic, and efficient global trading network."

Attendees of the Global Trading Web meeting representing e-marketplaces based on the CommerceOne-MarketSite-Portal solution included: Artikos (Latin America), British Telecom (United Kingdom), Cable and Wireless Optus (Australia), Citigroup, CommerceOne, Com2 Business (Taiwan), Concert (AT&T and BT joint venture), Covisint (automotive industry), Deutsche Telekom (Germany), Endesa (Spain), Hong Kong Consortium, Metique (metals industry), NTT Communications (Japan), PeopleSoft, SESAMi.com (Singapore), Swisscom (Switzerland), TD Bank (Canada), and Tradecom (Portugal). A representative of PricewaterhouseCoopers, a CommerceOne global technology implementation partner, also participates in these events. Each global trading portal is independently owned and operated by a leading market maker in a region or industry—resulting in the greatest choice for all trading partners. Currently, CommerceOne and more than 77 partners develop and operate regional and vertical portals worldwide, including exchanges for the automotive, aerospace, energy, and telecommunications industries.

Consolidation in the Market by Alliances

With IBM taking on an increasingly aggressive role with regard to their partnerships, even with past competitors, and the increasing role of infrastructure providers including Cisco and CommerceOne, the role of application service providers will inevitably be strengthened through these extensive relationships, which are aimed at sharing market and technology expertise. The partnerships defined here are admittedly of the largest corporations, yet they are provided to show the extent companies have to make alliances and partnerships.

As the partnerships, alliances, and mergers mentioned here show, the net effect for customers is the continual generation of greater value and lower costs. There are literally hundreds of partnerships, alliances and mergers taking place every day in the Internet and, more specifically, e-business arenas. The continual development of these approaches to bringing value to the customer shows the growth trajectory of e-business for years to come.

Implications for a company or organization looking to partner with either a single ASP or a series of ASPs shows the importance of seeing a company with a cohesive partnering strategy in place. In evaluating ASPs to work with, the depth and breadth of their partnerships are critical to your success long-term. The focus on ASP has on a strong partnership with a database provider (Oracle, for example) will very often dictate the extent to which an ASP can assist you with legacy migration issues. Partnerships are a barometer of the ability of an ASP to be flexible in meeting your needs. Ultimately the partnerships your ASPs of choice have are your choices as well.

Case Study: Cisco's Alliances and Acquisitions Drive Internet Growth

Cisco believes that having a wide range of flexible and evolving partnerships—even considering competition—is essential for being an effective e-business company. Within Cisco, partnerships are initiated across both regional and business units. Generally, partnerships have a market focus (example: sales and marketing), but more often they also include joint engineering efforts and aim to represent all interests.

Cisco already has a wide range of cross-industry strategic alliances but expects to build its alliances and investments across all regions. In Asia/Pacific, it has both global and local partnerships.

In searching for a strategic partner or for a company to create an alliance with, these are the common attributes Cisco looks for:

- Understanding of intellectual property
- Understanding of telephony
- Understanding of convergence
- Understanding basic application areas
- Consulting resources

Strategic Alliance Partners

Cisco has a wide range of strategic alliances with major information technology vendors including software, wireless technology, and solutions integration and e-business solutions. Table 8.2 profiles the various alliances Cisco has today.

Table 8.2   Cisco's many strategic partnerships are exemplified by the major IT vendors partnerships which are active today.

Company	Scope of Alliance
EDS	The alliance aims to deliver Internet solutions that help companies improve their global business performance through e-business. EDS and Cisco are focusing on three areas of collaboration: legacy transformation, Internet commerce, and telecommunication services
Hewlett-Packard	HP and Cisco are cooperating to deliver end-to-end network-enabled solutions that allow customers to optimize and reduce the complexity of their network. Together the companies are working on bringing together computing and networking, data and voice, and UNIX and Windows NT.
IBM	IBM and Cisco are partnering in two main areas: in deploying networking applications—allowing businesses to migrate to an Internet infrastructure—and in creating and delivering end-to-end e-business solutions. Together, they will work on areas such as Internet Infrastructure, e-business systems, and e-business services to deliver end-to-end Internet business solutions.
KPMG	KPMG and Cisco leverage KPMG's consulting and solution development expertise together with Cisco's networking technology. The two companies plan to jointly develop innovative, repeatable, end-to-end solutions for their clients.
Microsoft	Microsoft and Cisco have a broad technology alliance focusing on areas such as multimedia, security, and directory services. Cisco and Microsoft are developing network services and infrastructures to enable Internet commerce, secure networks, and make it easier to manage networks.
Motorola	Cisco and Motorola are developing a framework for fixed and mobile wireless networks based on an IP backbone. The two companies are developing an open architecture integrating data, voice, and video services over both fixed and mobile networks, providing users with wireless access solutions for the Internet.
NEC	Cisco and NEC have partnered to promote a best-of-breed convergence program based on Cisco's AVVID platform. NEC will act as a Cisco Gold Partner to deploy Cisco's voice and data convergence products alongside its own PABX systems.

Table 8.2   Continued

Company	Scope of Alliance
Nokia	Nokia and Cisco are co-developing a framework for Cisco's wireless data solutions that incorporate data, voice, and Internet technologies. This deployment will enhance Nokia's capability to offer extended data services over its wireless networks.
PeopleSoft	PeopleSoft and Cisco are developing and marketing enterprise application solutions. These solutions aim to improve performance, security, and availability of applications over the network. The companies have agreed to develop enterprise applications that give high network priority to mission-critical business applications.

An Alliance with IBM

IBM and Cisco had been traditional competitors in the networking market with their individual ranges of networking hardware. However, these competitors have now become partners, and both companies have sizeable teams allocated to the partnership. In 1999, IBM and Cisco announced initial details of their alliance, which also involved IBM selling the patents for its networking products to Cisco, and effectively withdrawing from the IP and Ethernet-based networking hardware market. Cisco has taken IBM's technology on board, and is now in the process of converting IBM's customer base to its products, and focusing on IBM's top accounts.

The two companies have an ongoing technology alliance, and together plan to deliver highly available, high-performance and scalable technology foundations for e-business solutions. The aim is to produce solutions that will reduce the complexity of e-business infrastructure and the speed of deployment. The alliance has already announced two solutions, one that combines IBM's servers and software with Cisco's networking products, enabling the system to distribute the workload and increase availability and scalability. The second solution enables the server and the router to time priority transactions for e-business.

The future of this alliance will see further announcements of jointly developed solutions. Cisco will also produce complementary efforts to IBM's branding in the coming months.

KPMG

Cisco made a $1 billion investment in KPMG's consulting business in 1999. In return, KPMG Consulting agreed to add 4,000 Internet consulting professionals over 18 months to help support Cisco's enterprise and service provider customers, and enhance Cisco's professional services capabilities. The company made it clear this was the first of several strategic investments in professional services firms to ensure it had the coverage that it needed.

While the partnership between KPMG and Cisco is concentrated in North America, the ramifications to competitors and customers are expected to be realized in Asia/Pacific as well. KPMG aims to add value to Cisco's clients, and offer business consultancy, rather than only undertaking network or solution deployment. The companies combine KPMG's consulting and solution development expertise with Cisco's leadership in enterprise infrastructure solutions. KPMG and Cisco will jointly develop innovative, repeatable end-to-end solutions that will focus on e-commerce and sales force automation solutions.

NEC and Cisco

Both companies have launched a partnership for converged eBusiness communications. The program has elevated NEC to a Cisco Gold Partner for systems and paves the way for Cisco to deploy its AVVID architecture alongside NEC's PABXs. This partnership has been launched in North America and Australia and is expected to be extended throughout Asia/Pacific over the next few years. The benefits to the vendors' customers are an easy and supportable migration of their NEC PABX systems to a converged voice and data platform.

Hewlett-Packard, EDS, and Cisco

The ongoing global alliance between Cisco and HP is focused on both enterprise and service provider markets, and uses Cisco's networking products together with HP's business critical enterprise solutions and telecommunications management expertise. The two companies are working together to deliver end-to-end network-enabled solutions that will allow customers to optimize and reduce the complexity of its network.

The global partnership is engineering-driven and intends to align computing and networking, data and voice, and UNIX and Windows NT to harness the Internet. Some of the alliance initiatives include IP usage management, Internet commerce, Web QoS, high availability, security, and network management.

All three companies have developed and launched an Interactive Commerce Alliance aimed at promoting e-business in Asia/Pacific, following a similar alliance in the US last year. Together, the three companies offer a range of solutions in the areas of e-procurement, security services, and I-billing. EDS provides the systems integration, project management and process management, whereas Cisco and HP provide the systems and solutions.

In summarizing the Cisco strategy, it's interesting to profile their strengths and weaknesses relating to their e-business strategy. Cisco, already a recognized leader in the field of e-business, is further strengthening the value they can provide to customers by increasing the breadth of their participation with companies that were once competitors and now are complementary in terms of their common goal of increasing value for customers. Table 8.3 provides a comparison of the strengths and weaknesses of Cisco's e-business strategy.

Table 8.3   **Comparing the strengths and weaknesses of Cisco's e-business strategies**

Strengths	Weaknesses
Cross-industry partnerships give Cisco a wide range of customers to sell in Cisco products.	Too many cross-industry partnerships can lead to issues of overlap and loyalty problems.
Partnering enables Cisco to concentrate on their core business, which is making network equipment.	Cisco partners will always be at risk of being taken over by Cisco competitors and this can leave them with gaps in their offerings.
Cisco's partners enable it to be more agile and nimble, and it can be faster to market with solutions than building everything internally.	As the competencies are not in-house, this gives Cisco less power over the technologies, solutions or services, and it could become dependent on its partners.
The partnering model essentially provides Cisco with more capabilities and more opportunities to satisfy its customers.	The partnerships will always be dependent on relationships and company cultures and could become high maintenance in terms of time and effort.
With the Cisco offerings of e-business advice, it is building important mindshare in the e-business market.	Cisco makes the assumption that people already understand or are doing e-business and this might not be the case.
Cisco providing an Internet vision is a really important part of the company being recognized as a thought leader, and worth listening to for e-business solutions.	The Internet vision that Cisco provides might be seen as too visionary and not grounded in reality, which could be off-putting for some potential customers.

Acquisition Strategies of Leading ASPs and e-Business Providers

The reliance on partnerships is already making the difference between the success or failure of ASPs. Extending the reach of a company, building a strong infrastructure, and even completing the transaction processing for customers needing to complete e-commerce transactions all are reasons why partnerships are happening daily in the e-business arena.

When an ASP decides that the potential partnership is so central to their business, an acquisition results. Several companies are well known for their capability to make strong decisions about who they acquire and when. Presented in the following series of profiles are companies who have built a successful track record when it comes to acquisitions.

BroadVision

In examining how BroadVision makes decisions on which companies to acquire, their recent purchase of Interleaf illustrates how they are actively making decisions to create a foundation for the next stage of growth in the company. Interleaf is an e-content company, a separate Interleaf business unit dedicated to the development, marketing, and sale of XML-based content management tools. These tools enable the creation, publication, management and re-use of dynamic, intelligent content for Web and wireless applications. The e-content company comprises nearly 70% of Interleaf's approximately 400 employees and has been the most significant area of Interleaf growth and investment over the past two years.

Subject to conditions, under the terms of the agreement each outstanding share of Interleaf common stock will be exchanged for .3465 of a share of BroadVision common stock and will be accounted for as a purchase transaction. In addition, BroadVision will assume all outstanding options and warrants to purchase Interleaf common stock. Based on basic shares outstanding as of January 25, 2000 and both companies' closing price as of that date, the transaction represents approximately a 40% premium over Interleaf's current value. On a fully diluted basis, BroadVision would issue approximately 5.6 million shares of its common stock, having a value of approximately $877 million based on BroadVision's closing stock price on January 25, 2000.

The transaction is intended to be tax-free to the Interleaf shareholders. The transaction, which has been unanimously approved by both the Interleaf and BroadVision boards of directors, is subject to approval by Interleaf's stockholders. The transaction is subject to certain other customary closing conditions, including Hart-Scott-Rodino antitrust clearance and other regulatory approvals. The companies expect to close the transaction by May 31, 2000.

"Through the acquisition of Interleaf, BroadVision will be able to quickly expand our leadership in delivering personalized e-business applications across multitouch points such as Web and wireless," said Dr. Pehong Chen, President, CEO, and Chairman of the Board for BroadVision. "With our combined customer base of more than 2,500 blue-chip and dot-com companies, both firms have the proven ability to meet e-business demands for a fast time-to-market, easier integration with content sources and back-end systems, and high performance and scalability. We look forward to leveraging the strengths of both companies to provide increased benefits for customers and shareholders."

"At Interleaf, we have spent the past three years repositioning the company around new XML and wireless technology," said Jaime Ellerston, President, CEO, and Chairman of the Board for Interleaf. "This past year we have successfully penetrated the e-business marketplace by delivering state-of-the-art XML-based e-content management tools. We believe strongly that these tools and our initiative into the wireless market make us a unique fit with BroadVision's strength in Web applications and with their strategic objectives. Both companies see XML content proving itself to be of particular importance for the fast growing business-to-business e-commerce market. Therefore, the combination of our e-content management tools integrated with BroadVision's e-business applications make a powerful end-to-end solution for the B2B market while further extending these applications to the emerging wireless market."

Benefits of Acquisition for Customers

The combination of the suite of BroadVision One-To-One personalized e-business applications and Interleaf's XML-based e-content management tools will create one of the most comprehensive, end-to-end offerings for companies needing to manage content-rich and transactional e-businesses for delivery over the Web and wireless devices. Gartner Group estimates that by 2003, 80% of application-to-application traffic passing over public networks will be in XML (Gartner Group, October, 1999).

Specific benefits of the combined offering will include those mentioned in the following sections.

Less Time and Lower Cost for e-Content Management

The integrated offering combines Interleaf's XML-based e-content management tools and BroadVision's real-time instant publishing tools to shorten time to production for content. This lowers the total cost of ownership for companies by enabling publishers to more easily create, publish, manage, and re-purpose transactional content. Additionally, the integrated offering is differentiated by its support for the publication of XML-based documents from Microsoft Office applications, greatly expanding general business users' ability to publish Web and wireless content.

Automating B2B e-Commerce through Intelligent Content

The integrated offering will enable the automation of B2B e-commerce by enabling companies to improve their operations via the use of intelligent content. Intelligent content is personalized, re-usable and dynamically assembled in real time to increase collaboration and communication among commerce partners. Unlike static content, intelligent content automates interactions and transactions among participants, creating a highly productive information value chain.

Expanded e-Business Reach

The integration of Interleaf's X-WAP (Wireless Application Protocol) and XSL (eXtensible Style Sheet Language, which enables content to be separated from data so that content can be shared across any number of XML documents) technology will enable BroadVision customers to deploy e-business applications that enable access to dynamic content from mobile and other wireless devices, such as digital cellular telephones, pagers, personal digital assistants and e-books. End users will be able to access in real time personalized product information, inventory, price, and catalog data and to execute orders from Web sites and wireless devices via BroadVision's capability to deliver e-business anywhere, anytime. The Yankee Group has estimated that wireless subscribers accessing the Internet will grow from 669 million in 1999 to 1.26 billion by 2005 (The Yankee Group, November, 1999). Therefore, BroadVision believes the integration of Interleaf's X-WAP technology will be a significant benefit for companies implementing e-business applications capable of providing dynamic, personalized content to the growing number of users of wireless devices.

The BroadVision and Interleaf Fit

The two companies share a vision for enabling e-business through a common commitment to an XML backbone. Interleaf, a thought and industry leader for XML-based e-content management, brings people, tools, and technologies that are completely complementary to BroadVision's applications. For example, Interleaf's employees represent the world's largest XML talent pool. And Interleaf's technology leadership in XML and WAP are technologies that supplement those of BroadVision. Additionally, Interleaf has a worldwide base of more than 2,000 customers who are potential users of BroadVision's e-business applications.

Key Technologies

BroadVision will fully integrate Interleaf's e-content management tools based on XML into BroadVision's full suite of e-business applications. Interleaf's key technologies include:

- **BladeRunner**—A scalable, comprehensive XML-based content management tool that enables companies to create, manage, and publish structured e-business content that is targeted, timely, personalized, intelligent and medium-aware. With XML as its technology backbone and Microsoft Office integration used for content creation, companies using BladeRunner are able to apply intelligence, structure, and style to content for e-business applications.

- **X-WAP Technology**—Interleaf's X-WAP wireless application technology transforms XML into HTML, WML, PDF, ASCII, and raw text into intelligent business content for delivery to wireless devices.

- **QuickSilver**—A full-featured high-end authoring and publishing product with an extension to enable the generation of XML-based content, QuickSilver enables users to manage XML- and non-XML-based content in one integrated system.

Cisco

Cisco Systems, Inc. is the worldwide leader in networking for the Internet. Cisco hardware, software, and service offerings are used to create Internet solutions so that individuals, companies, and countries have seamless access to information—regardless of differences in time and place. Cisco solutions provide competitive advantage to our customers through more efficient and timely exchange of information, which in turn leads to cost savings, process efficiencies, and closer relationships with their customers, prospects, business partners, suppliers, and employees. These solutions form the networking foundation for companies, universities, utilities, and government agencies worldwide.

The company was founded in 1984 by a small group of computer scientists from Stanford University seeking an easier way to connect different types of computer systems. Cisco Systems shipped its first product in 1986. Since then, Cisco has grown into a multinational corporation with more than 20,000 employees in more than 200 offices in 55 countries.

In 1999 Cisco agreed to invest $1.5 billion for a 20% stake in KPMG's consulting business, and it teamed with Motorola to acquire the fixed wireless assets of Bosch Telecom, forming joint venture SpectraPoint Wireless to provide high-speed networking services to businesses. However, most of Cisco's acquisition directly fortified its position as the king of networking gear. In its largest acquisition to date, Cisco bought Cerent (fiber-optic network equipment) for $7 billion. The company also snapped up several smaller networking companies, including Sentient Networks (ATM products) and GeoTel Communications (call-routing software). Cisco has agreed to buy Aironet Wireless Communications (wireless LAN products) for about $800 million. Also in 1999 Cisco and Qwest Communications agreed to collaborate on what will be the biggest Internet-based network in the US.

In early 2000 Cisco teamed up with GTE, Whirlpool, and Sun Microsystems to develop the *home gateway*, an answering machine-sized device that will facilitate high-speed networking of multiple PCs, as well as upcoming *smart appliances*, over a home's existing phone lines. The company also bought Perilli's fiber-optic telephone equipment operations for more than $2 billion.

Cisco has been acquiring networking companies at a rate of one every month or two, and Chambers expects this pace to continue for several more years.

Here are some of these past year's acquisitions:

- Internet: TGV Software, Network Translation, Internet Junction
- Workgroup/LAN: Grand Junction, Nashoba Networks, Granite Systems
- Remote Access: Combinet
- WAN: StrataCom

Cisco is quite good at acquisitions. They know how to select companies with complementary technologies and a shared vision and culture, and companies that give them a significant time-to-market advantage over internal development. They also know when to buy and how to integrate the operations and products smoothly.

This acquisition strategy has helped Cisco build a complete enterprise solution. A few years ago they didn't have the resources to develop everything in-house. The acquisitions give them a running start in the small but explosive growth markets; for example, the purchases have allowed them to go from no presence in ATM and frame relay to a strong presence very quickly. It would probably be more accurate to say they've employed an intelligent mix of acquisitions, internal product development, and strategic alliances; although the acquisitions receive most of the attention, about two-thirds of the development is done internally.

Acquisitions are never completely risk-free. The biggest challenges are usually product line integration, operations integration, and the risks inherent in entering new markets.

By and large, the company has had a lot of success with acquisitions. Granted, a few didn't work out as planned. For example, the value of the Lightstream acquisition was greatly reduced by the subsequent StrataCom purchase, due to technology overlap. But such failures are a rarity for Cisco.

StrataCom, by far the largest acquisition they've ever undertaken, seems to be going smoothly so far, but they're not out of the woods yet.

Another concern with an acquisition strategy is the dilutive effect it can have on earnings per share. For example, the total number of Cisco shares outstanding increased by 100 million (almost 20%) from 1992 to 1996, and the StrataCom purchase was paid for with 80 million shares. Although this is not necessarily a negative, it is something to monitor, since it means earnings per share won't grow as quickly as earnings.

CommerceOne

In assessing the direction of CommerceOne, the following key trends can be seen:

- More focus on strengthening partnerships with infrastructure participants including Cisco and Microsoft. CommerceOne is also a charter member of the XML/BizTalk Steering Committee.

- Acquisition strategies showing focus on content acquisition tools and commerce-based with the purchase of Mergent Systems purchased this month (January). The flagship product of this company is the iMerge content development tool. On December 13, CommerceOne announced the availability of CommerceOne Auction Services, based on the technology obtained from the acquisition of CommerceBid.com.

- Global strategy is becoming increasingly fulfilled with joint venture Banacci of Mexico City for coverage of Latin America. In addition CommerceOne has a joint venture with eMediate in South Africa for coverage of state and local government in that region.

- GM's stake in CommerceOne, now worth approximately $3 billion given recent stock price growth, is in turn leading to new opportunities for e-procurement sales into the automotive sector.

- Segmentation focus is now becoming apparent in the marketing and sales strategies of CommerceOne, with the forming a new division to focus on providing federal, state and municipal governments and universities.

- Increasing focus on vertical industries starting with healthcare. On December 14, CommerceOne announced a partnership with empactHealth.com to offer hospitals a comprehensive electronic marketplace to conduct business more effectively and at less cost.

- Supply Chain integration success stories are continuing to develop, including the endorsement of GUESS? clothing for the CommerceOne MarketSite application.

Interliant

The evolutionary path of Sage Networks into Interliant (NASDAQ: INIT) is an aggressive one. Sage Networks began an acquisition strategy in 1997, and has since added 18 companies. In acquiring these companies, Interliant Corp. spent $85.2 million during 1998 and 1999. Interliant Texas was one of the acquisitions, and Sage Networks took the name Interliant for the entire corporation. March 10, 1999 the transaction for the purchase of Interliant by Sage Networks was complete, and Sage subsequently changed its name. Unprofitable both for 1998 and to this point in 1999, Interliant continues to adhere to an acquisitions strategy and a reliance on software vendors for their outsourced products. The revenue mix of this competitor shows a reliance on applications outsourcing as a revenue, yet has many challenges ahead due to the strategic direction they have taken with their distribution, pricing, and product strategies. Major shareholders include SoftBank Technology Ventures with 3.3 million shares or 9.6% of total shares outstanding. Table 8.4 provides a list of 18 acquisitions completed by Sage Networks (now Interliant). These statistics are taken from the various documents that Interliant has filed with the Securities and Exchange Commission, in addition to their annual report.

Sage Networks acquisition strategy has yielded 47,000 customers representing more than 79,000 Web sites. The majority of these sites are not enabled with electronic commerce. The Interliant Texas acquisition brought Sage Networks thousands of Notes-enabled applications. Today Interliant claims 1,300 customers in the e-commerce and e-business market segments. The company has 516 employees and 19 full-time contractors.

Distribution of revenue for Interliant is as follows for 1998:

  28.0% from Web hosting offerings

  51.3% from application hosting product offerings

  14% from consulting services

  6.7% from customization and training services

Distribution of revenue for Interliant is as follows for Q1/99:

  31.4% from Web hosting offerings

  44.8% from application hosting product offerings

  16.0% from consulting services

  7.8% from customization and training services

Interliant relies on three data centers, located in Houston, Atlanta, and Vienna, Virginia. Each center is capable of handling co-located servers. Houston is the largest and most sophisticated, with Vienna being a start-up data center online since late summer of 1999. A total of $2 million was invested in the Houston facility. Interliant expects to invest $1.3 million in the Atlanta facility.

In interviews, the CEO for Interliant has mentioned his top priorities for the company:

1. Build the Interliant brand.

2. Continue aggressively pursuing an acquisition strategy.

3. Develop multiple sales channels.

Table 8.4   How Interliant's acquisitions strategies show growth plans toward regional strengths in chosen markets

Date Acquired	Company Name	Primary Focus
February 13, 1998	Omnetrix, Inc.,	Web hosting
April 7, 1998	Clever Computers	Web hosting
April 30, 1998	Server & Network connectivity assets from Knowledgelink Interactive	Web hosting

Table 8.4   Continued

Date Acquired	Company Name	Primary Focus
May 1, 1998	Tri-Star Web Computer	Web hosting
June 10, 1998	HostAmerica, a division of HomeCom Communications	Web hosting
June 29, 1998	All Information Systems	Web hosting
July 1, 1998	DevCOM	Web hosting
July 30, 1998	BestWare, Inc.,	Web hosting
August 31, 1998	B.N. Technologies	Web hosting
September 16, 1998	GEN International (Global Entrepreneur Network)	Web hosting
December 17, 1998	Dialtone, Inc.,	Web hosting
February 4, 1999	DigiWeb	Web hosting
February 4, 1999	Telephonetics International	Multimedia
February 17, 1999	Net Daemons Associates	Consulting
March 10, 1999	Interliant Texas	Application hosting
May 4, 1999	Advanced Web Creations	Web hosting
August 31, 1999	Daily-e Corporation	Application hosting Piloting
October 7, 1999	Joint development with SoftBank and Vivendi via AtVisio	Application hosting in Europe

Benefits to Your e-Business Strategy

Clearly the acquisitions of Cisco are going to pay dividends well into the future with an enhanced infrastructure that is operating system independent. The continued media and analyst coverage of the ASP model is also driving acquisitions at a quick pace, despite fluctuations in capital markets. With all the change that is occurring nearly on a weekly basis, the implications for your selection of an ASP based on their partnership levels can be perplexing. Here are several factors to keep in mind when working with a service provider who is in the midst of being acquired or acquiring companies.

Find Out the Nature of the Transactions by Looking into S1s and Annual Reports

This sounds almost too focused on the health of the company you are looking at to see how they are acquiring companies, but an S1 can tell you a lot about the company you are going to partner with.

Determine Whether the Acquisitions They Are Making Are Consistent with Your Roadmap of Needs

This is fundamental to the direction of your e-business strategy, so make sure the acquisitions are going to provide the necessary applications that will give you flexibility in fulfilling your e-business objectives.

Summary

Alliances and acquisitions are driving innovation into the ASP marketplace. Companies including Cisco and Interliant are aggressively acquiring companies to fulfill a vision each company has for their companies. For Cisco, the vision of building a cohesive infrastructure is now in full progress, and for Interliant, the building of a full-service ASP is also in full development. Acquisitions initially look to be events that consolidate an industry, yet in the end they are the beginning of additional value being added into the total service offerings of ASPs.

III

Architecting and Perfecting e-Business Strategies

9

Planning for Security with Your ASP

U NLIKE PHYSICAL SECURITY SYSTEMS, which have motion detectors, card readers, vibration sensors, and closed-circuit televisions, security on the Internet is not an exact science, bounded by the laws of physics. It's much more of an evolving challenge/resolution type of scenario, where the challenges are posed and the various organizations involved with the Internet need to resolve them. Knowing when a security breach has happened is much harder to track in an online world than in a physical one. Service providers vary significantly in terms of their ability to deal with denial of service attacks for example, and other threats of electronic vandalism and theft.

In planning your e-business strategy, security is an area in which there needs to be the highest level of performance possible from the ASPs you choose to deal with. The fact that many ASPs regularly have security companies test their hosting centers with simulated attacks shows a commitment to ensuring customers' data stays secure. ASPs that are security-conscious take the approach that it's best to continually test firewalls, authentication, and the identity of servers located behind firewalls within the network operations centers.

This chapter provides insights and specific questions you can use to qualify ASPs from the standpoint of how savvy they are about security. If you are completing an e-marketing site in which your brochures and marketing materials are online, the steps required minimizing hacking your site or stealing your URL are what is most needed. Alternatively, if you're going to have data hosted by the ASPs you choose to work with, the fullest extent of the questions and survey provided at the end of this chapter would make a good screening tool for the ASPs you are considering working with regarding your e-business strategy. Finally, the issue is not one of being paranoid; it's about being focused on what really matters for your organization and the information assets it has. Truly, in the world of security the best defense is an informed and smart offensive strategy to protect your data.

Case Study: How CyberSource Minimizes Online Fraud for GUESS?

GUESS? is one of today's most recognized and influential fashion brand names. After almost 20 years in the traditional retail channel, GUESS? opened an online store in March 1999. This was a big step for the fashion leader, but it was time to bring its GUESS? brand jeans, apparel, and fashion accessories to customers via the Internet.

A Hot Brand Attracts Cyber Thieves

The launch of the GUESS? online store was a big success. Unfortunately, the GUESS? online store also caught the attention of cyber thieves. Shortly after opening, GUESS? found that online fraud was becoming an issue. "Our online business was doing great, but the growing number of fraudulent orders were becoming a problem. Fraud was starting to cut into our bottom line," explained Jennifer Makkar, e-commerce manager at guess.com. "With the 1999 holiday season promising to be even bigger than last year, we could not afford to be in a vulnerable position," continued Makkar in a recent customer testimonial published by CyberSource on GUESS?

GUESS? Turns to CyberSource

CyberSource had a solution to the fraud issues that GUESS? needed to address. CyberSource Internet Fraud Screen enhanced by Visa offered a secure infrastructure to make online transactions safe and easy for GUESS? and its customers. CyerSource and GUESS? announced their working together and the quotes provided here in a success story originally posted to the CyberSource Web site in the first four months of 2000.

GUESS? heard that CyberSource has the Internet's most effective weapon against online credit card fraud and decided to implement its services. CyberSource Internet Fraud Screen enhanced by Visa has a proven record of being able to reduce online credit card fraud to less than 1%.

As soon as GUESS? implemented CyberSource Internet Fraud Screen enhanced by Visa, it saw results. "From the moment it was up and running, we saw our instances of fraud drop," said Makkar. "We have continued to see the number of fraudulent orders decrease, even after the initial drop. With CyberSource Internet Fraud Screen enhanced by Visa, we do not have to divert valuable personnel to manually chase down fraudulent transactions," Makkar continued.

CyberSource's Fraud Screen

CyberSource Internet Fraud Screen enhanced by Visa screens e-commerce transactions and measures the level of risk associated with each order, returning a related risk score back to the merchant in real time. This automated risk assessment service calculates the risk associated with an order, based on unique Internet order variables and other transaction characteristics, and returns a *risk score* to the merchant. A risk score is a metric that actually communicates the level of authentication associated with the party making a purchase. This metric communicates back to other systems what the relative level of fraud potential is. Taking an index of over 30 different factors, this metric is produced and is used for flagging potentially fraudulent transactions. The system leverages Visa's fraud modeling expertise and CyberSource's Internet fraud reduction experience and, historical transaction database. The score gives merchants added insight into the persons they are selling to online.

Internet Fraud Screen enhanced by Visa merchants maintain full control over their risk tolerance and final acceptance or rejection of the order.

Payment Processing Compatibility Essential

To provide customers with a rapid and secure checkout and payment experience, GUESS? also implemented CyberSource Credit Card Services. Designed to meet the needs of high-volume online stores, CyberSource Credit Card Services deliver 99.98% payment processing uptime and a quick, three-second response—even during peak sales periods.

GUESS? was anxious to get up and running with the CyberSource services and was pleased with how quick and easy the implementation process was. "It was a very simple procedure," explained Makkar. "We were able to implement the services on our own, without anyone from CyberSource coming on site. CyberSource was very easy to work with during implementation and continues to be very responsive to our needs."

International in Scope

CyberSource services are designed to support international sales. This is important to GUESS?, which plans to open its online store to international markets. "CyberSource is prepared for international e-commerce," said Makkar. "This is a big benefit for GUESS?. We are preparing to expand our online operations to international markets, and with CyberSource we do not have to rethink our back-end systems," continued Makkar.

All CyberSource Credit Card Services enable secure, reliable, multicurrency payment processing in local currencies worldwide. CyberSource Credit Card Services support real-time international trade in more than 170 currencies worldwide. CyberSource also provides robust tax calculation services to support the thousands of ever-changing taxing jurisdictions that exist worldwide. With CyberSource Tax Calculation, merchants are able to calculate Value Added Tax (VAT) in real-time to support sales in more than 18 countries.

Additionally, CyberSource Policy Compliance Services help online merchants, which do business outside of the United States, comply with corporate, partner, and government policies for sales. CyberSource uses a sophisticated combination of geolocation technology and artificial intelligence to validate the information provided by the purchaser and screen for compliance. With Policy Compliance, merchants can limit product or service distribution to specific territories, thereby maintaining marketing policies or distribution agreements. Also, with Export Control, merchants can ensure that they are in compliance with U.S. government export regulations by monitoring order acceptance against a changing list of denied countries or persons.

"GUESS? has a highly visible brand name and a reputation for customer satisfaction to protect. Our use of CyberSource services ensures that our customers are able to check out quickly and securely, as well as helps GUESS? prevent fraudulent transactions that take away from our profits," said Makkar. "Additionally, CyberSource has helped GUESS? gear up for end-of-year online sales and made fraud less of an issue for us. Its suite of high-performance payment processing and comprehensive fraud screening services has already helped GUESS? protect its profits and will be a real asset, particularly during the holiday season," concluded Makkar.

Your Data in Your Building Versus in a Network Operations Center

Whether your site is aimed at primarily selling products over your Web site, or if the e-business plans you have in mind also include e-operations applications, the need for security increases with the potential for increased revenues and reduced costs. As the breadth of your e-business plans increase, so does the need for a robust security strategy in the context of an e-business approach your organization is taking.

The levels of security vary by the types of activities you are trying to accomplish. Table 9.1 shows a comparison among various applications by the level of security needed.

Table 9.1 **Comparing typical applications by security approaches shows the pervasive role of firewalls**

Applications	Access Control	Firewall	Software Import Controls	Encryption	Incident Handling
Remote Access	X	X		X	
Electronic Mail			X	X	
Info Publishing	X	X			
Research	X	X	X		
Electronic Commerce	X	X	X	X	X

The fundamental question in working with an ASP is whether your organization has the security expertise to administer access controls, firewalls, software import controls, encryption, and the ability to troubleshoot incidents. Clearly if your organization also has remote access, there is a security issue from dial-in access being compromised. With many of the certification programs today focusing on security, system administrators in your organization might already be learning about firewalls and how to ensure encryption throughout your own complex of servers. IT organizations are increasingly either hiring security experts or getting their existing staff up to speed on how to work with firewalls and complete incident handling. The skills for keeping your own data safe in your own organization are increasingly focused on how to repel hacker attacks. International Data Corporation recently completed a survey of 1,000 technology companies that shows that the majority of companies spend the majority of their time working to resolve or repel viruses on both workstations and servers. This graphic shows the relative level of time a given company spends on troubleshooting security-related events. Figure 9.1 shows the distribution of how time is used by the representative companies in the study in completing security tasks.

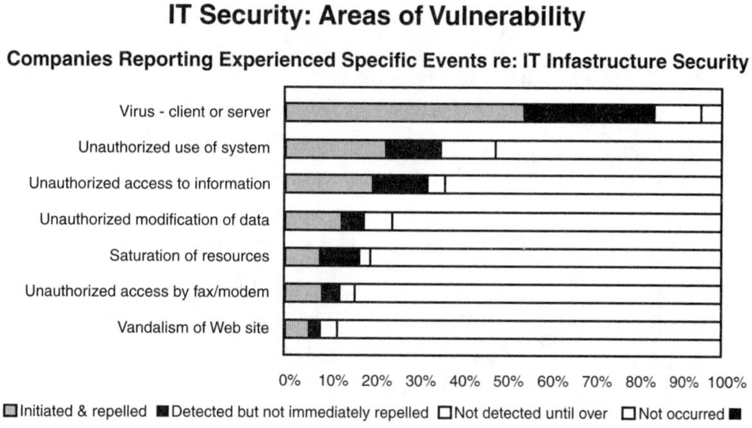

IT Security: Areas of Vulnerability

Companies Reporting Experienced Specific Events re: IT Infastructure Security

Figure 9.1 IT areas of vulnerability as defined from a recent study from International Data Corporation show the breadth of skills needed for protecting an enterprise-wide computing system.

The fact that the majority of the security issues center on viruses typically sent through email shows the need for strong administration of the messaging systems in and outside of organizations. That's one of the reasons, in addition to several other excellent security issues, that many ASPs have their hosting centers located in secured buildings that are completely separate from the daily operations of their businesses. Zland.com, for example, uses the hosting services from Exodus Communications, one of the leaders in offering security services for their hosted clients. Exodus has a series of levels of security services for ASPs. These are backed up with technologically advanced security engineering from the Exodus subsidiary Arca Systems. Arca has many interesting white papers on their Web site on the subjects of Internet security overall and the application of security engineering specifically. You can find Exodus Communications at www.exodus.com. There is a comprehensive series of documents on the Exodus site that describes their offerings in depth, with a summarized set of the data provided here.

Clearly the need for hosting providers to replicate the most advanced functionality a Fortune 1,000 company can produce is essential if the hosting company is going to expand its business. Exodus Communications has created a series of packages for companies, depending on their needs for security, taking the approach of replicating the functionality found in organizations, and then creating various levels of security that can be applied by both Fortune 1,000 companies and application service providers, many of which host their applications at remote, secure locations away from ongoing operations.

An example of each level of security pack offered by Exodus Communications is briefly listed here:

Security Service Pack Basic—Site Assessment

Provides an independent, ongoing assessment of the site security posture.

Package includes

- Semiannual Security Architecture Reviews to provide ongoing assessment of the customer's overall site protection strategy.
- Quarterly Internal and External Vulnerability Scans to detect potential site weaknesses from inside and outside the site's firewall. Exodus Security Engineers use industry-leading tools such as CyberCop Scanner from Network Associates, Inc. and proprietary software to assess site risks.
- Ongoing Alert Reports to provide timely information on known security vulnerabilities.
- Eight hours of Incident Response Assistance per year to reduce the impact and duration of a security attack

Security Service Pack Enhanced—Site Lockdown

Focuses on hardening a site and its perimeter, and establishing a foundation for responding to security incidents.

Package includes

- All features of the Security Service Pack Basic-Site Assessment.
- Security Account Manager (SAM) to offer a central point of contact for ongoing management of security requirements.
- Server Hardening to give hands-on assistance with configuring hosts for maximum protection against hackers.
- Incident Response Preparation to permit fast and easy identification of files that have experienced unauthorized modification.
- Incident Response Training to educate customers on how to respond to an attack.
- 16 hours of Incident Response Assistance per year to reduce the impact and duration of a security attack.

Security Service Pack Pro—Site Shield

Offers site assessment, hardening, and customized management for the highest level of security assurances.

Package includes

- All features of the Security Service Pack Enhanced—Site Lockdown.
- Customized Intrusion Detection System Configuration to optimize the effectiveness of these systems.
- Monthly Firewall and IDS reviews to provide on-going analysis and customization of these systems.
- 40 hours of Incident Response Assistance per year to reduce the impact and duration of a security attack.

The potential cost savings often dictate the trade-off of keeping an application in-house relative to contracting with an ASP first, and security is also a top priority, or at least a close second. The entire Application Service Provider industry realizes the need for accurately setting security expectations, and as a consequence the rapid evolution of hosting companies is taking place today. Figure 9.2 shows an example of the hosting center within Exodus Communications. You can also visit an interactive map of this center at `http://www.exodus.net/idcs/idc_diagram.html`. If you are not familiar with hosting centers, this is worth a few minutes to see how various aspects of security are dealt with in a data center.

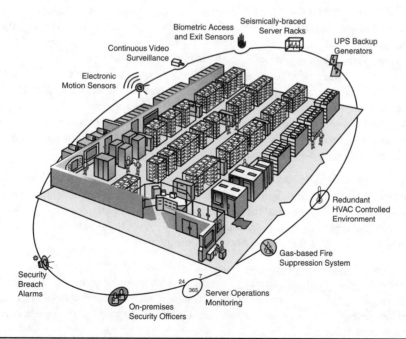

Figure 9.2 What a state-of-the-art-hosting center looks like. This is the Exodus Communications Internet Data Center.

Security Technologies to Keep Current On

With the FBI stating recently that Internet security is one of the top priorities, and in England with legislation pending to have government generated usernames and passwords so that email that compromises both their nation's security and industries is not sent outside the country, Internet security is now debated in Parliament regularly. One of the foremost law professors at Pepperdine University is also now the architect of a course purely on e-law, the law of e-business. There are emerging technologies just becoming available that any organization considering an e-business strategy needs to keep in mind.

Comparing Latest Developments by Industry Leaders

IBM Corporation announced in 1999 its second version of SecureWay FirstSecure technology, which is focused on providing architecture for secure e-business. This solution emphasizes strong authorization and authentication for enabling secure transactions with customers, partners, and suppliers. It also addresses strong firewall filtering and antivirus protection, two of the best-established security technologies in use today. Because manageability can be a major issue in complex e-business environments, the SecureWay technology builds on a Policy Director that eases deployment of applications that operate within defined policy.

Similarly, Hewlett-Packard has invested heavily in bringing together a variety of security technologies under the Praesidium label. The VirtualVault is a commercial version of its military-grade secure UNIX system, which helps protect Web servers through greater protection than standard perimeter security offers. The latest version of Praesidium VirtualVault is Version 4.0, which HP has repriced to make it more affordable for a wider range of industry segments with the hope of seeing its adoption outside the financial services industry. With its latest release of the VirtualVault, HP emphasizes support of multiple platforms and Web-based applications from multiple vendors. HP has added technology to make it easier to use its product to protect servers and applications that are running on servers from IBM, Compaq, and Sun as well as those running on HP servers.

Sun's security technology has been centered on network screening and secure communications via encryption. Sun Microsystems now has a close relationship with Network Associates, a company focused on security technologies. SunScreen SecureNet interoperates with Network Associates' Event Orchestrator to provide better security manageability and control on Sun networks.

The Microsoft approach to security reflects its desktop and workgroup server origins. Microsoft Windows NT security begins with a totally open, unprotected model of computing. Security hinges on electing to use the security features within the basic server operating system. For more control and security, users add specialized security products from those offered by the huge array of Microsoft partners. Each version of the NT Server operating system and its Service Pack have added more usability features to facilitate better security management and audit. The Microsoft Internet Information Server (IIS) is an example of a set of security technologies that are better integrated with a base server environment. IIS 4.0 extends Windows NT Server file security to protect data via file and Web permissions and to control access at basic or enhanced security levels.

There are hundreds of companies offering security products; the best-known names certainly include Axent Technologies, Network Associates, and RSA Security. Because all three companies have grown through acquisition, each offers a wide range of products that address perimeter protection, virus protection, access control, and data security. More importantly, all three companies have done some degree of integration across their diverse product sets to ease manageability of large installations. Selecting a suite of products rather than single offerings generally reduces the amount of customization and integration work that must be done in house.

Network Associates grew, both in size and in scope of the products it offers, through heavy acquisition in the late 1990s. It has spent the past months integrating these tools into easier-to-manage suites. The Net Tools Secure suite of tools combines perimeter protection, antivirus technologies, encryption, and intrusion detection. Communications between the component products occur through a secure, authenticated, standards-based central event manager, Event Orchestrator. This method, which uses hubs and spokes, facilitates central security policy and event management.

Axent Technologies has also grown through acquisition and acquired one of the major firewall vendors, Raptor Systems. The Axent Enterprise Security Manager, like the product suite from Network Associates, brings together a variety of technologies with centralized and simplified management. Enterprise Security Manager agents can reside on each system for managing, controlling, and reporting on the security status of the system. The solution also provides an overall manager that controls groups of agents and collects and stores the security audit data. Enterprise Security Manager supports combinations of managers and agents from a variety of systems. For example, a manager running on an HP-UX system can control agents on NetWare, Windows NT, Solaris, and OpenVMS systems.

RSA Security brings together two established names in security: Security Dynamics and RSA Data Security. Recognizing digital certificates as an important component of many Web-based applications, the company offers RSA Keon PKI as a solution that works with digital certificates from a variety of suppliers.

Axent Technologies, Network Associates, and RSA security top the list of security vendors, but there are a variety of other important players in the field, including Internet Security Systems (ISS), Entrust Technologies, CheckPoint Software, Cisco Systems, and Lucent.

Developing an e-Business Security Strategy on Your Own—Defining What's Needed

When selecting to pursue an e-business security strategy on your own or to outsource it, the following points, during a series of security conferences, are worth checking into.

Enterprises are rushing to keep pace with the e-business imperative, integrating suppliers and customers over public network infrastructures. Protecting valuable corporate assets while opening up these e-business opportunities raises serious security concerns in companies expecting to manage a substantial portion of their business over intranets and extranets. Organizations are concerned about the direct economic risks of compromised security. They also fear a severe loss of business through compromised Web presence. The stakes are high.

This security model for e-business addresses the conflicting goals of providing open access and the continued need for strict asset protection. The starting point is a secure infrastructure that permits low-level anonymous Web access with high-level transactional security. The greater the level of authentication and authorization control desired, the more sophisticated an e-business security architecture must be. IDC recommends identifying these requirements early and building the security framework before moving applications to the Internet.

The essential steps to building security architecture are constructed on up-front planning and ongoing diligence:

1. **Staffing up to do the job right**—Security does not come free. Staffing is as essential as the security products themselves.

2. **Establishing strong physical security**—IT security technology must be backed by strong physical protection of assets. All the IT security in the world is wasted if the fundamentals of protecting assets from physical disasters and theft are forgotten. Essential steps include
   - Inventory and actively manage all physical assets.
   - Protect all servers from unwanted access, theft, or mischief.
   - Invest in redundant systems, where appropriate.
   - Install locks, alarms, fire protection equipment, and the like, wherever appropriate.
   - Revisit physical security needs periodically, especially as business or geographical needs change.

3. **Data and user classification**—Understanding the essential assets of the enterprise and who should have access sets the groundwork for defining a policy that

can be put into practice. Before companies can effectively protect their systems and networks, they have to put a value on their intellectual property. Some enterprise resources, such as information that would go into an advertisement, might require only protection from unwanted manipulation, and other information, such as employee records and financial data, might require multiple levels of protection. A business that understands what is valuable has an edge in knowing where to deploy security technologies.

4. **Documenting a security policy**—Security crosses organizational boundaries to embrace not only the IT staff but also the executive, financial, human resources, and legal teams. A workable security policy usually requires involving all the organizations that must help enforce and maintain the policy.

5. **Piloting tools with that policy**—Because of the complexity of many IT security tools and the training that might be required first, pilots are often more practical than wide-scale implementations.

6. **Ongoing monitoring and feedback**—Security is as dynamic as the e-business environment it enables, and it demands monitoring and fine-tuning as conditions change.

Focusing on Security in Small and Mid-Size Companies

Many e-business strategists are keenly aware of the potential havoc that can be wreaked on their enterprises by hackers or virus attacks. The recent ILOVEYOU virus attack was a resounding warning to CIOs, security officers, and other enterprise executives. Executives clearly want to know what measures their enterprises are taking to secure Internets. Moreover, small and mid-size enterprises, which often do not have the security resources of large enterprises, are doing more business on the Internet, so their networks are increasingly exposed to security breaches. Gartner discusses the defensive actions required to protect such enterprise networks.

Any server connected to the Internet makes it and the rest of the network vulnerable to access from unauthorized and malicious users. An issue faced by small and mid-size enterprises is that many cannot afford, or do not attract, experienced security personnel. As a result, part-time employees or personnel with less than top-notch qualifications manage key enterprise servers (such as Web or email). Moreover, small and mid-size enterprises often use regional Internet service providers that provide unknown levels of security.

By 2003, 50% of small and mid-size enterprises that manage their own network security and use the Internet for more than email will experience a successful Internet attack (0.7 probability). More than 60% will not know they have been penetrated. Gartner identifies potential security holes and provides advice on how to plug them.

Start with a Security Checkup

Small and mid-size enterprises connected to the Internet should consider contracting with an outside security company to conduct an audit and risk-assessment of their networks. The effort should include an internal network security audit and an external penetration test. Consulting companies should have certified their security consultants.

External vulnerability assessments should be performed whenever an enterprise makes major changes to its Web site or firewall, at a minimum on an annual basis. Increasingly, security vendors will offer low-cost self-service vulnerability assessments, such as the offering by myCIO.com, which labels itself as Your Chief Internet Officer. Those types of tests can be cost-effective for small and mid-size enterprises but will require experienced support to address reported security problems.

First Line of Defense

Precautions must be taken to ensure a proper firewall configuration to offer the best possible protection for the enterprise. Firewalls are deployed to prevent unauthorized external users from accessing the enterprise network while permitting internal users to communicate with external users and systems. Firewalls also provide a central point for logging and auditing Internet traffic. Enterprises should focus on firewall appliances such as Watchguard Firebox, Nokia FW-1, and SonicWall that provide a base level of security without requiring detailed security knowledge.

By 2003, the dominant means of deploying network security technology will be through the use of appliance technology. Enterprises should request quotes for managed firewall and intrusion detection services from their own Internet service providers and companies such as ISS/Netrex, RIPTech, and GTE Internetworking. Those services will generally cost less than the equivalent salary of a half-time firewall administrator.

Other Safeguards to Consider

Other safeguards include

- **Boundary Services**—Virus scanning of incoming email is a critical security control. It can be done by using desktop antiviral protection, but it is often difficult to keep desktop signature virals current. Server-side antiviral protection (for example, from Trend Micro or FinJan) provides protection against incoming viruses and hostile ActiveX or Java applets. Enterprises should take immediate action to disallow relay and halt the entry of spam into their environments.

- **Web Security**—The major vulnerability in Web servers is attacks against Common Gateway Interface scripts and other active code. It is generally impossible for enterprises to assure that active server code does not contain security vulnerabilities. Enterprises that develop and host their own Web servers should deploy products such as Tripwire by Tripwire Security or Entercept by ClickNet to detect and prevent hacker attacks.

- **Consolidated Remote Access With Strong Authentication**—Enterprises that provide dial-in access to email and other corporate systems should eliminate desktop modems and use consolidated modem pools and remote access servers. Enterprises should require the use of hardware tokens such as RSA Security SecurID or Axent Defender to authenticate remote users.

- **Extra Protection**—The measures identified so far will satisfy the security needs of two-thirds or more of small and mid-size enterprises that use the Internet. Small and mid-size enterprises that must manage more highly sensitive environments must plan for additional precautions.

Additional Security Measures

Additional security measures include

- Virtual private networks for secure remote access over the Internet
- Intrusion detection to alarm the enterprise of internal and external attacks
- Firewall log analysis and email content filtering to detect misuse of the Internet connection by employees or business partners

Small and mid-size enterprises often have too low a usage level for managed services to be cost effective. That makes small and mid-size enterprises candidates for implementing remote access virtual private networks with the firewall acting as server.

Dealing with Emergency Security Situations

The ILOVEYOU virus, which spread so rapidly throughout the world, is a derivative of the Melissa virus and affects only Microsoft email systems. That incident highlighted why enterprises must have a plan for responding quickly to malicious code incidents. The plan should include a coordinated team, particularly the antivirus, firewall and backup people involved, and predefined procedures, including emergency powers such as blocking Internet email, and—as a last resort—shutting down email servers.

Presented here are standard security measures for enterprises dealing with emergency security situations:

- Have a security response team in place. Many companies have a security team that is organized into two main areas of expertise to facilitate immediate response, the virus team and the firewall team.
- Block all Internet email until the virus fix is applied.

- Have communications and security response team procedures in place. Each hour counts in identifying and stopping viruses and hackers. Early detection and communication are vital. Enterprisewide emails and warnings about the event rapidly restore an infrastructure to a secure state. Enterprises must have specific responses mapped to either virus or hacker attacks.

- Connect the security response team with the rest of the IT department. When the security response team is in place and reports directly to the CIO or chief security officer, other IT teams that maintain the supply chain and customer relationship management systems can be updated immediately about any impact to vendors and customers.

Bottom Line

- The amount of security required should be weighed against the degree of risk associated with doing business on the Internet.

- The sensitivity of information, productivity of users, and impact on revenue should all be assessed to determine the safeguards required. Enterprises that fail to pay attention to Internet security issues will experience significant losses as a result of attacks on their networks.

Qualifying the Level of Security Performance Your ASP Can Deliver

GartnerGroup estimates that the IT and personnel costs of securing Internet-exposed applications are three to five times that of equivalent internal applications. Application service providers (ASPs) provide one potential method of reducing the cost of providing secure service over the Internet—if they are up to the security challenges.

Provided here is a set of critical questions enterprises should ask when evaluating ASPs. A No answer to any of these questions represents a serious vulnerability that will put applications and data at risk. Given the difficulties in switching ASPs, a candidate answering No to two or more questions should be eliminated from consideration. Note that many ASPs outsource their data center and network facilities to hosting providers, but they should still be held responsible for meeting these requirements.

Network Layer:

- Does the ASP require the use of two-factor authentication for administrative control of all routers and firewalls?

- Does the ASP support 128-bit encryption and two-factor authentication for the connection from the customer LAN to the ASP production backbone?

- Does the ASP provide redundancy and load-balancing services for firewalls and other security-critical elements?

- Does the ASP perform (or have an experienced consulting company perform) external penetration tests on at least a quarterly basis and internal network security audits at least annually?
- Can the ASP show documented requirements (and ASP audit procedures) for customer network security to ensure that other ASP customers will not compromise the ASP backbone?

Platform:

- Can the ASP provide a documented policy for hardening the operating system under Web and other servers?
- If the ASP colocates customer applications on physical servers, does it have a documented set of controls it uses to ensure separation of data and security information between customer applications?

To surf the buzz surrounding the ASP industry, many entrants will rush to market with impressive facades propped up by flimsy, unproven security infrastructures and processes. Requiring potential ASPs to get an A on the GartnerGroup ASP Security quiz will ensure that an enterprise and its ASP will not show up above the fold in the Wall Street Journal as the subject of the latest successful hacking attack.

Summary

Security and the study of how to make the entire ASP model more secure is crucial to the growth of e-business. The challenges of completing secure transactions are being overcome with security engineering now taking place in Arcas Corporation, a subsidiary of Exodus Communications, in addition CyberSource, IBM, Hewlett-Packard, and the market leaders mentioned in this chapter. In building your e-business security strategy the issue of security is one that needs the utmost focus in terms of qualifying the ASPs you plan to work with. Presented in this chapter are checklists for ensuring the companies you partner with can provide secure hosting and application leasing for you.

10

Developing a Scalable
e-Business Strategy

With the advent of e-business, system scaling to meet increasing requests for transactions and fulfillment of information needs has become a hot topic at conferences and seminars. Intel even has Application Service Centers where applications are measured by how well they scale when enabled over the Web. Jeff Bezos at Amazon.com credits the scalability built into the initial fulfillment systems as being responsible for handling the sudden influx of orders for Amazon.com when the Web site started getting thousands of customers from Yahoo! and *Wall Street Journal* listings. All the e-business focus on scalability is the outgrowth of lessons learned in operations and logistics during the last 10 years as both the speed and number of transactions has increased significantly due to e-commerce applications and tools.

Scalability has been defined typically as the capability of a computer application or product (hardware or software) to continue to function well as it is changed in size or volume to meet a user need. Typically, the rescaling is to a larger size or volume. The rescaling can be of the product itself (for example, a line of computer systems of different sizes in terms of storage, RAM, and so forth) or in the scalable object's movement to a new context (for example, a new operating system). An example of this is presented by John Young in his book *Exploring IBM's New-Age Mainframes* in which he describes the RS/6000 SP operating system as one that delivers scalability ("the ability to retain performance levels when adding additional processors").

Another definition of scalability that is being actively promoted in the context of e-business is the capability of a server, application, or Web site not only to function well in the rescaled situation, but also to take full advantage of it. For example, an application program would be scalable if it could be moved from a smaller to a larger operating system and take full advantage of the larger operating system in terms of performance (user response time and so forth) and the larger number of users that could be handled.

Scaling upward is usually easier than scaling downward because developers often must make full use of a system's resources (for example, the amount of disk storage available) when an application is initially coded. Scaling a product downward might mean having to achieve the same results in a more constrained environment.

Why Is Scalability Important?

Being able to consistently deliver performance to your applications and others' applications is an essential characteristic to look for in the application service providers you intend to work with. Scalability is the assurance your e-marketing, e-commerce, or e-operations applications are not compromised in terms of performance as another of the ASP's customers increasingly accesses a site stored on the same server your site is located on. The promise of e-business is fulfilled when servers running applications also scale and simultaneously handle hundreds of thousands of users at literally the same time, providing responsive handling of requests. Intel, Microsoft, Sun Microsystems, IBM, and many other companies are all investing heavily into providing greater levels of scalability as the level of e-business traffic increases. From a partnership standpoint with the ASPs you choose to work with, scalability is the technology behind providing responsiveness to your customers.

It is important that scalability be built into your e-business strategy because it is the assurance of responsiveness to your customers that matters. Although the ASPs you are considering need to be on top of the latest trends in technology, including server and operating system developments, be sure to keep up with the major developments in this area to see that your ASPs are staying current with scalability technology.

One of the most perplexing problems for companies that embark on an e-business strategy and achieve success beyond their expectations is the part scalability plays in the growth of their companies. This dynamic of growth for companies with e-commerce strategies is highlighted in Table 10.1, which shows the exponential nature of the number of hits received on a Web site relative to the number of transactions. Based on data from a Forrester Research interview, this table highlights how scalability needs to provide the room for growth that is so essential for customer responsiveness and service. Without scalability these companies would have "hit the wall" and turned away customers without even knowing it.

Table 10.1 Transaction Site Growth and Architecture shows the scalability needed to sustain a growing e-business

Page View Growth (Monthly)	Number of Page Views (Daily)	Commerce Transaction Growth (Monthly)	Number of Commerce Transactions (Daily)	Average Transaction Value (Monthly)
400%	87,000,000	400%	30,000	$175,000
53%	3,684,000	96%	12,700	$13,400
19%	30,000	33%	1000	$90
0%	10	0%	10	$18

When asked how these companies are dealing with the loads placed on them by the increased transactions, many mentioned using load balancing and mirroring approaches to manage their server architectures. Figure 10.1 shows a bar chart comparing the various techniques used for minimizing the amount of load on a server and maximizing the capability of the system to scale.

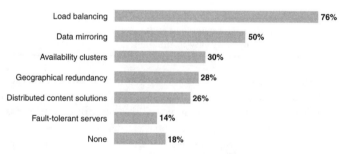

Transaction Site Growth and Architecture

"Do you use any of the following technologies in your commerce site infrastructure?"

Load balancing — 76%
Data mirroring — 50%
Availability clusters — 30%
Geographical redundancy — 28%
Distributed content solutions — 26%
Fault-tolerant servers — 14%
None — 18%

Percent of online companies doing transactions
(multiple responses accepted)
Source: Forrester Research

Figure 10.1 Forrester Research has found that the majority of companies, including hosting providers, consider using load balancing technologies and disk mirroring for alleviating potential slow-downs and increasing scalability.

The need for developing more robust applications, which ensure higher levels of scalability than is possible with an existing architecture, is the highest priority for companies facing scalability challenges. Hosting companies also need to constantly work with ASPs to ensure the latter's hosting applications are easily scaled. Figure 10.2 shows results of the surveys completed on how companies face scalability dilemmas.

What Will You Do to Deal with Increasing Scale?

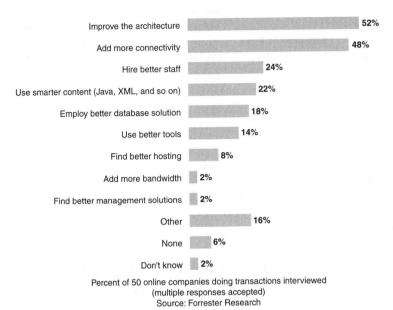

Improve the architecture — 52%
Add more connectivity — 48%
Hire better staff — 24%
Use smarter content (Java, XML, and so on) — 22%
Employ better database solution — 18%
Use better tools — 14%
Find better hosting — 8%
Add more bandwidth — 2%
Find better management solutions — 2%
Other — 16%
None — 6%
Don't know — 2%

Percent of 50 online companies doing transactions interviewed
(multiple responses accepted)
Source: Forrester Research

Figure 10.2   Developing a new architecture and adding connectivity are two common approaches to getting scalability to the highest levels possible.

Ultimately, the performance of your Web site speaks volumes to both first-time and repeat visitors to your site. One of the key tasks of an e-business strategy is to turn visitors into customers. Assuming your site has answered the questions a visitor has on the products provided and has made the navigational elements easy to work with, the most important aspect of visitors purchasing again is the stability and scalability of your site. Forrester Research completed an attitudinal survey of first-time visitors from a site relative to site-loyal visitors (those who had been to the site multiple times before) and found that the latter group can accept, to a point, an outage. The former group, the new visitors in the majority of instances, do not come back a second time. Figure 10.3 shows the results of the survey.

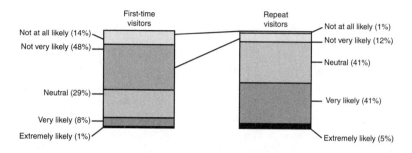

Perception of Site Availability

"Would you try to buy again from a site that was unable to respond to your first attempt?"

First-time visitors / Repeat visitors

Not at all likely (14%)
Not very likely (48%)
Neutral (29%)
Very likely (8%)
Extremely likely (1%)

Not at all likely (1%)
Not very likely (12%)
Neutral (41%)
Very likely (41%)
Extremely likely (5%)

Figure 10.3 Scalability brings responsiveness, and responsiveness brings new customers. This graphic shows the relative levels of behavior for new visitors relative to repeat visitors.

Introducing Capability Statistics

Server manufacturers look at the entire Internet arena as an opportunity to further differentiate themselves from each other by bringing measurable statistics, or benchmarks, on their relative levels of performance to potential customers. These benchmarks are the basis by which hosting companies decide on which servers to purchase for their data centers. Of course this is just one of many factors that go into the purchase decision. Service, support, prior experiences, and the capability of a manufacturer to provide insights into how to deliver the best performance for the given application is critical.

How Benchmarks Work

Benchmarks are typically artificial applications that are designed to stress an operating environment and the hardware upon which it runs in ways that are similar to some specific application or mix of applications. Because they are artificial, the benchmark software seldom matches the application profile in any given environment. This software is designed to give IT management a *standard* vantage point from which to view and evaluate hardware and software configurations offered by many vendors.

The Transaction Processing Council's (TPC) family of benchmarks, for example, is meant to simulate an environment having a relatively small number of tables in the database and a certain mix of read, write, and update operations. If the application profile of a specific organization's environment has little similarity to this mix of size and complexity, then the benchmark results by themselves will offer little guidance in determining what level of performance the organization will experience running their applications.

Competition in the server arena on benchmarks is one of the basic factors that drive new product development efforts and marketing efforts. It is entirely common to see specifications between manufacturers show over time that their solution is the most scalable in their class. Even if the benchmarks are run weekly and communicated via press release or article, server companies are very competitive on the topic of scalability as defined by benchmarks. This battle is not only between the various UNIX suppliers (Compaq, HP, IBM, and Sun) but also between UNIX and Windows NT.

Both Microsoft and Sun Microsystems are constantly working to show that their respective operating systems and server components have the best possible performance and scalability. The TPC benchmarks are the metrics used for communicating the relative level of performance between servers, taking into account differences in operating systems and processors. The TPC benchmarks are the most often used, and can be found at www.tpc.org. Figure 10.4 shows an example of how TPC benchmarks quantify performance relative to cost over time.

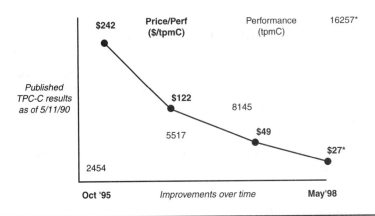

Price/Performance Leadership

Figure 10.4   TPC benchmarks compare server performance over time.

Many hosting companies that provide data centers for ASPs, and ASPs who are building their own data centers, typically evaluate the true performance of their corporate applications by running them on an in-house "test bed" of servers. In this way, they can gather their own statistics about performance and throughput under the actual workload they intend to run on the platform under evaluation. Often, such hosting companies are among the "early-release" evaluators who get operating-system code before it goes into a full-production release. In addition, many computer systems vendors have special test facilities where customers can bring their inventory of applications and databases for testing over a period of days or weeks.

Scalability Checkpoints

To have a strong understanding of how scalability works and its implications for your outsourced applications, consider the following points. These considerations show the issues surrounding scalability performance of your applications over time. Both Gartner Gray and Forrester Research have done much work in this area. From their conferences and interviews with analysts, I've developed these considerations for clients, networks, and applications relating to scalability.

Client-side considerations:

- The type and extent of operating systems and platforms supported
- The performance offered by the client

Server-side considerations:

- The number of users or clients to be supported
- The number and type of server operating environments being used
- Whether a single server supports a given application or whether different application services are provided by different servers

Network considerations:

- The network media being used
- The network protocol being used
- The number of intermediate nodes typically located between the client and the server

Application complexity considerations:

- The size of the applications
- Whether the applications are processing-intensive or I/O-bound
- Whether the application services are offered by different machines in the network and, if so, how many systems must work together to support the application
- The number of tables in the database
- The size of tables in the database
- The data types of items in each record (for example, voice and image)
- The number of joins or file accesses required when accomplishing a given transaction
- The number of databases being used in a given environment

The type of applications in a given organization's application profile is also significant. This is critical, for example, in companies that have widely distributed offices throughout the U.S. and the world. Here are additional considerations to keep in mind for the type of applications your organization is running:

- Data legacy requirements at regional offices to successfully serve customers and maintain relationships
- Availability of graphically based data, which takes an inordinate amount of storage space online
- Manageability of network security for a widely dispersed network
- Connectivity and the ability to provide reliable e-mail systems throughout all offices

Monitoring Performance and Scalability Metrics

Given the importance of scalability metrics to the sales of servers, and ultimately to the growth of e-business, the major operating systems vendors are increasingly bundling in tools for tracking the relative level of scalability of their solutions. Both Sun's Solaris and Microsoft's Windows 2000 Server operating systems continue to offer tools for measuring the level of scalability possible with respective servers running their operating systems.

The ASPs you are working with need to have a strong knowledge of both the Sun and Microsoft tools now included in the baseline configuration of their respective operating systems. In the case of Microsoft, the Performance Monitor has become recognized as the easiest to use and most efficient at tracking overall performance metrics. Obviously, you don't need to run these metrics yourself (that's for your ASP to do); however, you do need to know that Performance Monitor is available and so pervasive today that the ASP and hosting company together should be able to quickly isolate any scalability issues before any application-threatening events occur.

Performance Monitor has been included in all versions of Windows NT and now, Windows 2000 Workstation and Server versions of the popular Microsoft operating system. Performance Monitor uses an object/counter approach to defining performance variables, and the relative level of performance that the system should be accomplishing. Figure 10.5 shows an example of a Performance Monitor tracking memory and network usage on a dual-processor Intel-based Xeon server.

Make sure the ASPs you are considering are actively using Performance Monitor if the server complex is running on Windows 2000-based systems. If your ASP has its own data center, ask to see the relative performance data over time for the servers in the center. You can learn how the data center is run by seeing the data and also by seeing whether the data is available at all.

You don't have to be an expert on systems scalability when contracting with an ASP, but it is important to have the right questions in mind as you qualify one. There are additional tools for gauging relative system scalability that you should ask the ASP if it is using or planning to use. One of the more popular is the BlueCurve DynaMeasure application, which has the capability to measure throughout, response time, and processor use. BlueCurve is tightly integrated with Microsoft applications, including BackOffice, Exchange, and SQL Server.

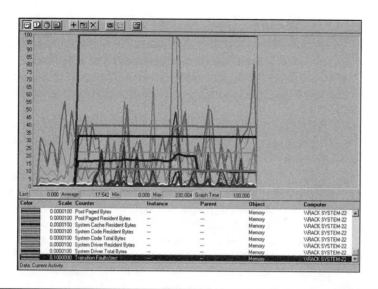

Figure 10.5   Using tools such as Performance Monitor gives your ASP the chance to predict whether the scalability issues serving multiple customers will dictate the need for additional hardware and network resources.

The ASP Plan for Scalability: Plans for Testing Applications

Any service provider actively creating suites of solutions is concerned with scalability. Because the essence of the ASP model is about taking an application and serving many customers with it, the one-to-many approach inherent in this model stresses systems and can, if left unmanaged, drive overall system responsiveness down. Conversely, a company that can actively manage the scalability of its applications and ensure responsiveness over time has a decided competitive advantage in the ASP arena. Scalability for the ASP ties directly back to its capability to provide superior service as a differentiator.

Taking the ASP route to share applications requires diligence on your part to make sure the partners you choose have tested their applications for scalability and load. Clearly, if an ASP has not completed this level of analysis using its application services, you should reconsider that ASP; the unpredictable nature of Internet traffic and your ASP's capability to respond to it have a direct bearing on your ability to serve your customers. The following sections describe a series of tests that your ASP needs to be running to ensure the robustness of the applications it offers.

Simulated Load Testing

Load testing is perhaps the best-known form of performance testing. Although load testing provides very useful information about the scalability of an application in a controlled environment, today's widely distributed systems are making it more and more difficult for this test to provide an accurate representation of just how scalable an application is.

Active Load Monitoring

Active load monitoring involves periodically sending a dummy transaction through a production system and carefully measuring response time. The advantage of this approach is that it operates against the production system and therefore can provide important real-world information about the performance of an application. Thresholds can be set so there is generally adequate warning of an impending disaster. Mercury Interactive's Topaz is a good example of an active–load-monitoring product. Although this approach approximates what can be accomplished in the more sophisticated *Predictive Performance Analysis (PPA)* segment, it is limited by being both a discrete monitoring activity and unsuited to the analysis of the many different dimensions of application performance that need to be assessed.

Predictive Performance Analysis (PPA)

PPA combines elements of real-time monitoring and predictive analysis of monitoring data to forecast potential performance problems both with considerable accuracy and with more lead time and intelligence to address solutions (manual and automated) than currently exist in active load monitoring. Although PPA products do not currently exist in the ASQ (Automated Software Quality tools) space, similar products are surfacing in the system management market. Computer Associates has been especially active in this arena with its Neugent technology.

PPA analyzes ongoing application loads with several objectives in mind. First, there are many ways in which scalability can become a problem due to the many components in applications today. Although system monitoring is a core activity in the system management space, its focal point is the system, which often means hardware. The focus of PPA is the monitoring and analysis of information, choosing the application instead of the system as the center of gravity. Although many of the metrics defined to monitor the application will be similar to those used to monitor systems, the frame of reference is very different.

PPA goes beyond simple analysis and develops trends based on recent data that is continually refreshed. When measured against available system capacity (overall capacity minus other projected workloads), this data provides a more accurate view into when scalability limits will be reached.

PPA should also work in conjunction with system management control software to redirect workload should a scalability problem be anticipated.

Unlike PIA (Predictive Integrity Analysis), for which there are no current product initiatives, the activities of PPA bear a close relationship to those activities and products that already exist in the system performance monitoring and system management space. To speed time to market for products, ASQ vendors should rapidly seek to partner with system management vendors and collaborate to provide solutions that offer the best attributes of system management functionality applied to application performance management.

Tying in Scalability with Your e-Business Plan

Driving your e-business strategy forward, scalability needs to definitely have a series of metrics associated with it so you can work directly with your ASP to either get even higher levels of performance or correct problems with the existing performance. The key metrics, as defined in Figure 10.6, show the impact of measuring your ASP's performance over time in relation to the customer loyalty generated from being responsive and having the type of content a visitor is looking for.

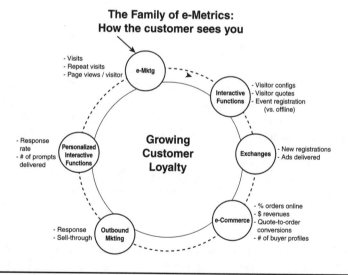

Figure 10.6   How metrics affect the growth of customer loyalty to your Web site.

When developing your e-business strategy, setting specific targets for each of the metrics shown in Figure 10.7 provides your ASP with direction concerning how you want to measure the performance of the Web site over time. These metrics can easily be included in a table that is made part of the overall contract with your ASP.

The entire area of scalability and performance begs the question of setting minimal quality levels of performance based on the Service Level Agreements.

Exploring Service Level Agreements and Assurances of Performance

Some industries mature extremely rapidly although others are continually defined through the interaction of customers and suppliers over time. The burgeoning ASP industry is quickly being defined by the level of services provided to customers, yet the quantification of these performance guarantees has been less forthcoming. The purpose of the Service Level Agreement (SLA) is to define the minimal acceptable performance metrics for an ASP you work with. The industry is still waiting for this practice to take hold in a broader context than it is today.

A Service Level Agreement is actually a commitment from the ASP you are working with to provide minimal levels of uptime, performance, and accuracy of transactions from e-commerce sites. These SLAs are evolving, and like many aspects of the ASP model, are being influenced by the role of early adopters in this marketplace. The continued growth of outsourcing is driving the development of these SLAs into documents that are actionable.

When creating your specific Service Level Agreement, quantify key performance variables and their allowable ranges. If you are familiar with the tools used for managing scalability, be sure to use the metrics associated with those tools in your SLA Agreement.

Defining Key Success Factors for Scalability

The key success factors to include in a series of metrics for your Service Level Agreement are profiled here. Keep in mind that with a Service Level Agreement you can structure the contract to list and quantify your expectations for performance. Although many ASPs are not yet to the point of providing a month's free services if servers hosting your applications are inoperable on a Monday morning from 8–12, for example, you can stress the need for concessions based on performance.

Set required performance levels to define the key attributes that a SLA needs to meet to fulfill contractual agreements. The most important is the percentage uptime metric.

Percentage Uptime

The majority of hosting companies and ASPs can provide this metric, and many specify 98%. With many of the larger Web sites hosted internally to companies, uptime is hovering around the 99% range. The statistics provided here are the minimum quality standards. You should hold an ASP to at least the same level of performance.

Quality of Service

This metric measures how long your ASP takes to solve technical problems and work through the development of modifications to its applications. The integration of legacy data and the extent of its functionality also provide a measuring stick for the level of quality of service provided by the ASP.

User Satisfaction

Taking the initiative to understand your customers and their experiences on your site is critical for the long-term growth of your business. Gauging how many visitors become customers and how many customers become repeat purchasers is a metric closely tied to the scalability of the site. Agree with your ASP to set a minimal customer satisfaction ranking through a mutually agreed methodology to ensure your customers get the service they expect.

User Expectations

Using the metrics of uptime and response to requests, in addition to the metrics of how your company is perceived by customers, can be directly written into the SLA Agreement. A typical agreement for service quality levels is rather broad and global. Strive to get individualized metrics into the SLAs you write with your ASPs. It's critical to have those targets in place before a site or application goes online.

The Future Direction of ASPs Regarding Scalability

Clearly, the range and depth of statistics available on performance of e-business sites worldwide needs to be increased. Industry associations such as the ASP Industry Consortium have pioneered the development of Service Level Agreements, adding performance incentive clauses in addition to creating templates for companies to use in creating their agreements with customers.

There is also the continued development of metrics from other areas of the Internet, which have direct impact on the ASP model. These include the Web metrics measurement applications that define bandwidth for companies and the relative level of traffic a company is having over time based on its use of promotional offers. The entire aspect of load balancing will eventually migrate into metrics that will be listed in Service Level Agreements.

Just as in the product development area of the ASP model, there continues to be a focus within the area of scalability on the role early adopters are playing in defining the industry. Taking the initiative with the ASPs you have chosen to work with can pay dividends down the road as the performance of your Web site is quantified and unequivocal with its performance.

Case Study: Sun's SunTone Program for Ensuring Scalability

Customers expect Internet services to be available 24 hours a day, 7 days a week, 365 days a year. There is little tolerance for downtime, planned or unplanned. Bad news travels at the click of a mouse, and at a time when customers have more choices than ever, there is no room for mistakes. The market is driving up customer expectations because there are more service providers to choose from every day. Seeking to differentiate themselves, service providers are pushing the standards bar higher. Customers now demand guarantees for availability and performance, both from their service providers and their in-house IT departments. Sun's focus on SunTone is thoroughly described on their Web site and was launcehd with much press coverage. VARBusiness, for example, ran an article on January 11, 2000 detailing much of the SunTone program.

Although customer expectations have never been higher, the task of providing continuous Internet services has never been more challenging. Many variables must be successfully managed to deliver reliable, predictable, customer-focused services. There can be no weak links.

Service providers must be able to effectively forecast and manage demand for their services at a time when overall Internet traffic volume is increasing by 1,000% a year. Although the market is growing rapidly, service providers must position themselves for growth and agility to handle increasing numbers of subscribers, additional services, and more challenging workloads. Having system architectures that can meet, and change with, these demands is critical to continued success.

Introducing the SunTone Certified Program Overview

Sun created the SunTone certification and logo program to recognize and promote investments in process, methodology, and infrastructure—elements that promote the delivery of secure, reliable, and predictable Internet services. Using the SunTone Certified logo as a guide, customers can quickly and confidently choose services that have met high standards—quality standards aimed at making Web tone as reliable as a dial tone.

The SunTone Certified program offers two certifications:

- **SunTone Certified service**—SunTone Certified services meet established requirements for hardware infrastructure, security, and operational processes. Additionally, in deploying SunTone Certified services, service providers follow a recommended methodology for building services, enabling predictable service levels, and promoting reliability and scalability.

- **SunTone Certified application**—SunTone Certified applications conform to requirements addressing scalability, availability, security, and management practices. SunTone Certified applications are optimized and tuned to run on the SunTone architecture.

Specifics on the SunTone Certified Service Program

The SunTone Certified service program has been developed based on high-level guidelines (for example, implement services using an n-tiered design). These guidelines, and the corresponding result measures, provide a specific means to assess a service as SunTone Certified. Service providers having services that meet or exceed all standards listed in the specification earn the right to use the SunTone Certified logo.

Three SunTone Certified service levels are planned, each raising the bar on the standards set:

- Level I certification, the topic of this chapter, is focused on ensuring that service operations and infrastructure are capable of supporting customer SLAs.
- Level II certification will specify increasing availability and security levels and architecture, which supports failover and greater scalability.
- Level III certification will focus on quality of service measures.

SunTone Program Objectives Explained—Heavily Scalability Focused

Level I of the SunTone Certified service specification ties customer needs to network design principles, which are then applied to eight dimensions of the service delivery environment. The result is a specification for the following:

- **N-tier Architecture**—SunTone Certified services specify functional decomposition by service, task layer, and special function to enhance reliability, availability, security, and scalability. These architectures provide for carefully controlled firewall access between separate subnetworks.
- **Platforms and Applications**—Key components of SunTone Certified services run in the Solaris operating environment, promoting robustness, reliability, and high availability. SunTone Certified services are backed by vendor SLAs. Service providers establish the capacity of key platform elements and monitor performance statistics to ensure SLAs with their customers are met.
- **Scalability**—SunTone Certified services specify a strategic growth and capacity plan that is regularly monitored. Functional components are shared across services, and vertical database scaling is supported.
- **Service Policies**—SunTone Certified services specify a standard suite of protocols, enabling implementation portability. Resource availability and performance are promoted by insulating resources provided to each customer. Service providers with SunTone Certified services provide secure remote provisioning for hosted customers and applications.
- **Availability and Reliability**—SunTone Certified services specify continuous service components for which any interruption is unacceptable, and resilient service components for which availability and reliability are predictable. Disaster,

recovery, and restoration strategies are provided for, and database availability is ensured using specific protection mechanisms.

- **Security**—Protection of SunTone Certified services begins with comprehensive security policies that are regularly reviewed to keep pace with security requirements and the demand for customer access to services. SunTone Certified services address security through network design, and support standard access control mechanisms (for example, certificates) to carefully control traffic across multiple subnetworks and protect customer privacy.

- **Operations**—People and process errors account for most service downtime. SunTone Certified services specify operational strategies and practices that promote quality service delivery. Such practices include standards for data center operations, change control, user support, back up and recovery, software migration into production, network management, and disaster planning and recovery.

- **Technical Competencies**—Service providers offering SunTone Certified services are required to have experienced personnel who have demonstrated technical competency in specific areas that are essential to the delivery of highly reliable and available services.

Summary

Hosting companies coming online today will need to differentiate themselves in the scalability area as convincingly as possible to establish a market presence. The technical aspects of scalability are indeed worthy of entire books. The intent of this chapter is to provide you with a set of guidelines for defining the expectations you and your customers have for ASPs you are either working with today or planning to work with in the future. Scalability metrics are essential in your e-business strategy for getting a continual high level of responsiveness for your customers.

11

Pulling It All Together into an e-Business Strategy

Taking the approach of looking at e-business as a means for strengthening your ties with your customers, generating revenue, and decreasing costs is the essence of a sound strategy. In defining an e-business strategy it is essential to specify metrics that measure progress. For example, the metrics of scalability show the need for being consistently responsive to customers and ensuring that responsiveness through the metrics is defined in service level agreements.

Ultimately the need for providing your customers with better service than your competitors is going to force the issue of an e-business strategy today. It's important to really talk with your customers about e-commerce and e-business in general. See what their needs are and how you can fulfill them with the Web sites you are contemplating building with an ASP. Taking the services that an ASP provides and turning them into a competitive advantage for your company is truly where the ASP model is going to contribute most to its customers.

It is essential to have a clear direction on e-marketing objectives and a definition of applications for staying in touch with customers. The development of e-commerce applications in ASPs is starting to reflect a depth of functionality over broad coverage of many features at a tertiary level. Your e-business strategy also needs to include metrics that define the role of e-operations tools in decreasing the costs of transactions and of completing business in general. Metrics across e-marketing, e-commerce, and especially e-operations need to be in your e-business strategy.

Pulling together the three dominant aspects of e-business and creating a cohesive strategy is the intent of this chapter. Think of the percentage of emphasis your company wants to put into each area of e-business, whether that is e-marketing, e-commerce, or e-operations. If your organization is one that values the quantifiable metrics of performance and holds metrics as a measure of return on their investment, e-operations deserves attention in your strategy.

If, on the other hand, your company is relatively new, and is planning on creating a Web site for getting your brand known, then going to an e-marketing emphasis makes the most sense. In previous chapters there has been a thorough overview of what e-marketing is and how to bring customers into your company. Many articles and even some presenters at conferences have shown brochures simply turned into HTML. Called brochureware, this approach to e-marketing robs you of the opportunity to interact with your customers. Regardless of the e-business strategy you adopt, staying focused on the customer and their needs through interactive tools is the best approach to get visitors to your site to become repeat customers. Many presenters at conferences are quick to point out how their companies were able to get online very quickly, or, in the case of ASPs, how they were able to help other companies make a rapid transition to doing business online. Yet for all these claims of quickness it's imperative to dig deeper into the true value-add of the ASP. Taking the content and key positioning within a brochure and forming a stronger message using the communication mechanisms of the Internet is the real payoff of a strong e-marketing strategy. Coupling this strength of communication with an interactive experience for customers takes the marketing to an entirely new level.

Surveys completed by International Data Corporation show that the majority of companies engaging in e-commerce today are generating between 10% and 20% additional revenue in the first quarter of operations. Higher sales is just part of the e-business strategy. One of the key messages of this book is that an e-business strategy needs to be balanced. With the high expectations for e-commerce, for example, there has to be a corresponding commitment to creating or leasing e-operations applications that have the potential of driving down logistics costs and driving up response times.

Clearly the integrated approach to an e-business strategy is necessary to bring in visitors, sell to them, support customers, and fulfill their requirements and expectations for service. Even with the fluctuations of capital markets such as NASDAQ, it's very important to realize that those e-operations applications including e-procurement, e-logistics, and Customer Relationship Management all have a common trait—they quantify the contributions they make to an enterprise. In creating an e-business strategy, many of the world's largest corporations have already focused on the quantifiable benefits—those areas of the Internet that are trackable and easily defined in terms of their progression of relative performance. None of the leading and most successful e-business strategies are running on pure hype. In fact the market fluctuations simply underscore the fact that components of the e-business strategy that deliver consistent value and have the potential to contribute to the bottom line, survive. ASPs that singularly focus on the quantifiable benefits of their models often excel and thrive in enterprises of all kinds. Be sure to check into the capabilities of your ASP and see examples of how you can get the metrics you require.

Considering e–Business Experts for Execution of Your Strategy

When creating an e–business many people think they should take the entire initiative in-house. There are millions of businesses throughout the world doing this today and many are successful at it. Mostly these companies doing all their e–business work in-house are creating experts on their own because the market for e–business professionals is one where demand exceeds supply. The entire labor shortage today is one of the key factors driving the adoption of the ASP model in general as well.

A survey was completed by Gartner Group on the most critical e–business competencies IT Managers look for when staffing internal projects. The traits listed in Figure 11.1 were the most popular.

Most Critical E-Business Competencies	Number of Responses	Percentage of Total
Business Strategy	34	81%
Business Process and Requirements	30	71%
E-commerce strategy	30	71%
Project Planning and Management	13	31%
Web Marketing	7	17%
Technology Architecture	5	12%
System Security Management	4	10%
Application Intergration	4	10%
Web Design and Development	3	7%
System Availability	3	7%
Network Architecture	2	5%
Extranet Technologies	1	2%
Electronic Data Interchange	1	2%

Source: Gartner Institute

Figure 11.1   IT Managers rank the most preferred attributes for new hires in their organizations who will be working on e–business projects.

Clearly, to be an e-business professional, one must understand business strategy, and business processes and requirements, and be able to discern when and where e-commerce and e-business aspects of a solution should be included. The IT Managers interviewed also mentioned that the ability to manage several projects to completion were crucial for the long-term contributions of the e-business initiatives.

The implications of the findings in Figure 11.1 show that in the definition of your e-business strategy there needs to be distinct and clear ownership for the e-business initiatives underway, as well as project management and the ability to execute and implement e-business projects. Figure 11.2 shows the evolution of customer-based service when it comes to e-business practices.

Most Scarce Competencies	Number of Responses	Percentage of Total
E- Commerce Strategy	33	79%
Application Integration	19	45%
Business Strategy	17	40%
Project Planning and Management	16	38%
Java Programming	15	36%
Web Design and Development	15	36%
Web Marketing	14	33%
Business Process and Requirements	14	33%
System Security Management	13	31%
Technology Architecture	12	29%
Data Mining Technologies	12	29%
Network Architecture	11	26%
Electronic Data Interchange	11	26%
Extranet Architecture	9	21%
Payment Technologies	5	12%
System Availability	5	12%

Source: Gartner Institute

Figure 11.2   The evolution of e-business service and support needs as defined by IT Managers.

Which Competencies Should You Look for First with an e-Business Expert?

Increasingly ASPs are facing the same hiring and staffing dilemmas as you are when it comes to finding and hiring e-business experts. In such critical areas as e-commerce project management, e-business strategists capable of reading the signals in client companies as to what needs to be done are in short supply. The role of the strategist in the ASPs you choose to work with need to have this expertise on staff to assist in the planning and implementation of your e-business strategy. For the most involved projects, the creation of the strategy typically precedes the actual cross-functional meetings with the ASPs you want to complete specific aspects of the e-business strategy.

These questions are what ASPs look for when it comes to creating a team of e-business experts who will work in conjunction with you on your e-business strategy. For many ASPs it is not surprising that business strategy is high on the list. Business strategists ask the following questions:

- In which businesses and markets should the enterprise compete?
- What are the competitive pressures?
- What have you found to be the strengths of your e-business strategy?
- What is the best possible mix of attributes a successful e-business expert should have?
- Describe your most successful e-business consulting experience. Why was it successful? Were customer metrics involved?
- Describe the toughest e-business client situation that involved you. What went wrong and how did you assist in a solution?
- Describe the most important lessons learned from working with clients in terms of managing their expectations?
- How do you quantify a client's expectations to ensure they are met?
- Have you ever had a situation where someone in the company you worked for had overcommitted to a client and you had to handle the situation? How did you handle it and what steps did you take with the client?
- Many CIOs are reading all they can on e-business. How do you manage the technical aspects of an ASP relationship without trying to sound like a technical expert instead of an e-business expert?
- Why are you an e-business expert? What attracts you to this work?
- What is more important in being an e-business expert: passion for serving customers or technology expertise? Why?
- What's the best possible approach for ASPs to take in ensuring responsiveness and support?
- What are your thoughts on how an ASP can re-engineer itself to be more responsive to the needs of a client?

- Is an ASP in the products business, distribution business, or service business? What's the best approach to take with all clients for consistency?

Those kinds of questions are an essential part of most e-business projects and will definitely bring the best possible performers into an ASP, as these questions are what many senior management teams of ASPs are asking themselves today. Even at this early phase of e-business, it is clear that business models vary in terms of their adaptability to the Internet. For instance, online publishers that rushed to the Web found that it was difficult to count the number of readers who visited their sites to the satisfaction of advertisers. While they could count Web "hits," few online publishers sufficiently thought through the challenge of identifying exactly who was hitting their Web sites.

Clearly, e-business requires a closer alignment between the business units and the role of Information Systems in planning the integration of back-end systems. A cross-functional team that comprises business unit leaders, IT staff, and the ASP implementation team is all-critical for the long-term success of the project. ASPs are also looking for business strategists who can lay out the business models that will be successful on the Internet. To do that, they must be familiar with the kinds of e-business models that are already in the market, and they must have a high-level understanding of current e-business technologies.

Making Sure Your ASP Team Can Go the Distance

In creating the team that will drive the development of the ASP solutions for your company, there are several attributes to look for when creating the cross-functional team to drive the integration effort. Here are the guidelines that can increase the chances of success for your ASP project:

- **Seek out technical extroverts**—These individuals, who publish in trade journals and speak at conferences, will probably have the mix of technical and behavioral skills that e-business jobs require. This may seem counterintuitive to you, yet realize that ASPs are clearly in the services business in that they enable the delivery of technology. It's important to have the right mix of emotional and social intelligence with technical acumen since the most important task these experts perform is serving individual clients.

- **Individuals with adaptability**—Individuals' ability to adapt is essential to e-business because of the short project life cycles. The individuals' adaptability will also help them shift their focus quickly from technical to business issues.

- **Marketing and finance experts, as well as experienced project managers and IT consultants, are good choices for converts from business to e-business**—For each of those groups, much of their basic business knowledge will be easily transferred to e-business roles. The many research projects completed by Gartner Group on e-business recruitment have found an interesting mix of individuals—everything from former software sales executives to Big 5 consultants—running e-business projects.

- **Have a fast-track training program for e-business candidates**—This is a challenge because not much courseware about e-business is available, and e-business encompasses so many technologies that it would be impossible to give each trainee a solid grounding in all of them. Therefore, trainees should attend an e-business fundamentals class that covers the broad spectrum of technologies and gives them a basic understanding of how e-business projects are planned and managed.

- **Accountability starts at home: get strong project managers**—The worst shortages of e-business skills will be in areas that are most critical to project success, such as business strategy and project management.

- **Developing your own e-business experts**—Enterprises should identify individuals within the enterprise who can, through a rapid training program, supplement their business knowledge with e-business fundamentals.

How ASPs Enable Data Integration

The most challenging aspect of any project with an ASP is getting your previous data recognized and quickly useable on your new Web sites and through the Web-enabled applications. The key aspects of bringing data into applications from legacy systems is best handled by working through cross-functional team members who have the core competency of being able to import data from other platforms.

ASPs have varying names for the department responsible for this function, with some calling it Custom Engineering, Customer Support, Engineering, or even Field Service. Because the integration and management of this data is central to the success of your project, be sure your ASP can meet the majority of the following questions and challenges. If they have had experience integrating legacy data before and have success stories they are proud of, that's a good sign:

- **Strategy experience**—The ability to build and sustain a strategy with you is one of the strongest differentiators among service providers. Look for an e-business expert to have the experience with defining strategy as it relates to each component of your e-business plan. Having expertise in how to make the e-marketing goals work for you, taking the extra costs out of e-commerce to maximize your sales and minimizing costs, and integration expertise for e-operations are all skill sets an ASP needs to execute strategies effectively.

- **Extent of Operating Systems Knowledge**—At the most basic level of being able to integrate legacy data with their applications is a thorough knowledge of operating systems, including certifications for Sun Microsystems and Microsoft's Windows NT and Windows 2000 operating systems. It's essential that the ASP you are working with has the ability to work at the TCP/IP level of these operating systems and integrate their functions together for sharing data.

- **ODBC expertise**—The ability to work with the various tables inherent in the ODBC database interfaces within operating systems is also a needed expertise. Having the ability to map file names and their applications for easier use by database applications is critical for the success of integrating applications into a total e-business solution.

- **Rollout of integrated sites**—Each time an ASP rolls out an integrated site it learns more about how to make its internal subsystems work with legacy applications. Check to see how many sites the ASP has done that needed to integrate several of their applications in addition to using legacy data. Ask for success stories in this area; this will tell you the ability of the ASP to scale its functions internally to meet the unique challenges of customers' e-business strategy.

- **Scalability success stories**—A significant success story will help you determine the ability of a specific ASP to scale sites to your increasing needs.

- **Specific product knowledge**—It's critical for your integration efforts to find a team member on the ASP partner side who has expertise in the development and support of their core applications. The need for a product expert is especially critical when creating larger e-business implementations.

- **Customer service attitude**—Last and certainly not least the willingness of your ASP to go the extra mile for you can be assessed from their repeat business evident from their success stories.

Virtual Private Network Considerations in Your e-Business Strategy

Companies are increasingly outsourcing functions such as Marketing Communications and PR, and very often Engineering. In response to the need for communicating throughout workgroups, companies often create *Virtual Private Networks (VPNs)* with the majority of an outsourced function offsite.

In looking at what's driving the development of VPNs, the majority of demand is being generated from the following two market trends:

- **Telecommuting**—With an increasing number of functions outsourced, telecommuting is increasingly being seen as the best approach for enabling online communication between cross-functional groups. The shortage of technical talent is increasingly turning the labor market into one where the sellers— the technical professionals in this case—can work from anywhere in the world they want. With the advent of VPNs entire companies are now forming where individual contributors are located in various cities worldwide.

- **Extranets**—With the increasing focus on bringing in suppliers, customers, and consultants into cross-functional teams of organizations, extranets have become one of the highest growth areas of VPNs. One of the areas where ASPs are adding value to the extranet implementation plans is the development of interoperability tools with other networks. Just as users today may use one or more carriers for legacy and data networking, in the future they may use multiple carriers for VPN services. This will enable carriers to obtain best-in-class VPN services from complementary service providers.

In selecting an extranet as part of your e-business implementation strategy, the two most important issues you need to address are security and network reliability.

Exploring VPN Security

If the greatest strength of the Internet is its pervasive use and availability, then its greatest weakness is security. Security and VPNs are often mentioned in the same breath, and the issue ranks at the top of the list of concerns for many companies contemplating building one.

Today, most of the VPN providers offer authentication via protocols such as PAP/CHAP or RADIUS for dial-up users, or authentication services via firewall technology.

Encryption is offered, but not as extensively as authentication. Some providers offer encryption from the remote client using either an encryption device from a hardware provider such as VPNet Technologies or software from a supplier such as CheckPoint Software Technologies. A barrier to VPN acceptance has been customer fear of becoming locked into a particular provider with a proprietary security approach. Many companies look at VPNs and are concerned about the security issues. Upon investigating the security options, many companies stop on VPN efforts when the decision needs to be made between encryption and authentication.

Essentials of Network Reliability

One of the most competitive issues in the VPN sector today, and the focus of many service providers, is the ability to ensure network reliability. Many have found an effective shortcut to meeting the criteria for some sort of service guarantee: simply extending their Internet access service-level agreement (SLA) to their VPN products. However, the more aggressive service providers such as Concentric and GTE Internetworking have pioneered VPN-specific SLAs. SLAs are more demonstrative than effective but can prove a service provider's commitment to service.

An aggressive pioneer is GTE Internetworking (GTEI). Its SLAs apply to both dedicated and dial-up connections. In addition, GTEI offers identical remote access SLAs for both its domestic and international services. SLAs for international dedicated services are based upon geographical zones around the world. GTEI also has SLAs that apply to the availability of VPN gateways for extranets when GTE doesn't provide the connectivity.

As another example, Concentric provides premise-to-premise SLAs with its "Concentric QoS" service, its premier VPN suite of services based on VPN equipment from Xedia. Concentric offers three dedicated SLAs: availability, latency, and packet loss. The availability guarantee promises 100% premise-to-premise, including the local loop for dedicated connectivity as long as it is ordered through Concentric.

Extranet Essentials

For larger ASP project implementations, extranets are commonly created. This is especially true when a company has a distributed series of locations throughout a region or country. With the distribution of offices and the sharing of information across broad geographic areas, the need for security is tantamount. If you are planning an extranet, consider the security issues surrounding that configuration.

e-Business extranets demand robust authorization and access control management services to support commerce while maintaining security. To help enterprises determine which security architectures will be safe and usable for e-business, Gartner Group, the research company, has created one of their magic quadrants for mapping this market area.

As the use of the Internet for e-business continues to ramp up, successful enterprises will find the balance between the traditional needs of the corporate security groups (keep out everyone except employees) and the demands of the business units (let in everyone who might buy something). The time to market will always win out over waiting for security perfection, so the balance now includes intrusion detection and vulnerability assessment tools.

Gartner predicts that by mid-2003, increased demand will upset this balance by requiring support for anonymous activity in some areas and by requiring enterprises to protect consumer data and, more importantly, support a variety of privacy models, such as opt out, opt in, or selective release. This will require much stronger mechanisms for protecting stored information and authenticating users.

The role of the industry is driving the uncertainty of security out of extranets. Although Web vandalism is widespread, the problem and its cure are well known. Compromised Web sites could have been protected using security technologies, including hardened operating systems, firewalls, intrusion detection systems and wise administration. The complexity of those technologies has led enterprises to ignore them and hope for safety. Skyrocketing security salaries and expensive tools, magnified by frequent and massive Web site changes, mean that vulnerabilities will exist and quickly be found by automated hacking tools.

Despite the attention given to bulk stealing of credit cards for ransom purposes, long-term credit card fraud in business-to-consumer Internet systems will focus on large numbers of small-value fraudulent transactions and use theft to make purchases with stolen credentials. The media is the network security manager's friend. Every day the CIO reads about hacked Web sites "above the fold" in the mainstream press, which makes spending money on firewalls and intrusion detection easier to accept. As the press loses interest, security managers will have to make better use of audit and reporting tools, and co-opting of business unit funds to maintain a sufficient level of security.

Except for firewalls, by 2003, 40% of security solutions will be funded from business unit budgets, requiring security managers to be much more responsive to the business unit.

An extranet Web site typically evolves from a dominant series of applications that are accessible through an exchange or portal for the internal use of associates. The eventual use of these exchanges by customers is eventually going to be pervasive for geographically dispersed businesses. As the number of applications increases in extranet or portal, users are often required to remember and enter multiple passwords, and system managers must maintain and synchronize multiple access control lists. Gartner Group has defined extranet access management products as solutions that provide a unified mechanism to manage the authentication of users (including single sign-on) and implement business rules determining their connections to applications and data. These business rules may be authorizations in a security sense, entitlements in a legal/contractual sense, or personalization in a marketing sense.

Gartner's Magic Quadrant analysis for this market shows that there are a number of viable vendors, but more than the market will support in the long run (see Figure 11.3).

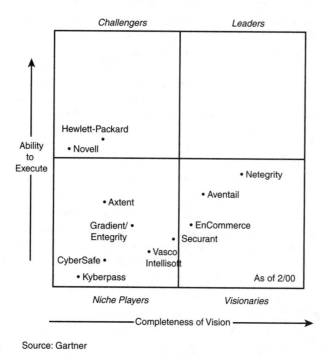

Figure 11.3   The Gartner Groups' Magic Quadrant Analysis of Extranet providers.

In summary on extranets, here are several key aspects of these communication methods to keep in mind when planning one:

- The complexity of managing multiple disparate access control lists to manage extranet users can increase security vulnerabilities and cost of ownership.

- Extranet access management solutions should be selected based on their ability to implement business rules and integrate with high-value business applications.

- By 2002, 50% of e-business extranets and portals will use consolidated authentication and authorization systems.

- By year-end 2002, 40% of extranet user management vendors will be acquired, merge with content personalization vendors, or go out of business.

ASPs and Strategy Definition

An e-business strategy is made possible through the partnerships chosen to implement it. ASPs that have a wealth of partnerships will be on track for delivering more functionality at a lower cost than if you put the entire series of relationships together by yourself. In creating your e-business strategy, there are several areas where an ASP can assist you in generating your goals into categories. Many companies, for example, want to have a balanced approach to brand building yet also want to have a lead generation program that will provide the sales force opportunities to close sales. ASPs can assist you in defining objectives and giving you paths to their accomplishment. Presented here by area of an e-business strategy is a description of how an ASP can provide that assistance for you.

Business Case for the e-Business Initiative

At the heart of any e-business strategy is the idea that ultimately the efforts will yield higher sales, lower costs, and in the end, more profits. The reason for applying metrics so heavily throughout an e-business strategy is precisely for this purpose—quantifying the contribution of a strategy is critical. When a client visits an ASP based purely on hype there is too much room for a disconnect with regard to profit expectations. When creating your e-business strategy, always have metrics for each area so you can unequivocally describe the performance levels delivered to your customers via the ASP or ASPs you choose to work with.

This ties back to the fundamental business case for the e-business initiatives underway. If the fundamental goal is cost reduction, then the e-operations aspects of the strategy's extensive metrics are best applied to the e-business strategy statements—preferably in the executive summary to ensure everyone's expectations are on target. Conversely, if the objective is for brand awareness, first the objectives will be focused more on the contributory nature of the Web site you're building to drive the name of the company to the target segments.

In terms of an e-commerce strategy the entire series of metrics having to do with transactions and the level of responsiveness is critical for the e-business strategy. Communicating expectations to your ASP partners in quantitative terms makes the direction of the project clearer and drives the development of strategies on the part of the ASP to tailor the implementation to accomplish the goals.

Managing Expectations

The Internet being so pervasive and the alacrity with which companies get online makes the entire e-business arena look instantaneous in implementation. This is obviously not the case. Anything on the Web that looks easy has hundreds, if not thousands, of hours invested in it. If you are the information strategist primarily responsible for making the ASP relationships bear fruit in regard to the e-business strategies, be sure to consider the following ideas for level-setting expectations with your internal teams. Your ASPs should also be able to assist with these tasks because it is in their best interest to show progress yet also not fall into an overcommitment trap from lack of communication. With the beginning of a new project there are both high expectations and uncharted waters that need to be crossed in the completion of the tasks. Constant communication provides feedback as to the progress of the project relative to goals. Of course when a project starts everyone sees the objectives as just a matter of time to fulfillment. The opportunity to set even higher targets once the first ones are easily achieved can lead to even greater gains. Conversely, if a project encounters delays and challenges, then the continual flow of information is critical. If there is a lack of information in this second instance, expectations may need to be delicately managed.

Have Monthly Lunch Meetings to Discuss Progress and Show Results

Lunch meetings are a great approach to keeping everyone involved with the project informed, and if yours is a smaller division of a larger organization, chances are there are going to be associates interested in the progress of the project even though they don't have responsibility for its completion. In the early stages of the project, as the Web sites you are creating with an ASP are taking shape, it's a good idea to have these lunch meetings to provide an update on progress. This is essential so that you give the ASP a chance to get feedback from the individual associates who know certain aspects of your business better than anyone else. You will also lessen the resistance and increase the ownership of the project at an organizational level. Resist the inclination to not share anything until it is done—that is one of the worst things to do. Be sure to share the development's progress and actively look for feedback. You increase the chances of success for e-business initiatives by harvesting feedback from the beginning. This will help you create a sense of shared ownership as quickly as possible.

Develop Beta Versions at Password Protected URLs as Quickly as Possible

In the world of the Web you want to communicate speed of development as often as possible—as often the converse is true. Projects get bogged down and feature creep sets in, sometimes paralyzing a project. What you need to do with the ASPs that you work with is set a reasonable but aggressive pace of development to have a deliverable to show for the investment relatively quickly.

You need to build support internally and keep support going for the program. An excellent way to do this is to get the feedback of your peers and superiors on what they think. Once a beta version is available, get the URL and password out to each functional lead in your organization for their feedback. Think of this as the initiative marketing done internally before it goes live. Inevitably there will be changes, but making them mid-stream is a much better approach than having an element of the Web site or Web-based tools be launched and not fully meet the needs of those around you. Be sure to take the versions as quickly as possible and get feedback to make sure it is meeting the needs of your customers internally.

Develop an Opt-In Email Distribution for Those Interested in Progress

As the e-business initiative continues, be sure to create an internal newsletter—nothing fancy—just an email that describes what is going on with regard to the project's status. You can make this opt-in by providing a specific location where users can enter their email addresses for further HTML or ASCII-formatted mailings.

Beta Test with Real Customers Is a Must!

Many e-business projects that have quickly progressed through initial development have not launched or even thought to launch a beta test. It's the most important aspect of any e-business initiative—it provides feedback from the customers that the sites are being built to serve. Don't stop short of doing a beta test for the Web sites you are creating.

Collectively these recommendations for managing expectations might seem like a lot of work for little return. The reality of many e-business initiatives is that the teams sometimes lose track of the internal and external customers they are creating Web sites to serve. Staying focused on just the deliverable needs to guide the development overall and not letting feature creep invade the sites, yet being responsive, is the balance that needs to be achieved.

Architecting the Implementation of an e-Business Strategy

Earlier in this chapter extranets and the concepts of a VPN were discussed in terms of the market drivers that are modifying the approach many companies are taking to architecting their solutions. If your focus is primarily on creating trading and commerce exchanges between you and your trading partners, then an extranet definitely makes sense as the architectural element supporting commerce online.

Another example of companies that are actively developing extranets are those with a heavy emphasis on the direct sales model, where the majority of their sales force either operates out of regional offices or their employees' homes. IBM's direct sales force, for example, has regional managers working out of homes, as does Gartner Group with certain industry-specific analysts. The need for creating an architecture flexible enough to serve the information needs of sales people at diverse locations is driving many ASPs to become vertically focused as well. Since there is a need to differentiate what is relative to competitors on a core competency, this verticalization of ASPs is going to become even more pronounced as time progresses.

With this differentiation for ASPs and due to market dynamics, the focus on architectural structure is increasingly going to be vertically focused. Ask your ASPs you are working with what the dominant approaches are to managing the information flow between distributed members of an organization. There needs to be focus on keeping everyone informed through the online tools and applications being developed in your e-business strategy. Relying on a simple dial-up access to the Web site works for specific companies. Yet, creating an extranet can increase cost savings and enable issues to be resolved through more accurate information communicated online.

In developing the components of your e-business strategy, look for the expertise and core competency of the ASPs you are working with to provide recommendations on the use of VPNs and extranets. Your IS organization may already have plans for one, yet the security issues may need to be resolved before implementing one. If your company has a widely distributed sales force, taking the approach of creating an extranet makes sense. The value of having an extranet is accentuated if you are moving from an e-business strategy standpoint to creating an online trading exchange with your trading partners. If you are, for example, working in several international markets, a VPN can greatly reduce lag times caused by the time zones differences.

e-Marketing Goals and Direction

The basis for any excellent e-marketing implementation is giving visitors and customers the opportunity to have an interactive dialog with you about products, services, and even the company's strategic direction. Here are several metrics by which an ASP can assist you in setting objectives for performance for your company:

- **Search engine hits**—An essential element of your e-marketing site objectives needs to have a metric associated with the percentage of customers who are using your search engine relative to the total visitors to the site. This tells you whether the content headings and the design of the site are providing what's essential for the visitors and customers.

- **Content analysis of search engine hits**—Content analysis determines which content is being accessed by the search engines on your site. This needs to be included in all reports of the performance of your sites, and in fact needs to be an iterative measure of how your Web site is being tailored to the needs of your customers.

- **Page views/visitor**—Answers the question of how far visitors go into your site to find what they are looking for. This metric provides a barometer of how interesting and valuable your site's content is for the visitors. This can also be interpreted as the relative level of searching that your customers go through to get the information they need. Providing a search engine on the front page of your Web site to alleviate the need for continued searching makes this metric a relief to the frustration of trying to find information.

- **Opt-in email requests**—The first step in creating an interactive marketing campaign is giving your customers the chance to learn more about who you are and what your products and services mean for them. The idea of opt-in email requests for periodic updates of information ensures you have a chance to capture email addresses of people interested in your products. It also addresses the point of permission marketing. Opt-in is by definition the giving of the rights for distribution.

- **Demographic analysis of email requests**—In conjunction with the opportunity to get opt-in email on your site to initiate communication with your customers, having the customers respond to several questions on their demographic profile can also assist you in getting more helpful data. Check to make sure the ASPs you are considering working with have the ability to take demographic data and complete an analysis of it quickly, and that they can save the data in a format you can use for further analysis.

- **Reference URL locations**—Be sure to get an understanding with your ASP that you want to definitely know where the visitors to your site are coming from. With many companies taking on affiliate programs to drive traffic to their sites, it's important to get a metric going as to how effective these programs are at driving traffic to your sites.

- **Single hits and no activity**—If a visitor arrives at your site and doesn't continue on for further information it's important to find out why. Check to see whether the ASP you are considering working with has the ability to show the subject area from which the visitor came and where they went.

- **Click-through rates on banners**—This single statistic is the cornerstone of many business plans and strategies on the Web today. All those dot coms whose business model is based on advertising revenue rely on this metric above all others. Click-through rates on banners can also tell you the propensity to generate leads from specific banners.

- **Linked-to address growth**—In planning an e-business strategy, an essential component is the development of a partnership and alliance program. This is the statistic that tells you the strength of your alliance program and its growth over time. Many alliance programs are based on the fact that their specific URLs are linked to each other as part of the Affiliate Marketing campaigns. Amazon.com's Affiliate Marketing campaign for example is considered one of the most subscribed to, with Expedia.com and Monster.com having impressive subscription counts.

Exploring Affiliate Marketing

Just reading over the Securities and Exchange Commission (SEC) documents, which define the strengths and weaknesses of a company when they are going public, can provide a great deal of interesting information and insight into setting your own strategy. The SEC is a very rigorous regulatory agency when it comes to companies telling the truth about their business models. The SEC provides information, like the periodic statements for companies such as Amazon.com, that reveals fascinating statistics about their Affiliate Marketing campaigns. Admittedly these campaigns are just as much a marketing variable responsible for increasing brand awareness and global name recognition as the advertisements the company provides. In recent documents (which can be accessed via jump points to the Edgar database from the Amazon.com site), Amazon.com reports a significant increase in those companies participating in their Affiliate Marketing programs. Over 300,000 companies are now registered with Amazon.com within the Affiliate Marketing programs.

Clearly the role of Affiliate Marketing is to drive additional brand recognition and allow business growth through having a pervasive message, as simple as a branding button, on as many complimentary sites as possible. The recent successes of HitBox.com are another example of how the metrics of Affiliate Marketing can quickly accumulate. Visiting HitBox.com shows the power of metrics quickly as the numbers of customers are displayed on the front page of its Web site. Nothing connotes credibility as quickly as metrics do! Yet another example of this is the Sun Microsystems site with the download count of the StarOffice products. The count continues and is unequivocal in the role Sun is playing in gradually leveling the playing field in the office suite marketplace. Figure 11.4 shows an example of the Sun Microsystems Web site with the clear message of how successful are the StarOffice product branding and resulting downloads. StarOffice is a series of applications that is directly competitive with Microsoft's Office offerings.

As e-marketing and e-commerce sites seek ways to expand audience reach and generate additional revenues, many of them are turning to Affiliate Marketing as a viable solution. Amazon.com and its Associates program popularized Affiliate Marketing. The company remains the benchmark for any site launching an affiliate or associates program. Amazon.com's nearly 300,000 affiliates make it the envy of any other e-commerce merchant. As a result of Amazon.com's success, hundreds of merchants are turning their attention to Affiliate Marketing programs. It's now apparent that virtually any e-commerce merchant site can generate revenues by paying an affiliate Web site for referrals that result in sales.

Quite simply, Affiliate Marketing involves a merchant firm creating a network of affiliate sites that offer the merchant's product by creating a hyperlink to the merchant's site. The user is taken from the affiliate site directly to the merchant's site, where all electronic transactions take place. A software tool tracks the user and notes the affiliate site referral so that the merchant can then pay the affiliate a predetermined commission fee for the referral. Many ASPs have the capability of providing this service, and it should definitely be on your checklist for an e-marketing campaign. At the very least, this type of marketing approach needs to make it onto your roadmap.

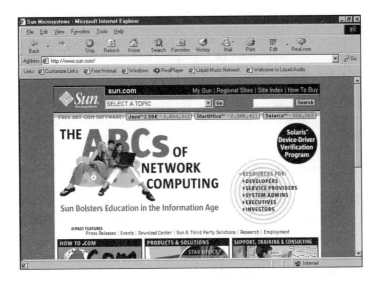

Figure 11.4   Sun's aggressive use of Affiliate Marketing is demonstrated by the free offer of StarOffice, their suite of office applications.

Given the affiliate programs' quickness in promoting sites and being an essential part of branding strategies, the need to quantify this marketing approach is obvious. The best estimates of the market sizing today and its growth for the future come from International Data Corporation, which has quantified the market with the figures shown in Table 11.1.

Table 11.1   U.S. consumer e-commerce affiliate sales, 1998–2003 ($M)

Affiliate	1998	1999	2000	2001	2002	2003
Consumer e-commerce spending	14,688.36	30,400.28	49,540.94	76,096.79	113,884.78	175,583.34
Sales from sites with affiliate programs (%)	22	31	40	48	53	56
Total affiliate merchant revenues	**3,231.44**	**9,424.09**	**19,816.38**	**36,526.46**	**60,358.93**	**98,326.67**
Affiliate sales (%)	20	22	24	26	27	27
Total affiliate-generated sales	**646.29**	**2,073.30**	**4,755.93**	**9,496.88**	**16,296.91**	**26,548.20**

Source: International Data Corporation, 1999

Two of the most alluring aspects of Affiliate Marketing are that it increases impulse buys and strengthens branding. This program is one of the most economical ways for accomplishing the following objectives, all starting with a basic e-marketing focus in your e-business strategy:

- **Increase revenues**—As the numbers of affiliates grow, so does the opportunity to increase growth with incremental revenues.

- **Extend audience reach**—Each affiliate added is just like bringing on an additional salesperson. You suddenly have additional salespeople at locations throughout the Web you could not reach on your own.

- **Pay for performance**—Commissions are based only on sales, which means there are no incremental marketing costs associated with each additional affiliate.

- **Alliance-building**—By establishing alliances with affiliates early on, merchants can create a lasting relationship that will continue to generate affiliate referrals over time.

Deciding Whether Affiliate Programs Make Sense for Your Company

With companies extending their reach and multiplying the chances of increasing sales, Affiliate Marketing seems to be a can't lose proposition. What does it take to be successful at affiliate programs? Here are the characteristics of companies that have successfully integrated Affiliate Marketing programs into their overall e-marketing campaigns:

- **Products that are mass-consumption items**—It stands to reason that Jaguar, the car manufacturer, does not have a renowned affiliate program while K-Tel.com does. The difference is obviously the premium-pricing strategy of Jaguar relative to the more common and everyday needs of the majority of users of the Web. Affiliate Marketing works best when a broad and distributed customer base is involved.

- **Focusing on recruitment of affiliates**—It is imperative to launch an aggressive campaign to recruit affiliates upon the introduction of an affiliate program, even if the firm is using a network-owned affiliate model from affiliate program providers.

- **Defining affiliate standards**—Defining the level of standards for affiliate participation will also dictate how much time will be taken with managing the program itself. The higher the standards, the more monitoring has to occur. In the case of a new company just entering a marketplace, the need for having a consistent branding message is crucial; therefore, the monitoring of activities needs to be thorough.

- **Strength of the incentives**—Having an affiliate that does not generate any revenues is of very little value. Consequently, the merchant firm must reward successful affiliates with appropriate incentives. Affiliates should have ongoing access to the site's latest marketing campaigns, special offers, and promotional content.

- **Tracking capabilities**—Your site must have the technological infrastructure to monitor affiliate click-through rates and sales generated by each affiliate in real time. In working with your ASP, it's essential to check and see that this type of data is available. It is the responsibility of your ASP to ensure that each affiliate should have access to the latest referral sales data, payment information, and performance benchmarks.
- **Making affiliate payments**—Your ASP needs to define the payment schedule and parameters for all affiliates upon sign up. As an affiliate program grows, the challenge of keeping up with payments for several hundred thousand affiliates can be quite daunting.

Seeking out an ASP with an expertise in this area is worth the investment, because the tasks associated with this type of program are significant. It's far better to have an ASP assist with the monitoring and administration of affiliate programs than trying to do it on your own. The great news is that it is a worthwhile use of resources in terms of expanding your company's presence and also generating potential sales leads and brand loyalty.

According to a number of merchants, affiliate programs often follow the 80/20 rule, whereby the top 20% of affiliates generates 80% of revenues. Consequently, the remaining affiliates only account for 20% of revenues. Therefore, it is recommended that merchants automate their affiliate programs for the bulk of affiliates while providing a dedicated account manager to work with the top tier of affiliate partners.

Where Affiliate Programs Are Headed

Clearly, there is significant opportunity to differentiate yourself from your competitors by using an affiliate marketing campaign. What is important is to find an ASP partner who knows how to handle this type of program and implement it for maximum results.

Banner advertising has been the primary method of drawing traffic to an e-commerce site, but many merchants recognize that banner advertising campaigns have been relatively ineffective and must be considered as only one piece of a broader marketing campaign. A wide-reaching, integrated marketing campaign in conjunction with an ASP will yield the most effective results for any company working to expand sales on the Web. Lowering the cost of customer acquisition, however, will remain a key challenge for all e-marketing and e-commerce sites.

Creating an affiliate network can be extremely time consuming, expensive, and technically challenging. Because most e-commerce merchants cannot afford to dedicate the time and money to develop these programs on their own, it is recommended that companies seriously consider third-party service providers.

e-Commerce Goals and Direction

With the set of metrics that will be used for describing clearly the goals of your e-marketing strategy defined, you are ready to begin the next step of your e-business strategy: to define an e-commerce strategy.

Starting with the basics of handling a transaction online and then progressing through the development of supply chains and the streamlining of transactions, e-commerce is the area of e-business that has the most volatility associated with it today. Clearly ASPs are needing to differentiate themselves now more than ever before, so expect to see the functionality and depth of features delivered with e-commerce applications become more robust over time. The major e-commerce application is the catalog. Where just two product generations ago this included only the ability to list products and pictures of them, today catalogs encompass links to legacy data, and several play a critical role in e-procurement application integration.

Just as much of a transformation is happening in e-commerce as well. The simple definition of an electronically enabled transaction is actually just part of the picture for e-commerce. According to the American National Standards Institute, the working definition of e-commerce from the user's perspective includes the following steps:

1. Information gathering
2. Engagement
3. Negotiation
4. Transaction
5. Fulfillment
6. Support

Whether the process occurs in the electronic or physical world, these basic processes are moved through during a complete transaction cycle. While in the physical world this sequence of steps is in linear order, it often is parallel in terms of online implementation.

Metrics Associated with e-Commerce

Defining the direction of your e-commerce strategy in terms of the measurable is one of the better approaches to managing your ASP to deliver the results you expect. Here are metrics that are commonly used for measuring the level of success step by step in an e-commerce transaction.

Information gathering:

- **Cumulative downloads of PDF files**   These are the brochures and product literature on your Web site. While this might appear to be e-marketing, this is one metric that can tell the level of interest by product area. Taking these results and correlating them back to actual product sales shows the effectiveness of your site at guiding customers to what they need.

- **Hits by product page**—Defines the number of hits by page for the specific products as well.

Engagement:

- **Pages of catalog accessed**—Defines the relative level of interest a visitor has with the products on your site.
- **Queries by product**—It is useful to cross-reference this metric back to the number of a particular product sold. This defines the close rate per product.

Negotiation:

- **Use of auction site by product**—In the case of using auctions, this metric defines how often a given product is bid on.
- **Compare function used**—If your existing e-commerce site does not have a comparison function included, consider adding it. Its functionality will save visitors to your site from leaving just to check another site. Of course there needs to be credibility in the product comparisons to drive incremental sales.
- **Percentage of time comparison function used**—Looking at how much time a visitor spends comparing products and shopping on your site can tell you which products need to have specials associated with them that will bring customers to your site.

Transaction:

- **Transactions attempted**—Defines how often a visitor tried to purchase from your Web site.
- **Transactions completed**—The number of transactions that are fulfilled and the product or service order.
- **Percentage of time a transaction is cancelled by user**—This will tell you whether the purchasing process needs to be modified to make ordering easier.
- **Reasons for transactions cancellation**—Provides an opportunity for the customer to explain why the transaction did not fulfill their needs.

Fulfillment:

- **Percentage of orders shipped on time**—This is a measure of how responsive your e-commerce site is to the needs of customers who ordered products.
- **Percentage of orders backlogged**—Looking at this metric by product tells you how to best manage the product inventories you have.
- **Returned shipments due to misshipment**—Shows the operational efficiency of the logistics systems handling orders.
- **Percentage of shipments by freight method**—Useful for determining opportunities for future alliances and asking for preferred pricing based on the level of activity.

- **Percentage of out-of-stock messages**—Defines the accuracy of product forecasting systems at being able to track what's needed by economic order quantity.

Support:

- **Emails per transaction count**—Defines the number of emails per order.

What to Expect from Your ASPs When It Comes to e-Commerce

In working with your ASPs to create an e-commerce solution, they should be able to handle ongoing management of the site, rapid development of the site itself, and the ability to manage tracking metrics to gauge performance. The ASPs you are working with should have the ability to monitor these metrics and provide a URL where you can track their performance at any time. Although some may not yet have instant access to the metrics, the trend in the market is definitely in that direction. The quantification of e-commerce performance is essential for the growth of your e-business strategy.

What's happening in the ASP marketplace is actually very fortuitous for companies thinking about outsourcing their e-commerce initiatives. The competition between Internet services companies and the traditional application service provider arena is intensifying the need to bring greater value to customers through excellent service. Although the need for e-commerce is large (and according to International Data Corporation, growing at 60% per year through 2003), there is still the competitive aspects of winning business—especially for many ASPs as they get up and running. For many ASPs, every customer counts.

In the context of the competitive differences between Internet service providers and ASPs, Table 11.2 shows the differences between their offerings.

Table 11.2   **Differences between e-commerce ASP and Internet services**

Internet Services	e-Commerce ASP Services
Custom-developed projects	Projects with minimal customization
Fees due in a lump-sum payment	Fees due on a monthly schedule over several years
Provides consulting and implementation services	Provides implementation and operation services
Longer projects	Shorter projects

Source: International Data Corporation, 2000

Even though e-commerce ASP services will be sold as a substitute to Internet services, don't expect it to always be so clear cut. IDC, for example, expects that as a result of the ASPs becoming a competitive pressure in the market, more Internet service firms will be taking on characteristics similar to those of ASPs.

e-Operations Goals and Direction

Cost reduction strategies are required for making e-business investments have an impact on the bottom line of a business. e-Operations metrics define a company by their ability to execute on logistics, CRM, and sales force automation strategies, as well as their payoff for taking an e-procurement strategy into action. The cost savings of the Internet are exemplified in the area of e-operations. Its streamlined logistics is one of the areas showing the greatest potential for contributing to the financial growth of a company.

Here are several key trends that are driving the adoption of e-operations solutions. Keep these in mind as you write an e-business strategy to provide a frame of reference:

- **Supply chain optimization plays a central role**—The value-adds of carriers no longer merely lie in physical-based truck and warehousing services but extend to engineering their clients' business processes. Furthermore, some carriers have chosen to develop their own proprietary technologies and software applications to assist them in redesigning and enhancing their clients' logistics business process.

- **e-Logistics emerge**—The Internet will have a profound impact on the logistics service marketplace. Increasingly, systems and services will be positioned as IP-based and Internet-centric to optimize the availability and distribution of the highly complex information and data that drive the growth and development of the logistics marketplace.

- **Global capabilities become more important**—As more and more United States-based corporations outsource their manufacturing activities and expand business opportunities overseas, logistics providers will be called on to serve expanded needs in a global marketplace. Thus, the logistics services players in the market will face a new set of challenges at many levels, including local government rules and regulations, infrastructure changes, human resource shortages, and cultural and language barriers.

- **Growth and consolidation are crucial**—For logistics providers to achieve the size and scale necessary to be competitive partnerships and alliances will clearly be critical. Currently, at least 20 large national players are in this space. If all the logistics, transportation and warehousing, and freight forwarding-related companies are considered, including regional players and hundreds of carrier-based organizations, there are many more potential companies to join in alliances aimed at providing more efficient e-fullfillment for businesses worldwide. Given the regional nature of many of these companies, the benefits of alliances and partnerships are clear.

Exploring e-Procurement Applications

In looking toward the development of an e-procurement component in your e-business strategy, the definitions of various classes of applications are essential for defining what you want delivered by your ASP.

The Internet procurement market is composed of four major segments:

- Buy-side applications
- Sell-side applications
- Catalog conversion
- Trading community

Internet Procurement Buy-Side Applications

The Internet commerce buy-side procurement application market covers software applications written to allow an entity to conduct business-to-business transactions over the Internet with another entity. Buy-side procurement applications are geared toward buying entities such as the purchasing department of a bank or a hotel.

Internet Commerce Sell-Side Procurement Applications

Though sell-side procurement applications have functions similar to those of buy-side applications, they are primarily marketed to sellers that want to automate the process of connecting to their business buyers. For example, a number of computer distributors install applications that allow their corporate customers to use the Internet to look up items, place orders, and settle payments under pre-negotiated contract prices.

Catalog Conversion Procurement Applications

The automation of supplier catalogs into an electronic format for the broadest number of user organizations is the domain of catalog conversion procurement applications.

Trading Community Procurement Applications

Applications that are designed to build either vertical or horizontal market portals are called trading community procurement applications. Think of this as "infrastructure" software, providing tools to build a trading community. Examples of this are Plastics.com and Metals.com.

CRM and Sales Force Automation Key Trends and Applications

The principal criterion for defining a successful partnership with an ASP that has the ability to deliver CRM and sales force automation applications is their ability to deliver value on each of the following aspects of their business models. Those ASPs capable of staying focused on their CRM applications will exhibit the following attributes:

- **Strength of partnerships**—With the evolution of the customer-centric economy, the CRM market is still at the beginning of ramping up to its true potential. Partnerships with strong firms are key for success in this market.

- **Breadth of geographic coverage**—Many of the leading CRM firms are currently located on the West Coast of the United States. Make sure your CRM vendor of choice and the ASP delivering the application has the ability to be globally focused.

- **Participation and success in vertical industries**—Currently, almost all of these firms have gone to the market focusing on dot-com clients; there has not been much of a vertical industry focus. Given that customer care issues tend to vary across vertical industries, there is significant potential for the development of specialized knowledge bases for vertical industries. For example, a financial services end user will require a lot more customer assistance than someone buying a book over the Internet.

- **Expertise in staffing**—Staffing contact centers and Call Center Representative training are important issues. With the advent of real-time communication, the CSR becomes the main point of contact between the client and the customer. Each of these customer interactions is an important opportunity to build brand and loyalty and to up-sell customers, dramatically increasing the pressure on the CSR. Recently there have been companies specializing in re-engineering call centers, alleviating the turnover in personnel, which has at times affected call center effectiveness.

- **Ability to meet client criteria**—Important criteria for clients choosing between systems include price, time to implement, scalability, ability to integrate, solution flexibility, understanding of the business, and in the case of customer interaction specialists, the quality of the CSRs.

- **Understanding of the customer life cycle**—Customer support and retention is becoming the most prominent part of the customer life cycle, with most of the customer interaction specialists profiled in this report providing one form or another of customer support.

- **Business to business (B2B) expertise**—B2B growth is one of the hottest phenomena seen in recent times. Forecasts for B2B growth are getting larger each year. Companies such as FaceTime have only just started exploring customer care in this market by developing products that facilitate communications between buyers and sellers, suppliers and distributors.

- **Value-added services**—Related services include companies' development of consulting and systems integration wings to help clients establish a customer care system that best suits their needs.

Conversely, check with the ASPs you are considering partnering with and see what their health is relative to the following threats now appearing in the CRM marketplace:

- **Excessive customer churn**—If your ASP is experiencing a high level of customer churn you definitely want to save yourself from being a statistic. Work toward understanding whether the ASPs you are working with have churned customers or whether they have worked in the CRM arena in the past.

- **Customer interaction repository problems**—It is key for ASPs to have the ability to integrate their knowledge bases with previously existing systems or with systems from other vendors. Some ASPs are just learning or barely getting by on this. Be sure to check, especially when customer data is involved, that the ASPs you are considering working with have this as an expertise that has been proven over time.

- **Imminent consolidations and acquisitions**—One of the more common reasons why ASPs sometimes have trouble delivering a CRM solution is because of a merger or acquisition of their firm. While many companies can stay focused during the ongoing development of new business, it's important to get the necessary support and accountability to ensure your project isn't slowed down.

e-Operations metrics for gauging performance

In creating your e-operations strategy there are many metrics that you can include for tracking the performance of applications leased from your ASP. Here are several of the key metrics that need to be included in your e-business strategy. Literally thousands of metrics in e-operations are applicable by the application used, so check with the ASPs you are working with for additional measures of performance:

- **Time to complete transaction**—In the world of e-procurement the ability to streamline performance on this metric is critical.

- **Average response time to query**—In the CRM and SFA areas this is the time taken to respond back to a customer's request for information through an automated means.

- **Average response time to logistics carrier request**—This is the average time for your carriers to service your customers (a measure of responsiveness you need to watch to ensure customer satisfaction).

- **Average lead-time by product**—This is an important statistic for telling how responsive your suppliers are in keeping your warehouses full of products. This is another important stat for checking in on customer satisfaction.

- **Net sales history per month by customer**—Relative level of sales productivity per salesperson.

- **Average sales history per month by customer**—Defines the relative level of growth, decline, or steady state of a customers' account.

e-Business Strategy Components

The development of a strategy for your e-business is in many respects identical to the one you would use for creating an entirely new division of your company. The focus on the electronic component of the strategy is what makes the entire process more urgent. Also, it accentuates the need for more accuracy. Following this outline provides you with the basis for creating the necessary foundation for going forward with an e-business strategy with your ASPs:

I.   Executive Summary

II.   Market Dynamics and Roadmap

Essential to define how the roadmap is based on the needs of customers.

Also defines the market assumptions and minimum metrics for the e-marketing and e-commerce sections of the Web sites planned.

III.   e-Marketing Plan

Defines the objectives for the e-marketing part of your Web site and the metrics associated with each of the interactive communications planned for the site. This section should also include a roadmap of when search, opt-in email, alerts, and affiliate marketing will be added to your site.

IV.   e-Commerce Plan

Defines the scope of the catalog being developed and the extent of the metrics defined earlier in this chapter. This section also has a specific roadmap for the e-commerce initiatives planned for the future.

V.   e-Operations Plan

Describes the objectives and the role of each component of e-operations, potentially including e-procurement, CRM and sales force automation, and e-logistics. This is a plan that also defines metrics of responsiveness with both customers and suppliers, which is critical to this procurement function. This plan also has a roadmap specific for e-operations enhancements.

VI.   Fulfillment Plan

Defines the steps of how the site will be delivered.

VII.   Launch Plan

Includes the entire plan for introducing the new site to the company and the outside world.

VIII.   Internet Product Strategy Roadmap

Companies are increasingly working to develop products that are orderable over the Web in a very efficient manner. Shaquelle O'Neill's `dunk.net` is an example of a site that is entirely focused on its product strategy toward athletic apparel and merchandise that is easily sold and fulfilled from a Web site. Mr. O'Neill's approach to blending content with commerce is what e-commerce sites will look like in the future, because consumers look for both interesting information and a chance to purchase products while enjoying the shopping experience.

IX.   Appendices

Financial Projects

Side-Stepping the Hype of e-Business

There are several common misconceptions about e-business that often lead to flawed e-business strategies. Channel conflict and a failed e-business initiative are common results. Gartner Group's analysts recently completed an analysis of the hype factor in e-business. Relying on metrics is the best approach for getting the unequivocal results you are looking for.

The combination of unprecedented media coverage and vendor advertisements regarding e-business has created an atmosphere in which otherwise intelligent business managers have developed strategies that have no hope of success. These strategies would pale in the face of traditional financial analysis, but because everyone is convinced they must operate at "Internet speed," traditional analysis is often bypassed. A top executive at one of the world's largest corporations announced the creation of a supply-side marketplace exploiting e-procurement (in itself, a very promising undertaking). The press also reported an offhand comment made by the executive that the corporation would no longer use its traditional business analysis procedures on e-business initiatives because e-business did not provide sufficient time for such practices. Such press reports have helped generate a propensity among business planners to leap before they look.

Last year, Gartner Group published the following SPA: "By 2005, e-business will account for as much as 10% of global GDP (0.7 probability)." It would have been logically equivalent to say "Through 2005, 90% of the global GDP will be generated without e-business (0.7 probability)." The latter is just as accurate and emphasizes the importance of protecting brick-and-mortar operations while integrating e-business into the enterprise.

The early coverage of Amazon.com also created misconceptions. Here was an Internet start-up that took on established competitors and was about to knock them out of the box. In reality, Amazon.com has yet to turn a profit (as opposed to Barnes & Noble or Borders Books). Amazon has recently indicated that its book operations are now profitable. However, it is hardly a pure Internet company anymore. It has more than three-million square feet of warehouse space and is making a substantial investment in IT infrastructure to automate it. By the time Amazon finishes creating its infrastructure and its brick-and-mortar competitors integrate e-business into their enterprises, it may be very difficult to differentiate Amazon from the competition. They will all be hybrid enterprises.

Nonetheless, the illusion that traditional retail outlets can be easily disintermediated has been created. Managers who do not understand exactly how this can be done believe that magic will occur "if we just know enough about e-business." They will sell all their products through this wonderful new channel called the Internet. Combine that misconception with the lack of fact-based financial analysis from the first misconception and the stage is set for trouble.

Bottom Line—Massive misinformation has caused managers to push into direct product sales over the Web in inappropriate situations. The lack of realistic financial analysis of the impact of channel conflict has led to flawed e-business strategies. Enterprises are advised to use quick but comprehensive quantitative analysis to evaluate the impact of e-business strategies on revenue and costs.

The experiences of publishing, as well as other industries, suggest a number of Internet axioms applicable across a range of supply networks.

Axiom No. 1: Inefficient Supply Networks Are at Risk

The story of the publishing industry demonstrates the degree of inefficiency that has accrued over decades, such as the practice of returning over-ordered books. The Web book retailing model eliminates the need for display inventory and improves forecasting of real demand. As a result, Amazon.com can deliver a book with inventory investments at 15% to 20% of a traditional player's, while lowering returns to 3% from around 30%. But to date, Amazon.com has only tapped part of the power of the model.

Axiom No. 2: First-Movers Gain Advantage from Scale

By attacking inefficient supply networks, the e-tailer has room to make mistakes in the early phases of startup. As Amazon.com showed, by tapping the pent-up demand for online buying, first-movers can gain market share and economies of scale. During this phase, the biggest challenge comes from other Internet startups targeting the same inefficient network rather than from traditional retailers. High on-time delivery represents a top priority during this phase. (For evidence, note that on-time delivery is one of three key metrics used to judge e-tailers by BizRate.com, the self-appointed e-business rating service. The other two metrics are an overall rating and the BizRate.com rebate percentage.)

Axiom No. 3: New Delivery Systems Require Big Investments

Scale and first-mover advantages help companies survive the shakeout phase. But eventually, the Web retailers must compete head-on with the well-established traditional retail model. For long-term survival, the e-tailer needs to deliver goods in a cost-effective and timely way. Although the Web model avoids the need for physical retail space, backroom operations don't just go away. Amazon.com, which now sells much more than books, operates over two million square feet of warehouse space—over 2.5 times the amount operated by Ingram, the largest book distributor in the United States—and more space is coming.

Axiom No. 4: Defining New Distribution Structures Is Vital

Because the Internet advantage manifests in distribution economics, the decision to build new capacity or buy existing distributors requires a rigorous strategic assessment.

Initially, startups may need only a single national distribution center. But as an operation grows, successful Web retailers will need regional distribution centers to optimize supply economics. For example, in 1999, Amazon.com built its sixth fulfillment operation in the United States: An 800,000-square-foot facility in McDonough, Ga.(a long way from its original 93,000-square-foot facility in Seattle, Washington).

Case Study: How Buy.com Changed Direct Sales with an e-Business Strategy

The growth of the Internet has dramatically changed the way consumers purchase goods. The limits of traditional business—limited operating hours and confined geographies are gone. They have been replaced by 24/7 online businesses serving a large, informed audience. Buy.com is the leading Internet superstore, offering a comprehensive selection of brand name items through their ten specialty stores. With the number of shoppers visiting their stores, buy.com needs a platform that drives their e-business by connecting the front-end Web site to back-end ordering, processing and shipping. With the help of Microsoft Windows 2000, buy.com can give their customers the best online experience.

"As we have grown from infancy to adolescence as a business, we are constantly reviewing our technical infrastructure," says Tony McAlister, vice president of information services for buy.com. "Buy.com needed a platform that is reliable, scalable and secure while keeping costs down. After an extensive research process, we decided that Windows 2000 was the best option."

Reliability is key in the realm e-commerce and Windows 2000 delivers for buy.com. "The beauty of the Internet is that if a product is for sale, you can find it," says Greg Hawkins, CEO and president of buy.com. "If your site is open and reliable, then your customers can count on you to be there. At buy.com, making products available 24/7 is our business model."

"We are driving toward a goal of 99.999% system uptime, up virtually 100% of the time," states McAlister. "Buy.com's consumers need to be able to come to our store 100% of the time." Windows 2000 allowed buy.com to develop an architecture in which they can perform maintenance on some servers while keeping the running site for online visitors. This flexibility will help buy.com achieve their goal.

"We currently have the system architected to 99.99%. With Windows 2000, we are hoping to achieve that other nine," says McAllister.

"Our decision was focused less on who could run our business today, but on who could partner with us down the road. Windows 2000 is a platform that gives us the tools we need to get our company to where we hope to be someday soon," says Hawkins.

Buy.com is a leading Internet superstore, offering a comprehensive selection of brand name computer hardware and peripherals, software, books, videos, DVDs, computer games, music, and surplus equipment at everyday low prices. Through ten online specialty stores, buy.com offers more than 850,000 products in a convenient, intuitive shopping interface that features extensive product information and multimedia presentations. Buy.com's e-commerce portal, www.buy.com, links all ten specialty stores and is designed to enhance the customer's online shopping experience 24 hours a day, 7 days a week.

Summary

Taking on the task of building an e-business strategy is easily accomplished by taking a modular approach to its development. The components of an e-business strategy are defined in this chapter, along with the necessary metrics for ensuring the best possible level of performance will be attained. With any e-business strategy there is also the need for getting the most out of the existing infrastructure and tying back metrics to existing systems performance to see the advantages of taking on an e-business strategy. This chapter is specifically developed in the context of a corporation taking on the task of beginning an e-business strategy without departing from the core strengths of a business beforehand. It is a point of contention that e-commerce experts argue that your whole company needs to be re-engineered and that e-business is not a bolt-on. This chapter is focused on the fact that an e-business strategy is not existing on its own, yet it can be complementary to the existing objectives of your business today. Collectively an e-business strategy is a series of tools for making the goals in your business more accomplishable at a faster rate. Subsystems and legacy data are always a concern, yet the emerging expertise in the ASP community is definitely showing strength in this area. It's not necessary to completely re-construct your company from the ground up; rather take the core competencies of today and extend them through e-business.

12

Knowing You Are Doing It Right: Measuring Results

EVERY BUSINESS ULTIMATELY COMPETES with itself over time to show growth, progression, and most importantly, an increasingly higher level of responsiveness and service to customers. Ultimately you will know the story of a business by reviewing its financial statements, customer counts, customer satisfaction levels, repeat customers, size of sales orders, productivity per salesperson, and net increase in sales from quarter to quarter.

When discussing metrics to gauge performance of an e-business initiative, two dominant thoughts emerge. The first is what gets measured gets better, as increased focus on a given area can greatly increase the chances for success. One of the great strengths of Intel Corporation, for example, is its internal cultural value of quantifying everything associated with a product and decision. Intel is a master at quantifying decisions.

The second dominant thought is that the only true approach you can take to competing with yourself is the measure of where you are as an organization today and where you want to be, in quantitative terms, in the future. Many individuals measure themselves by the pounds they lose right after the beginning of the year, and if they are in a sales role, very often how many sales they have generated during the last month. What gets measured is the basis of self-competition for the future. The best companies in the world acutely know they need to compete ruthlessly against themselves to make themselves stronger for competing with other companies.

Focusing on metrics takes any business away from the hype. Perhaps the greatest contribution of quantitative methods in business is that numbers, grounded in solid methodologies, illustrate the unequivocal reality of how a business is performing. Too often companies new to working with the Web take the seven- and eight-digit market figures and extrapolate market share and resulting sales, and then profitability. This is like taking the distance between Chicago and San Francisco and saying if you drive 80 mph you can make the trip in the perfect equation of 2,143 miles divided by 80 mph yielding trip duration of 26.78 hours. Although some college students might be able to go for 26.78 hours straight and stop only for coffee and Big Macs, most travelers would stop for sightseeing, side excursions, and spending a night or even two on the road. The point of this analogy is that the same metrics exist for the road warrior students as the middle-aged couple taking a leisurely pace—both cover the same distance, yet the pace and even the intention are widely different.

Metrics cannot be seen in isolation, but must be used as signposts along the journey a company undertakes to arrive at its e-business goal. The students might see themselves as true road warriors if they can get to Chicago in less than 30 hours from their departure point in downtown San Francisco, whereas the middle-aged couple will see a two-day drive and an almost vacation-like feel to the trip being next to nirvana. The metrics of e-business must be seen in the same way.

Thousands of dotcoms want to get their page counts to the multi-million count ASAP and see themselves as Web warriors, thereby creating a strong advertising model in the process. Given the rate of change, this is absolutely essential for companies with advertising-based business models; they must be Web warriors to survive. Yet for many other companies, the road to e-business success is managed as an essential part of their business with balance to both visitor-to-customer transitions being critical. Metrics are relative measures; however, they definitely bring the real situation to bear for a company, and the quantified performance of an organization is essential for it to grow and prosper.

Metrics of Success in e-Business: How ASPs and Their Customers Measure Themselves

Today the need for Service Level Agreements or SLAs is stronger than ever before in the ASP industry because performance to expectation is often a matter of verbal and written contracts that include explicit metric parameters, depending on the ASP offering the service. Strive for metrics of performance that ensure your e-business objectives generate a baseline of performance in your actual contract and your SLA with the application service provider. From this baseline of performance, you can create a strong sense of how you are performing at turning visitors at your site into repeat customers. Being committed to metrics provides you the roadmap to replicate your marketing, sales, and operations successes.

Too often companies that embark on e-business strategies need to experiment and do trial and error to see what works at a tactical level to accomplish their strategic objectives. Cutting through the trial and error by knowing the metrics of what has worked in the past can save a tremendous amount of time.

Ultimately the objectives of any e-business initiative are to generate incremental revenue and cut production costs. Figure 12.1 shows a visitor to your site progressing to repeat customer, and ultimately becoming a loyal customer. (Read the chart in the clockwise direction.)

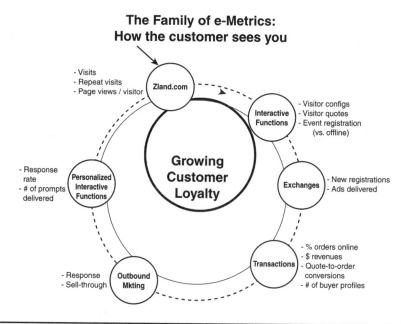

**The Family of e-Metrics:
How the customer sees you**

- Visits
- Repeat visits
- Page views / visitor

Zland.com

Interactive
Functions
- Visitor configs
- Visitor quotes
- Event registration
  (vs. offline)

- Response
  rate
- # of prompts
  delivered

Personalized
Interactive
Functions

**Growing
Customer
Loyalty**

Exchanges
- New registrations
- Ads delivered

Transactions
- % orders online
- $ revenues
- Quote-to-order
  conversions
- # of buyer profiles

- Response
- Sell-through

Outbound
Mkting

Figure 12.1   This graphic illustrates the progression of visitors to your site turning into customers and ultimately into loyal customers.

Notice the metrics around the outer parts of the circle. These metrics speak to the responsiveness level shown to visitors as they progress to become customers, and from customers to loyal and hopefully raving fans for your products and services. The quantified results of their repeated interactions with you are actually a collective barometer of how you are doing as an e-businessperson in concert with the ASPs you choose to work with to get the various tools in place for handling each of the information and product exchanges around the circle.

Review the family of e-metrics by briefly looking at each of the metrics associated with each step around the circle. Starting with your Web site, which would be in the circle titled Zland.com, the key metrics are to the left of the circle. Visits, Repeat visits, and Page views/visitor are the metrics initially used for defining basic traffic. Because there has been no previous interaction with the person visiting the site, the biggest challenge is to turn the visitor into a customer by providing compelling content on your site. As visitors progress around this circle in clockwise fashion, the content of the site actually becomes more tailored to their specific needs, and in turn gives you additional insights into their preferences. This circle then represents the progression of a Web site's product strategy away from a vanilla-like, one-size-fits-all site to a more personalized approach to delivering content and value. In many respects the Yahoo! and Amazon.com product strategies have pioneered the progression of visitors to their sites into customers, and in turn, loyal buyers.

The progression around the circle is actually a definition of the processes needed for building loyalty with your customers. Notice the Exchanges area, where new registrations and ads delivered are measured. This is a further step up from the Interactive Functions of a site, and leads to the actual completion of a transaction.

Taking the data from customers logging into the Exchanges area and tailoring a customized experience directly contributes to the Outbound Marketing steps shown in the fifth bubble. At this point the response rate and sell-through data for response rate information is collected and used for predicting adoption of the next step, which is the Personalized Interactive Functions. Metrics for measuring personalization continue to be taken to another level through the efforts of Amazon.com, Yahoo!, and in the financial services area, MySchwab.com. Clearly, personalization will be the differentiator in many e-commerce plans for the future, in conjunction with more focused and strengthened customer service and support.

In summary, metrics associated with the building of a transaction online actually embody the voice of customers as they progress from being visitors. You can learn a lot about your own levels of responsiveness and your ability to serve customers by using these metrics. Over time, you can also define minimum levels of performance for these metrics, even giving operations managers, departments, or divisions the autonomy of being creative about how to accomplish the metrics.

A final note on the progression of visitors to customers, and the effect of metrics on helping make the transition as effortless as possible is illustrated by the commitment of the United Kingdoms' transportation authorities. When you visit the London Underground, you will see that each of "the tubes" (as the underground transportation stations there are called) shows the percentage of trips that are on-time by location. This is a useful metric because it shows when you have the best chance to get to your destination by the stated times. A simple bar chart sets the expectations in measured performance over the last 90 days. It's a useful metric in terms of planning for using this popular form of public transportation. Despite the occasional delays, the Underground continues to attract the majority of commuters in London because the environment is kept clean, the metrics are accurate and real, and the expectations are communicated through a simple chart.

Ascertaining Return on Investment for e-Commerce Initiatives

Although personalization has become popular, there is some question as to its level of effectiveness. Generating a positive return on investment is actually contingent on several factors, many of which are defined by an ASP on a merchant-by-merchant basis.

ASPs that provide personalization options have consistently focused on assisting customers in accomplishing these objectives:

- Increase revenues per transaction (multiple product purchases per transaction)
- Increase the opportunity for cross-sell and/or up-sell of products (suggestions of specific products based on user profile/previous purchasing behavior)
- Increase the conversion ratio of visitors to buyers
- Increase repeat buyers (increasing the lifetime value of a customer)
- Increase ad-targeting effectiveness (customizing ads based on behavior or profile)
- Gain a clear understanding of users' behavior and preferences

Gradually, the Internet industry has begun to recognize that you can define a return on the resources (both monetary and non-monetary). The days of just investing in the Internet "because everyone else is" are over. It's all about having a strategy that you fully intend to see some traction from in your core businesses, and ultimately see an impact on your net income. Certain companies have the propensity to generate a higher return on investment more quickly than others. Take for example software companies that have a sales per employee in the $250,000 range or higher. This key metric of sales level and growth over time is a barometer as to the financial health of a company. Many companies have internal targets for the return on investment that are defined by both the CEO's expectations and the abilities of the company to drive revenue and margins profitably. The metrics associated with a company, in conjunction with the competitiveness of its products and the influence of a CEO's expectations all drive the minimum acceptable level of return on investment. Table 12.1 shows the results of a series of studies completed by International Data Corporation aimed at defining the feasibility of measuring Internet ROI, and what factors contribute to a greater ROI over time.

Given the phenomenal success of Dell Computers and Gateway, the direct model has proven itself the primary differentiator between companies that quickly get a return on their Internet investments relative to others. The ability to market online products with a mass appeal (books, computers, PC hardware and software) is also a major differentiator between those companies that get their velocity of transactions up and their costs down through operational efficiencies. Companies with a strong focus on a direct model to large audiences have a decidedly strong advantage relative to other companies.

Table 12.1 **Factors that contribute to faster returns on e-commerce investment**

Criteria	Weighting
Direct sales model	High
Popular industry products desired by a large number of consumers	High
Large potential customer universe	High

Table 12.1   **Continued**

Criteria	Weighting
Product lines that offer strong	Medium to high cross-sell and up-sell opportunities
No trial period required for	Medium to high purchase
Potential for high number of	Medium to high units per transaction sale
Opportunity for targeted marketing	Medium to high across multiple product lines
Many product offerings	Medium
Low pricing	Medium
Partial ad-based revenue model	Medium to low
Minimal sales assistance required	Low for purchase

Exploring Media Metrix: Hits Do Not a Customer Make

Media Metrix is a leading provider of Internet and Digital Media measurement products and services and has built a strong reputation as the standard by which Web usage is measured. Specifically, this company measures activity on the World Wide Web, proprietary online services such as America Online, software, and instant messaging applications, and other digital applications. Media Metrix has established itself as the leading provider of metrics in the industry today, and was the first in this market arena.

Since the introduction of its first reports on Web activity in January 1996, Media Metrix has established themselves as one of the leading providers of performance rankings for the industry. Their most well-distributed report is the World Wide Web Audience Measurement report, which has a widespread audience in the e-commerce, advertising, and technology measurement services provider industry segments. Media Metrix is one of the main companies used by companies to buy, sell, and plan advertising; support marketing and commerce initiatives; assess partnerships and distribution strategies; and analyze competitors.

Media Metrix collects Internet audience data by measuring Internet usage from representative samples, or panels, of personal computer users with proprietary tracking technology. The company maintains large panels of randomly selected professionals, reporting Internet usage at home and at work. Panelists are randomly recruited to participate in the Media Metrix sample. They are required to fill out a detailed questionnaire to provide background demographic information at the individual and household level. Panelists download and install Media Metrix tracking software onto their PCs. The tracking software tracks all PC usage at the individual user level. The tracking software follows the panelists, page-by-page, minute-by-minute, click-by-click, as they use their PCs. The usage data is then collected from the panelists' personal computers and transmitted to the Media Metrix data collection center for processing. The data are used to construct several databases, and they provide the foundation for the products and services offered by Media Metrix.

The unique interactive nature of the Internet has led to its rapid emergence as a compelling vehicle for advertisers and marketers. The Internet offers advertisers the ability to target people with specific sets of interests, users with desirable demographic characteristics, and populations within specific localities, regions, or countries. Timely audience and advertising measurement data has emerged as "must have" information to which Media Metrix has provided the necessary tools for defining market opportunities. You can find the Media Metrix site at `www.mediametrix.com`.

The Media Metrix Top 50 U.S. Web and Digital Media Properties listing is an often-quoted statistical listing in *The Wall Street Journal*, *Internet World*, and many other magazines. Media Metrix also publishes the listing on their Web site at `http://www.mediametrix.com/usa/data/thetop.jsp`.

The Media Metrix offerings include

- **MyMetrix.com**—A state-of-the-art client user interface with customizable reports and analysis based on vast database of trended audience measurement statistics compiled by Media Metrix, including cross tabulations, source/loss reports, and the ability to save client-specific parameters.
- **AdRelevance 2.0**—The industry's only online advertising tracking system now capable of monitoring and capturing ads from over 500,000 URLs.
- **AdAlert**—The first and only email service to deliver up-to-date online advertising competitive intelligence via email and cellular devices, alerting users when a company or site runs a new ad or launches a new Web advertising campaign.
- **AdContact**—An all-in-one online advertising sales prospecting tool.

ASP Solutions for Measuring Customer Loyalty

Developing ways to measure how to get the greatest return on your investment in an ASP solution takes the focus off the veneer and puts it more on the delivered functionality, even for first-time visitors. Taking the time to create the best possible solution for your specific business takes planning time with your ASP, in which the following stages of taking visitors to your site and turning them into a loyal customer are explained in this section.

As Figure 12.1 illustrated, there are several steps to creating a strong sense of loyalty with your customers. One of the most beneficial aspects of a relationship with an ASP is that it can assist you in attracting customers to your site. Your ASP needs to be your business development partner, in that its efforts to attract visitors to your site and move them to being loyal customers is one that requires extensive coordination with your other marketing and sales efforts. Your ASP needs to know you expect that of it, that it is your business partner, and that metrics associated with new visitors is just the beginning. How many visitors turn into customers is the most critical metric associated with having an ASP as a business development partner.

Suspect

A *suspect* is anyone who visits your site and has an interest in purchasing a product or service from you. Metrics include the number of page hits, visitor counts, and number of opt-in email offers. This is also the largest percentage of visitors to your site, and where the need for interactive marketing is at its greatest. For example, adding a quick questionnaire in which the respondent is offered the chance to win a new laptop or Palm V once a month is a powerful incentive for a visitor to turn into a customer.

Prospect

The use of opt-in emails is a great approach to qualifying what percentage of a suspect base will turn into prospects. Having newsletters readily available also gives you the flexibility to tailor messages to various sets of prospects. The key metrics in this area are the number of opt-in email acceptances, the number of newsletters read online, the number of times an email arrives for additional information, and the figures for the total number of requests for information from your email account for the site.

First-Time Customer

Metrics on customers include the net amount of the initial order, types of products purchased, and the time taken between the initial visit and the actual purchase. Clearly, after a prospect crosses into this area there are many additional metrics your ASP can provide.

Repeat Customer

Purchasing patterns provide some of the most telling statistics generated from the repeat customer. In addition, the amount of ancillary products, new products that are comparable to existing ones purchased, and brand loyalty by customers are all variables that can be easily measured at this level. Initial customer satisfaction with the experience of purchasing from your site, the quality of the products delivered, and the method of delivery are all variables that speak to the repeat customer.

Client

When a customer becomes so familiar with your site and products that the metrics associated with their actions are more in terms of brand loyalty, personalization options, and a definition of the future direction of new product offerings based on their preferences, the customer is considered a client. Clients are ideal for including in Customer Advisory Councils in which new product ideas are defined and tested.

Fan

When the execution of orders, development of key relationships, and personalization aspects of the site are consistent with, and even exceeding, the expectations of customers, fans are created. Delivering value and consistently over-serving customers by exceeding their expectations creates fans. Metrics associated with fans include the amount of times they use online specials, their contributions to your newsletter, increasingly focused feedback (for example, the book reviews on the Amazon.com site), and a higher level of responsiveness with online surveys and feedback requests.

Building Customer Listening Systems That Quantify Performance

An online customer feedback area that includes a survey for measuring customer attitudes and preferences on your products and services is an essential element for all Web sites created in an e-business initiative. It is worth your effort to create this area from the initial stages of development. In fact, many ASPs offer online questionnaires and entire customer feedback areas on the sites they build for clients because many businesses have asked specifically for these features. Questionnaires online are as good as the back-end systems used for gathering, analyzing, presenting, and taking action on the results. That's the fundamental difference between just having a questionnaire online that generates an email with the responses included in an ASCII file format for use later. ASCII is text-based and is easily entered into programs, yet capturing the quantitative feedback into an overall analysis system is much more efficient and powerful in getting feedback results.

Customer listening systems serve to quantify the behavior and expectations of customers, and are often constructed of both legacy data and real-time profiles of visitors to Web sites. A customer Listening System is an information resource in which modeling data and completing data mining are the primary reasons the systems are developed. For example, SPSS, Inc., which stands for Statistical Package for the Social Sciences, has created an extensive array of products that can act as the intelligent back-end processing area of a customer listening system. SPSS is one of the premier companies providing statistical analysis software for educational and business use. Check out the SPSS site at `www.spss.com` for free demo versions of applications and an entire series of white papers on how its software applications can be used for data mining and statistical analysis of customer data.

To be effective, a customer listening system needs to have the following attributes:

- **Commitment to constant feedback from customers.** Providing a way for customers to communicate with you is essential for your company to grow and prosper. You should include a predetermined amount of space on a Web page that leads to a series of pages of questions.

- **Rely on your ASP to provide a new survey periodically to continually generate additional insights into your customer base**. Many ASPs already have the capability to provide online questionnaires as part of their overall offerings. A second set of ASPs focus purely on creating online surveys as their only offering. One of the more popular ones is `www.hostedsurvey.com`. Pricing for a hosted-only survey is also very reasonable, so if your ASP does not have a specific application for completing online surveys, consider using a secondary ASP just for your survey work.

- **Flexibility in defining questionnaires**. The days of having a Web site developer or even your ASP create the questionnaire forms in HTML are gone. Instead, insist that your ASP create an approach that provides you with the most possible flexibility using CGI and Dynamic HTML scripting. Although you don't need to become a technical consultant to use an ASP for this work, it is good to at least stress the point that you want to have customer listening systems user interfaces all in CGI and Dynamic HTML so they can be changed easily. Don't settle for simple HTML representations, or you will have to pay for an entirely new page to be created for each survey. Focus on flexibility and drive your ASP to deliver on that.

- **Statistical analysis tools.** A robust set of applications that can quickly and easily work on incoming data is a crucial part of a customer listening system. Make sure the software used to power the analytical aspects of the system has the capability to generate trending analysis, and also the flexibility to create cross-tabulations of the data. *Cross-tabs*, as they are most often called, profile one variable against another. It's one of the more efficient ways to analyze data because you can get to insights in the data relatively quickly by comparing one variable against another.

  In addition to the need for cross-tabs, statistical modeling and prediction tools are also useful for taking the raw data from surveys and projecting market sizing and growth for a given product or service offered on your site. The growth in statistical analysis tools will make this easy to accomplish, and your ASP either can provide the routines via software back-end or contract with another company to provide it. If you are doing a large amount of advertising to drive visitors to your site, using the tools available in this approach is crucial, because you'll want instant feedback as to which media activities have lead to the most hits to your site.

- **Remote Administration through the standard ASP interfaces.** After you get up and running with an ASP, you will find that many have a specific approach to managing their sites through administration tools available to you as a customer. Be sure to have the survey and analysis functions passworded and accessible from these administration screens. Because you can manage your site from a single location, it will save you hours of extra work.

Case Study: How J.B. Hunt Logistics Uses Metrics to Streamline Customers' Operations

Taking the approach of serving customers to allow them to better measure and deliver on their courier businesses, J.B. Hunt Logistics assists customers with e-business initiatives tied back to logistics systems. Recently, J.B. Hunt Logistics and AutoZone, one of

America's leading auto parts retail chains, took on the task of automating key aspects of their supply chain infrastructure. International Data Corporation, in conjunction with AutoZone and J.B. Hunt, completed a thorough analysis of how the benefits of automating logistics processes benefited the automobile aftermarket retailer. AutoZone is facing significant challenges as they rapidly grow, thanks in large part to the increasing focus consumers have on doing everything from building decks to rebuilding transmissions on their own. AutoZone has grown from $800 million and 598 retail stores in 1991 to $4.12 billion and 2,763 stores in 1999. In 1995, AutoZone realized that the resources needed to grow new stores were also needed for sustaining business in existing store locations. Because J.B. Hunt is one of the most recognized names in logistics, AutoZone contacted the logistics division of the company in an effort to apply stronger focus on supply chain infrastructure issues through an e–business-based strategy. The results were very successful and established an entirely new series of metrics by which AutoZone could monitor, manage, and develop their core business.

Taking the concept of the localized presence and developing it on a national level brought AutoZone immediate success on a per-store basis; however, it also brought an entire new array of challenges and problems as the scalability of its systems was tested at levels not experienced by the company before. One of the most dominant challenges was getting in control of the inbound logistics processes. The thousands of products handled by the company needed to be more efficiently handled during the incoming process, because the inventory management tasks were cutting into the liquidity of the company. With a higher rate of inventory turns generated, there would be a great potential return on the funds used for financing product inventory. The biggest challenge of the company was getting in control of the logistics overall. Suppliers controlled 95% of the inbound shipments, and 85% of the incoming shipments were LTL (Less than Load) which had a direct bearing on longer cycle times, a lack of visibility, unpredictable delivery times, and overall a bottlenecking of core processes in serving individual stores. The net result was a slowing of growth as products were constrained from being delivered to individual stores. For the company to grow, the logistics had to be more aggressively focused on serving the customer instead of adhering to the scheduling and logistics of suppliers.

In analyzing the situation, J.B. Hunt Logistics realized that AutoZone had many challenging logistics issues, yet was able to centralize on the top three, as follows:

- Develop a strong supplier shipment strategy with vendors, ensuring that shipments went from prepaid to collect for better control and visibility.

- Increase the efficiency of the fleet of delivery vehicles the company uses for completing key delivery tasks for customers. There was the definite need to create e–business-enabled applications that could provide individual stores with insights into how the overall logistics system was functioning in real-time.

- Increase supply chain efficiency by at least 30% over previous quarters by working directly through e-logistics applications to drive increased information throughout the distribution and partner channels.

Prior to AutoZone's implementation of the supply chain center outsourcing efforts with J.B. Hunt, each supplier was shipping its products directly to each AutoZone distribution center. This resulted in the predominance of LTL shipments as inbound, which drove longer lead times, higher transportation costs, higher claims, and ultimately unnecessary inventory. It also resulted in confusion and missed communications between various participants in the supply chain process, including AutoZone merchandising, distribution, traffic, retail store operations, and suppliers.

The Results of an e-Business Solution Take Immediate Effect

With the new processes enabled by J.B. Hunt, the logistics and fulfillment processes were re-engineered through a series of steps that are briefly described here:

- Developing a logistics strategy and plan that involved logistics, merchandising, distribution, retail store operations, information systems, and AutoZone suppliers. In short, the members of the supply chain became parts of an entire trading exchange. This approach to streamlining operations has been well documented by International Data Corporation in their analysis of the AutoZone and J.B. Hunt results achieved.

- Developing the systems and communications needed to share supply chain information, such as point-of-sale, forecasts, purchase orders, shipment schedules and status, performance reporting, and measurement.

- Executing supply chain optimization procedures focused on quality, time-definite shipments while minimizing total logistics costs.

- Monitoring, reporting, and measuring the performance of suppliers, carriers, and AutoZone logistics.

When the enhanced features of the e-business solution were defined and implemented, AutoZone quickly saw the benefits as these processes took hold throughout the organization. Results of the change to a more automated approach to handling logistics included

- LTL shipments were consolidated into truckloads, shipped to the nearest distribution center, and then cross-docked to the servicing distribution center.

- Distribution center transfers to other distribution centers were now possible.

- A reverse logistics program was initiated for parts and spares.

- The redesigned network created backhaul opportunities to increase use of the AutoZone private fleet.

Because J.B. Hunt did such an outstanding job with the implementation, it remains today the single point of contact for AutoZone's logistics needs. By leveraging J.B. Hunt's industry-leading systems technology, its extensive shipper and carrier network, and its own assets, AutoZone has gained supply chain value that has made a major contribution to its growth and profitability.

The following factors influenced AutoZone's decision in selecting J.B. Hunt as its implementation partner:

- IT capabilities in optimization and transportation management systems (TMS)
- Capability to affect supply chain management and add strategic value to clients
- Resources and speed to implementation
- AutoZone representatives particularly impressed by J.B. Hunt's project methodology

Using Surveys and Research Tools on the Web

Taking a proactive role with your ASP to specifically create an online survey is something I have advocated throughout this book. It's an area that is growing rapidly, as companies are actively working to provide free online surveys with just the minimal amount of functionality in return for your loyalty as a customer. This is identical to the dynamics of the click-and-build marketplace, in which free e-marketing and e-commerce sites are being offered in the hopes that businesses such as yours will stay with the ASPs of choice and eventually purchase services.

In the context of your discussions with the ASPs you are looking to hire, focus on their previous experiences in building online surveys. Because you are working toward a comprehensive e-business strategy that is going to be enabled by a service provider, bringing in your requirements for an online survey is only incrementally challenging to an ASP. Given the technology challenges of creating more robust e-business solutions, the development of a questionnaire should be achievable for little incremental cost.

One of the leading ASPs in this area is Informative.com, which has a unique positioning strategy in that it focuses on creating marketing information and tools for helping companies stay in touch with their customers. Informative.com's mission is to empower companies worldwide with easy-to-use, cost-effective, Web-based solutions that collect and report mission-critical information over the Internet in real time.

Informative.com's flagship product is SurveyBuilder.com, which gives you the flexibility of creating your own surveys online, getting feedback as quickly as the information is available from respondents. The entire approach is focused on being as responsive as possible to the companies who need the feedback. The second offering Informative.com has is the ePerformance Solutions set that includes professionally designed templates, preformatted with industry-specific questions and methods of quantifying results, tailored to provide instant control over the variables being measured. Informative.com's offerings are rounded out with a full suite of value-added turnkey services supported by in-house experts to ensure that the research objectives of your studies are accurately accomplished.

Delving into how other customers of ASPs are using applications to meet comparable needs to yours is a valuable exercise. You need to dig deeper into the actual performance of the applications relative to other customers' needs as well. More often than not, the CIO- and CEO-level users of ASPs want to get right to the bottom line of financial performance and return on investment. The elegance and streamlined nature of applications has a direct bearing on the return generated from the investment. This is so critical for customer feedback and the metrics associated with it because the metrics based on what your customers think can be the most impressive set of stats and have the greatest impact on your company. Ultimately, the level of differentiation inherent in an e-marketing application and its ability to deliver value to your customers are what matters most.

The reason I am bringing up these points is that when you take a tour of Informative.com's questionnaire-building application, you discover a definite simplicity in how the navigation is handled, which contributes to higher productivity than is possible in HTML-based methods. This approach to building and revising the specifics of an application is what an ASP is all about. Figure 12.2 shows an example of an online questionnaire being built.

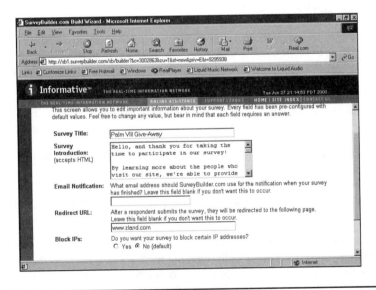

Figure 12.2   Using the features of the online questionnaire development tool from Informative.com is intuitive and a great time-saver for getting metrics back from customers on your performance.

Notice that you can tailor the questionnaire result distribution to any email address you want, and even point the respondent to your specific URL for further information. The capability to customize a message is also provided in the middle of this first configuration screen.

Taking Incentives to Your Customers in Internet Time

There are market research journals that routinely publish academic studies of the role of incentives for increasing the response rate to questionnaires. Increasingly companies are providing respondents the option of specifying a charity to which a contribution will be made. In the case of hostedware.com, for example, there is the option of defining varying dollar amounts for a survey, and also the option of defining which charity the donation is sent to. This is one of the more challenging aspects of creating an online survey with ASPs because the effort required to create the links back to charities is often an unknown for ASPs. Strongly consider using a charitable incentive and varying the amount by the value of the information to you. It's an interesting experiment that provides you with a glimpse at your customers' preferences for incentives and also greatly simplifies the administration of payments. After all, you will only need to write a few checks rather than hundreds to individual respondents to your surveys.

Looking to differentiate themselves from the other build-online questionnaire companies, Informative.com has built-in the capability to create incentives as your survey is being completed. Figure 12.3 shows an example of how the opt-in function works for building an incentive of $100 donation per completed questionnaire. This is a powerful feature because it can quickly be changed for each successive questionnaire that is developed. Companies in broader markets with environmentally aware consumers (for example, soap and shampoo makers) have successfully used this approach for providing a donation to the World Wildlife Fund.

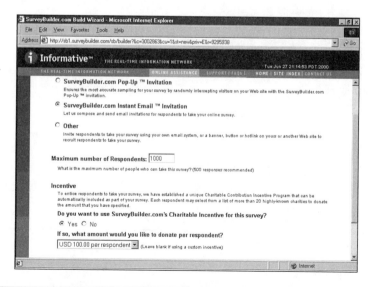

Figure 12.3   Configuring an online survey to provide an incentive of a charitable contribution is effective, and easily configured using online tools with ASPs.

The Informative.com interfaces for completing tasks are comparable to the tools used by ASPs internally for handling the production of e-marketing and e-commerce sites. What's invigorating about the direction the industry is taking is that this level of functionality is getting into the hands of the actual customer, giving you the chance to architect the e-marketing, e-commerce, and in this case, online questionnaires you want. This also presents the ASPs the unique and very real challenge of becoming even more focused on differentiation and increased value and performance of applications over time. With the wizard-like tools available from ASPs, there is really no excuse to rely totally on HTML-based efforts.

At the core of a questionnaire are the sequencing and content of the requests made to customers. With the velocity of change occurring in many industries, the ability to quickly switch questions in a survey and create an entirely new survey based on feedback from customers is very expensive when a purely HTML-based approach is taken.

Figure 12.4 shows an example of how the wizard-like interface for defining the contents of a questionnaire are easily navigated.

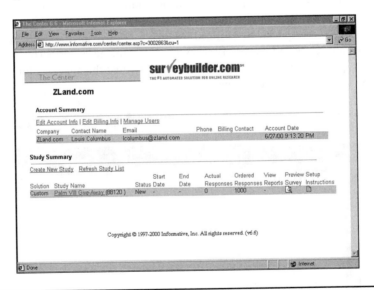

Figure 12.4   Managing an online questionnaire is easily accomplished with the latest set of tools from ASPs specializing in obtaining market feedback.

Tying It All Together with a Measurable e-Business Strategy

Getting your e-business strategy out of conjecture and anecdotal data into practical information based on real performance measures will mean the difference between success and failure. The fact that metrics provide you an opportunity to compete against yourself in the service of your customers is a critical distinction from the over-hyped nature of e-commerce today. Integrating metrics into each step of your e-business strategy ensures that your plan will generate a trail of successes and lessons learned over time, which will be invaluable for everyone following you in the organization's roles you participate in today.

Creating opportunities for interaction with customers is a goal that can be accomplished through e-marketing and creating a viable communications strategy. Being content with simple brochureware is unacceptable. Developing communications tools for getting the customer to provide a strong and relevant voice into your business is really the goal of marketing. It's much more than counting mouse clicks and developing metrics that easily scale to seven figures; it's all about building relationships with customers through responsiveness and being service-oriented in all activities. e-Marketing's role is to provide information in a package for easy consumption. Be that person in your industry who leverages the ASP model to its fullest in the service of your customers. You can take a leadership position in your industry by being the most responsive to customers, guided by metrics that show progress in service and customer satisfaction over time.

In the arena of e-commerce there are many options for creating and maintaining a Web site, yet the best have personalized accountability inherent in their business models and can go the distance with you as a customer. Don't think the easily taken paths of creating an e-commerce site with a free Web site provider is going to scale with your organization. These click-and-build companies face the challenge of extending their business models to deliver greater value over time by focusing on the e-operations and collaborative tools aspect of their offerings, which is many times absent. In the arena of e-commerce applications, the need for a vendor that is personally accountable to you is critical. The role of the world's largest Internet integrators is that of providing that service for literally millions of dollars. With market models that provide personalized service, there is the corresponding value of being able to revisit ideas and concepts over and over again. ZLand.com has an approach based on a franchise model to provide this personalized service so essential for building a stable Web site.

e-Operations include a wide array of applications and services, and is the one area of e-business where metrics are most extensively used and drive a very rapid impact on the bottom line of companies. What's impressive about the e-operations arena is that as companies go public—even in the midst of NASDAQ fluctuations—their values hold over time. It's because they are delivering quantifiable performance over time and have a definite impact on businesses adopting them. Be very thorough and stress metrics when working toward an e-operations solution with an ASP because you need the following: a strong set of solutions that scale with your business, the technical depth and scalability of your ASP to provide support for legacy data migration and integration, and most importantly, domain expertise to manage the integration of new features as they arise. Making the metrics that apply most to the profitability of your company the objectives of the ASP will drive instant accountability and provide a barometer of performance going forward with the ASP partner(s) you choose.

Summary

Taking the hype out of the e-business equation is possible by centering solidly on metrics and what they mean to your business. Drive your ASP relationships as you would any other outsourcing relationship, holding your ASP responsible for performance on metrics and building both incentives and penalties based on performance overall relative to plan. For your e-business plans to be successful, clearly communicate with your ASP that both of you are in the partnership for the long run and both will be measured on the results against quantified performance. Leveraging off the expertise in your ASP to develop an aggressive go-to-market strategy with an e-commerce and e-marketing solution is critical for your success. Just as there is success in many counselors, it's imperative that the direction of the partnership be centered on the business case objectives that lead to contacting an ASP in the first place. As the ASP industry matures, there is always the need for early adopters to contribute their vision of the market going forward, because many of these early adopters are actually the catalysts of growth in the industry today. Being focused on the direction of your customers and leveraging the ASP model gives you the freedom to focus on your core strengths, ultimately delivering greater value to your customer.

Bibliography

Chapter 1

"Comparing Online Office Suites." e-MarketDynamics.com. April 2000.

"Distributors Embrace ASP Model." e-MarketDynamics.com. February 2000.

e-Market Monitor Newsletter. e-MarketDynamics.com. April 2000.

"Is Sun Rising with Star?" About.com. 2 September 1999.

"Microsoft Announces Microsoft Office Online." *Start Magazine.* (`http://www.startmag.com/news_9911/99111518.asp`). November 1999.

"Microsoft Shakes Up the Personal ASP Market with Office Online." International Data Corporation Bulletin. November 1999.

"Microsoft Taking Office Online." PC World. 3 September 1999.

"Microsoft to Rent Out Office." *Network World.* 11 November 1999.

"Rent Microsoft Office Online." *Advisor Magazine.* 12 November 1999.

"The Role of Office Suites Online." *e-MarketDynamics.com Research Services.* December 1999.

"Why Personalized Content Matters." *International Data Corporation Bulletin.* December 1998.

"Will New Hosted Productivity Applications 'Off' Office?" *Summit Strategies.* April 2000.

Chapter 2

"Analysis of the Click-and-Build Marketplace." e-MarketDynamics.com. April 2000.

"Building Your Own Online Store." *WWWiz Magazine*. Q1 2000.

e-Market Monitor Newsletter. e-MarketDynamics.com. May 2000.

Kneko Burney Conversations on eBSP Marketplace. January–April 2000.

"Mom and Pop on the Web." *CNN Financial Network*. 23 May 2000.

"Ohgolly.com Helps Small Businesses Become Web Savvy." dbbusiness.com. 23 May 2000.

"Q1/00 eBSP Rankings." *Cahner's In-Stat Research*. June 2000.

"Q4/99 eBSP Rankings." *Cahner's In-Stat Research*. January 2000.

"Scorecard of Web Storefronts." *PC Magazine*. 27 October 1999.

"Setting Up Shop Online." *PC Magazine*. 27 October 1999.

"Top 10 Companies to Watch." *Red Herring Magazine*. May 1999.

"Zeroing in on the Low-Cost e-Commerce Providers." e-MarketDynamics.com. March 2000.

Chapter 3

"Assessing the Impact of Internet Integration on the Small and Medium Business Marketplace." *The Yankee Group Small Business Service*. 19 August 1999.

Columbus, Louis. Case studies written for Zland.com. February–April 2000.

Columbus, Louis. Personal notes and observations from IDC's Appsourcing Forum. San Francisco, CA. April 2000.

Columbus, Louis. Teleconferences with Eric Klein, Senior Analyst of SMB Research. September–December 1999.

"Who's on First—Supply or Demand SMBs Doing Business on the Web Teleconference Notes and Presentation." *The Yankee Group Small Business Service*. 11 November 1999.

Chapter 4

Columbus, Louis. Case studies written for Zland.com. February–April 2000.

"Early Adopters in the Small Business Arena." e-MarketDynamics.com. April 2000.

e-Market Monitor Newsletter. e-MarketDynamics.com. June 2000.

"e-Marketplaces Boost B2B Trade." Forrester Research. February 2000.

"Hands-Free: A New Trajectory for Business Apps." Forrester Research Brief. 24 January 2000.

"Partnering with ASPs: Licensing and Channel Strategies." *International Data Corporation Bulletin*. May 2000.

"Sizing App Hosting." *Forrester Research Report.* December 1999.

"Sizing e-Commerce Services." *Forrester Research Report.* October 1999.

"U.S. Small Businesses on the Internet: Market Forecast and Analysis 1999." *International Data Corporation Report.* March 2000.

Chapter 5

"Assessing the Impact of Internet Integration on the Small and Medium Business Marketplace." *The Yankee Group Small Business Service.* 19 August 1999.

Columbus, Louis. Case studies written for Zland.com. February–April 2000.

Columbus, Louis. Notes from e-business conference with AMR Research. May 2000.

"e-Business Strategy Needs Help." *Forrester Research Report.* January 2000.

"e-Market Monitor Newsletter." e-MarketDynamics.com. March 2000.

"e-Marketing Checklist." e-MarketDynamics.com. January 2000.

"e-Marketplace Hype, Apps Realities." *Forrester Research Report.* April 2000.

Eric Klein presentation for Zland.com senior management. *The Yankee Group.* March 2000.

"Europe's eZones." Forrester Research brief. February 1999.

"Partnering with ASPs: Licensing and Channel Strategies." *International Data Corporation Bulletin.* May 2000.

"Top 10 Companies to Watch." *Red Herring Magazine.* May 1999.

"U.S. Small Businesses on the Internet: Market Forecast and Analysis, 1999." *International Data Corporation Report.* March 2000.

Chapter 6

"Adding Value to Net Finance." *Forrester Report.* November 1998.

Columbus, Louis. Notes from e-business conference with AMR Research. May 2000.

e-Market Monitor Newsletter. e-MarketDynamics.com. April 2000.

"Europe's eZones." Forrester Research brief. February 1999.

"Global Cash Management Services for the Business Market: Strategic Positioning for the New Decade." *Killen & Associates Report.* January 2000.

"IT Strategies for Banking Delivery Channels in Europe." *International Data Corporation.* November 1999.

"Moving Banks onto the Net: Online Banking in Europe." *International Data Corporation* Report. May 2000

"NatWest and Razorfish Link Up on Digital Future." *Razorfish* press release. 6 October 1999.

"Online Banking Today." e-MarketDynamics.com. June 1999.

"Razorfish Expands Operations in Southern Europe: New Milan Office to Capitalize on Italy's Digital Boom." *Razorfish* press release. 10 May 2000.

"Razorfish Creates Global Portal for Financial Times." *Razorfish* press release. 14 February 2000.

"Show Me e-Money." *Wired Magazine*. 3 June 1999.

Chapter 7

"A Flea Market for Web Heads." James Lardner. *US News & World Report*. 10 October 1999.

"A Real Amazon." Rita Koselka. *Forbes*. 5 April 1999.

"Affiliate Marketing: The Enablers." International Data Corporation. August 1999.

"Amazon.com: The Wild World of Ecommerce." Robert D. Hof. *Business Week*. 14 December 1999

Columbus, Louis. Interviews with UPS and Federal Express Managers. October 1999–April 2000.

"e-Commerce ASPs: How Will e-Commerce Projects Become the Next Battleground for ASPs and Internet Service Firms?" International Data Corporation. April 2000.

e-Market Monitor Newsletter. e-MarketDynamics.com. April 2000.

"e-Marketing Checklist." e-MarketDynamics.com. January 2000.

Eric Klein presentation for Zland.com senior management. March 2000.

"Hands-Free: A New Trajectory for Business Apps." Forrester Research brief. 24 January 2000.

"How to Be a Great CEO." Geoffrey Colin. *Fortune*. 24 May 1999.

"The Inner Bezos." Chip Bayers. *Wired*. March 1999.

"Jeff Bezos." Q&A, Robert D. Hof. *Business Week*. 31 May 1999.

"Marketers of the Year: Jeff Bezos, Volume Discounter." Bernhard Warner. *Brandweek*. 12 October 1998.

Notes from Internet Summit 99 from *Industry Standard* magazine. Jeff Bezos presentation. Conference held July 17–20 1999 in Laguna Niguel, CA.

"Now It's One Big Market." Daniel Eisenberg. *Time*. 12 April 1999.

"Running Scared." James Daly. *Business 2.0*. April 1999.

"UPS: e-Logistics Initiatives and Competitive Position Relative to Federal Express." e-MarketDynamics.com. March 2000.

"What's Really Going On with Amazon?" Bethany McLean. *Fortune*. 3 August 1999.

Chapter 8

"The Art of the Deal." *Business 2.0.* October 1999.

"Cisco Competitive Analysis and Acquisition Strategy Assessment." e-MarketDynamics.com. April 2000.

"Cisco Dials Up InfoGear." *IDCFlash.* March 2000.

"Cisco's Secret for Success." *Red Herring Magazine.* 6 March 2000.

"Cisco Systems: Developing e-Business Opportunities through New World Ecosystems." *International Data Corporation Bulletin.* May 2000.

e-Market Monitor Newsletter. e-MarketDynamics.com. April 2000.

"Meet Cisco's Mr. Internet." *Business Week.* 13 September 1999.

"New Roles for Cisco Switches?" *Network World Magazine.* 21 February 2000.

"The New World of M & A." *Fortune.* February 2000.

"Patent Protection Weaving a Tangled Web on the Web." *Cisco World Magazine.* April 2000.

S1 document and amended documents for Cisco Corporation. Securities and Exchange Commission.

"Why Cisco Is on Top." *Fortune.* 28 March 2000.

Chapter 9

Columbus, Louis. Case studies written for Zland.com. February–April 2000.

"e-Business Strategy Needs Help." Forrester Research reports. January 2000.

"e-Commerce Software Applications Review and Forecast: 1999–2000." International Data Corporation report. June 2000

e-Market Monitor Newsletter. e-MarketDynamics.com. March 2000.

"Guess? Inc. Partners with CommerceOne and PeopleSoft to Launch e-Commerce Portal for the Apparel Industry." *Guess?* press release. 15 December 1999.

"Hands-Free: A New Trajectory for Business Apps." Forrester Research brief. 24 January 2000.

"Peoplesoft: Ready for e-business and Europe?" International Data Corporation bulletin. March 2000.

Chapter 10

Columbus, Louis. Case studies written for Zland.com. February–April 2000.

"Ingram Micro Rolls out Two New Sun Partner Programs—Provides Funding for Training, Certification, Marketing." *Computer Reseller News.* 20 March 2000.

S1 document and amended documents for Sun Microsystems Corporation. Securities and Exchange Commission.

"Sun Co-Founder, Top Scientist See Many Webs." *TechWeb*. 11 January 2000.

"Sun Delivers e-Biz Portal Solutions." *VARBusiness*. 29 February 2000.

"Sun Eyes Market Share with Program to Certify ASPs." *InfoWorld*. 11 January 2000.

"Sun Gives VARs Incentives to Buy Online." *VARBusiness*. 18 February 2000.

"Sun in Deal to Tie Stores to Websites." *ComputerWorld*. 31 January 2000.

"Sun Moves to Set Standards for Service Resellers." *Smart Reseller Magazine*. 11 January 2000.

"Sun Stamps ASPs with Seal of Approval." *VARBusiness*. 11 January 2000.

"SunTone Gains First Nine Members." *VARBusiness*. 14 January 2000.

"Xerox, Sun and iPlanet Team Up to Ease e-Billing." *ComputerWorld Magazine*. 13 March 2000.

Chapter 11

"Buy.com Launches Affiliate Marketing Program." Buy.com press release. 1 March 2000.

e-Market Monitor Newsletter. e-MarketDynamics.com. July 2000.

Eric Klein presentation for Zland.com senior management. March 2000.

"Forbes Ranking Buy.com 'Best of Web,'" *Forbes*. 8 March 2000.

"If You Build It, Will They Come? Electronic Commerce for Hardware Resellers." International Data Corporation bulletin. July 1999.

S1 document and amended documents for Buy.com Corporation. Securities and Exchange Commission.

Chapter 12

"AutoZone Finalizes Purchase Of Express Stores From Pep Boys." AutoZone press release. 21 October 1998.

"AutoZone Names Chief Content Officer." AutoZone press release. 4 May 2000.

"e-Logistics Business Process Outsourcing Industry Scope and Definition." International Data Corporation bulletin. September 1999.

e-Market Monitor Newsletter. e-MarketDynamics.com. July 2000.

"Logistics Business Process Outsourcing: Market Overview and Service Provider Analysis." International Data Corporation report. December 1999.

S1 document and amended documents for JB Hunt Corporation. Securities and Exchange Commission.

S1 document and amended documents for AutoZone Corporation. Securities and Exchange Commission.

Index